ARIGO:

Surgeon of the Rusty Knife

Also by John G. Fuller

FEVER!

ARIGO:

Surgeon of the Rusty Knife

John G. Fuller

Afterword by
Henry K. Puharich, MD

Hart-Davis, MacGibbon
London

Granada Publishing Limited
First published in Great Britain 1975
by Hart-Davis, MacGibbon Ltd
Frogmore, St Albans, Hertfordshire AL2 2NF and
3 Upper James Street, London W1R 4BP

ISBN 0 246 10856 8

Printed in Great Britain by
Fletcher & Son Ltd, Norwich

Author's Note

In this story, so strange, so incredible, there are undisputed facts, facts that cannot be denied, cannot be altered even by the most obdurate skeptic.

It is an established *fact* that Ze Arigo, the peasant Brazilian surgeon-healer, could cut through the flesh and viscera with an unclean kitchen- or pocketknife and there would be no pain, no hemostasis—the tying off of blood vessels—and no need for stitches. It is a *fact* that he could stop the flow of blood with a sharp verbal command. It is a *fact* that there would be no ensuing infection, even though no antisepsis was used.

It is a fact that he could write swiftly some of the most sophisticated prescriptions in modern pharmacology, yet he never went beyond third grade and never studied the subject. It is a fact that he could almost instantly make clear, accurate, and confirmable diagnoses or blood pressure readings with scarcely a glance at the patient.

It is a fact that both Brazilian and American doctors have verified Arigo's healings and have taken explicit color motion pictures of his work and operations. It is a fact that Arigo treated over three hundred patients a day for nearly two decades and never charged for his services.

It is a fact that among his patients were leading executives, statesmen, lawyers, scientists, doctors, aristocrats from many countries, as well as the poor and desolate. It is a fact that Brazil's former President, Juscelino Kubitschek, the creator of the capital city of Brasília and himself a physician, brought his daughter to Arigo for successful treatment. It is a fact that Arigo brought about medically confirmed cures in cases of cancer and other fatal diseases that had been given up as hopeless by leading doctors and hospitals in some of the most advanced countries in the Western world.

But none of these facts, all carefully brought together and examined, can add up to an explanation. And it is for this reason that this story is so difficult to write. The question keeps repeating itself in my mind: How am I going to write this story so that the reader will believe it —especially when I had so much trouble believing it myself until completing the research in Brazil?

Any understanding of the events here must arise from an understanding of the atmosphere and culture of Brazil itself. It is a country of contrasts, a country of vast wilderness and of bristling modern cities. São Paulo, for instance, is a city of nearly eight million, approximately twice as large as Chicago or Los Angeles. Belo Horizonte, in the plateau region northwest of Rio, is larger than Baltimore, Washington, or San Francisco. Yet it is a city little known to most people in the United States. Brazil is larger in area than the continental United States. Its population ranges from highly sophisticated intellectuals and scientists to primitive Amazon Indians.

Most important to understand in this story is the prevalence in Brazil of a willingness to accept paraphysical happenings as basic realities. This willingness cuts across all social and economic lines. In fact, it almost seems that the more sophisticated and educated the group, the more likelihood there is of acceptance of a philosophy known as Kardecism, springing from the writings of a nineteenth-century French mystic known as Allan Kardec, a French professor whose real name was Denizard Rivail.

The Kardecists flatly believe in the rational reality of

the spirit world, and in communication with and effective use of it. They believe in reincarnation. The Kardecists are known as intellectual "spiritists" who do not believe in ritual and paganism. They meet quietly, most often in private homes, and embrace most of the tenets of Christianity. They believe, however, that they can draw on the power and knowledge of the spirit world through mediums who are carefully trained for this purpose.

Some Kardec theorists who are knowledgeable about every aspect of Freudian theory believe that "possession" is a phenomenon that has been overlooked in the headlong development of modern psychotherapy, and that there is rational and viable evidence that many cases of psychosis from schizophrenia to dementia praecox could be ascribed to the phenomenon of "possession" by an alleged spirit that refuses to accept the fact that he or she is dead. The spirit, whether good or bad, is said to be "incorporated" in the living body of a receptive person.

This idea is mostly rejected by the modern pragmatic mind, and "possession" has been summarily dismissed by medical science without either positive or negative evidence being examined until recently. Catholicism has long struggled with the problem, but remains ambivalent about it.

"Possession" is a very heady concept for the materialistic mind to accept or cope with. Modern parapsychology is beginning to reexamine the concept, although gingerly. There are other signs on the horizon that foreshadow a reawakening of interest in this area, not only in Brazil but also in the United States. It may or may not have been an accident that the novel *The Exorcist* rode the best-seller lists for so many months. Many people do not realize that this story was based on an actual documented case of possession in the archives of the Catholic Church, and that there are many recorded cases similar to it.

Any serious exploration into this field in the United States is bound to raise eyebrows. There are many good reasons why it should. Charlatans and irresponsible writers have created so much static and high noise level, without any reliable documentation, that they defeat their own cause. Anyone exploring a strange phenomenon has to assume that the burden of proof lies on his shoulders. The more strange it is, the greater the documentation needed, and the greater the need for understatement.

No other so-called "psychic surgeon" in Brazil or the world has been confirmed and documented as thoroughly as Arigo. Many reports have come from the Philippines about feats of surgery by untutored and untrained psychics there, but there has been a constant exposure of trickery in their work. Further, their lack of cooperation with medical researchers has made their case untenable.

Arigo was unique. He cooperated in every possible way with medical science in the hope that he could discover for himself the strange mechanism that created his inexplicable powers. He defies classification. What he did was vividly real. *How* he did it remains a mystery and a challenge for science.

JOHN G. FULLER
Westport, Connecticut

List of Illustrations

**From *Time* Magazine
October 16, 1972:**

"Even before he died last year in an automobile accident at the age of 49, the peasant known as Arigo had become a legend in his native Brazil. Claiming to be guided by the wise voice of a long-deceased physician whom he had never known personally, the uneducated healer saw as many as 300 patients a day, diagnosing and treating them in minutes . . . He treated almost every known ailment, and most of his patients not only survived but actually improved or recovered.

"A few years ago, reports on the exploits of such miracle workers would have drawn little more than derision from the scientifically-trained. Now, however, many medical researchers are showing a new open-mindedness toward so-called psychic healing and other methods not taught in medical schools."

ARIGO:

Surgeon of the Rusty Knife

1

It was almost dark as the Volkswagen microbus twisted along the serpentine road from Rio de Janeiro, four hundred kilometers to the south, toward the village of Congonhas do Campo. The green mountains, rolling like a rumpled billiard table, had turned to a purple-gray as the hot Brazilian sun deserted them. The Rio highway, known as BR-3, favored the gentlest possible route through this mining country, where black gold and iron had magnetized the attention of European and North American exploiters since Brazil's earliest colonial days. At twilight, the bare emerald surface of the treeless mountains changes from stunning brilliance to an ominous aura that historically has engendered myths and legends.

Inside the microbus were four men: two interpreters, university students from the University of Rio de Janeiro, and two Americans of widely divergent backgrounds. Henry Belk, a rangy, congenial, fiftyish Southerner from North Carolina who was both a successful businessman and an intellectual adventurer, had been at the wheel for nearly ten hours, dodging overexuberant Brazilian drivers and maneuvering around the precipitous hairpin turns with considerable skill. Beside him was Dr. Henry K. Puharich (he rarely used his given name, Andrija), with a medical degree from Northwestern University and a specialty in bioengineering. He further had a proclivity for trying to fuse and consolidate his extensive scientific background with little understood psychic phenomena. An alert and articulate man in his forties, he had been drawn together with Belk in an exploration of the unusual faculties of Peter Hurkos, the medium whose ESP prowess had engendered considerable attention among both scientists and law enforcement agencies when he located missing persons and solved some knotty cases by clairvoyance.

But it was not Hurkos they were seeking out in these sweeping plateau highlands of Brazil. It was a man called Ze Arigo, a dynamic Brazilian of peasant stock whose fame had reached the ears of Belk in his own explorations of the paranormal. Belk had set up an extensive research foundation for just such inquiries. He had persuaded Puharich to join him in an investigation of Arigo, whose medical cures kept him on the front pages of Brazilian newspapers and whose exploits were rumored to border on the miraculous.

By the time dark had closed in, the bus still had not reached Congonhas do Campo, and it was after ten before they stumbled on the rather shabby little town of Conselheiro Lafaiete, a railroad-mining village on the plateau, twenty kilometers short of their target. A hotel in the village looked black and uninviting, and they decided to press on, late as it was, under the peculiarly brilliant stars that hung like lamps over the mountains, now chilled by the darkness.

Tired from the long drive, Puharich found himself wondering just what he was doing in this offbeat part of the world. He had reached that point in the expedition where he wondered whether he should ever have set out on it. Belk was finding his enthusiasm waning, too, although neither had yet cast eyes on the object of their inquiry, the man known as Arigo.

They had little enough to go on, but the clues were intriguing. In Rio, Dr. Lauro Naiva, a doctor who had studied medicine in the United States, had vouched for

Church of the Bom Jesus in Congonhas do Campo with the statues by Aleijadinho.

View from the church

Street scene in Congonhas. Arigo's "clinic" is in the center, the Hotel Freitas is next to it, and in the foreground, across the street, is the farmacia São José where many of his prescriptions were filled.

Henry Puharich, M.D. (right) and Henry Belk in Arigo's backyard during their first visit in 1963.

Views of the inside of Arigo's "clinic" during Puharich's and Belk's first visit. Arigo is writing prescriptions with the same pen he used for twenty years.

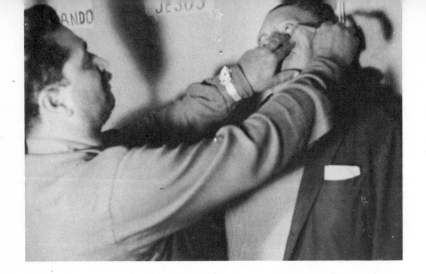

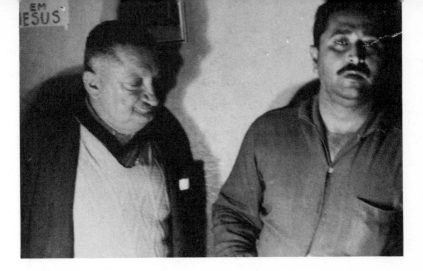

(opposite page and above) Arigo operating with a kitchen knife. Dr. Puharich observed in his notebook: "It was thought the patient's eye would be gouged out. But no pain was felt."

(below) Arigo and villagers in front of Hotel Freitas.

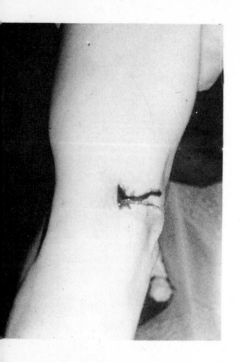
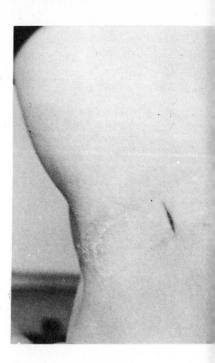

Operation by Arigo on right forearm of Dr. Puharich to remove a lipoma. *(above, left)* The arm immediately after surgery. *(above, right)* The arm two days after the operation. *(below)* The knife used and the excised lipoma.

À esquerda, o Presidente da Belk Research Foundation e o Prof. Henry Puharich, que pediu a Arigó um exame no ôlho (sem anestesia) e acabou sendo operado pelo médium... com um canivete! Ligado às pesquisas espaciais, Puharich é uma das glórias da ciência norte-americana.

Os cientistas norte-americanos estão maravilhados com os exames feitos com a ponta da faca. Mas não podem entender uma coisa: como os enfermos suportam uma faca no ôlho, sem anestesia. Incorporado no médium José Arigó, tenho diante de mim o Dr. Adolfo Fritz, espírito de um medico alemão falecido durante a Segunda Grande Guerra.

— Dr. Puharich gostou do que viu, hein? Aqui, a verdade é mostrada às claras!

— Os dois cientistas estão satisfeitos. Mas o Dr. Henry Puharich deseja sentir na carne o mistério mediúnico... Quer que o Senhor lhe examine o ôlho: com a faca e sem anestesia.

— Besteirra, respondeu o espírito-guia de José Arigó, com seu sotaque tipicamente alemão. Puharich não tem nada na vista. Pra que vou eu enfiarr bisturri no ôlho dêle?

— O cientista americano diz que para bem se entender um fenômeno é preciso "viver" êsse fenômeno Sem experimentar o bisturi no ôlho, êle não poderá explicar a falta de anestesia Está, pois, disposto a sentir as mesmas sensações dos enfermos.

— Esse cientista amerricano é corrajoso! Merrece uma exibição. Trraga êle aqui. Vou mostrar a êsse materrialista o que pode um espírito fazer Mas êle está certo, meu irmão. Um cientista tem de se arriscar a tudo. Pasteur não arriscou a vida com os microbios? Assim fazem os cientistas de verdade; e não os brasileiros, que têm mêdo até de vir a Congonhas. Trraga o Dr. Puharich aqui.

— Êle tem um lipoma no braço. Mas, o Senhor não esta operando

— Trraga êle aqui, insistiu Dr. Fritz. Vou mostrrar uma coisa que êle nunca viu nos Estados Unidos!

SEGUE

CIENTISTA AMERICANO OPERADO POR ARIGÓ

Texto de JORGE RIZZINI

A magazine article by Jorge Rizzini about the Puharich operation. The story was also carried by nearly every newspaper in Brazil.

ampolas de
Betmelve R. forte de
B-12-B
mil 3 vidro de
novazolon 4 vidr
de Pankreon 4 vi-
dros de Luizym

(top) The highly unconventional prescription Arigo gave Henry Belk for his back condition. The writing on top is Arigo's.

(above) Altimiro, Arigo's long-time assistant.

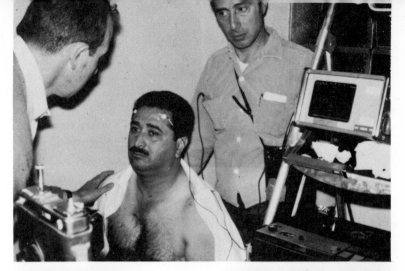

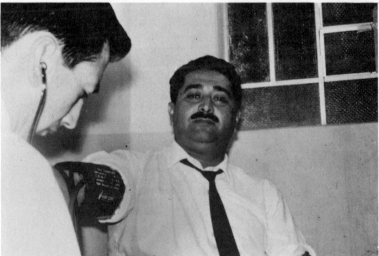

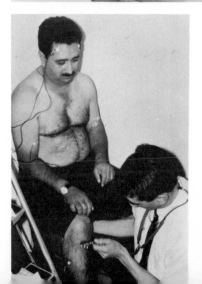

Members of the American Medical team in 1968 conducted a complete physical examination of Arigo, including brain wave tests with an EEG instrument.

ESSENTIA
RESEARCH
ASSOCIATES

STUDY
ARIGÓ
in
Congonhas do Campo,
BRASIL
May '68, Jan. '69

The pictures on pages 12-16 were made from the 16mm motion picture taken by the American medical team.

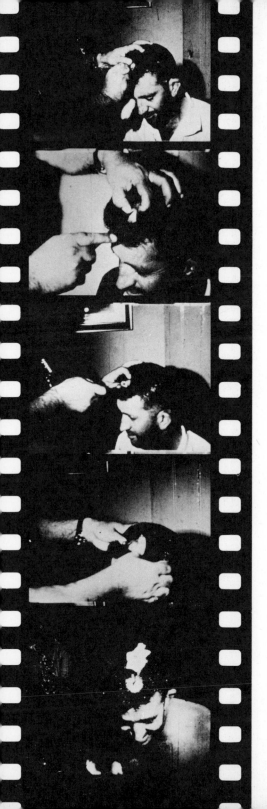

Arigo cutting out a scalp tumor.

A close-up of Arigo's hands writing a prescription.

(top) Patients waiting to see Arigo in his "clinic."

(middle and bottom) Arigo performing eye surgery.

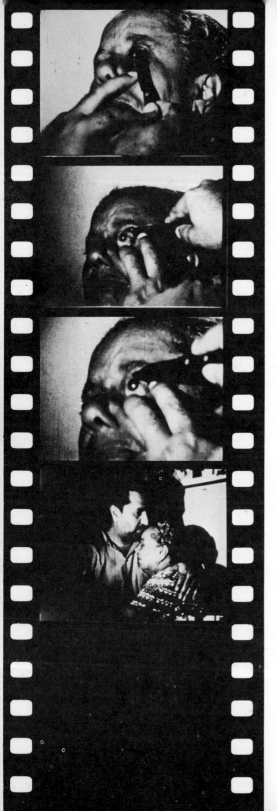

Arigo removing a cataract. In the last picture he is comforting the patient.

ARIGÓ MORREU NA BR-3

Zé Arigó morreu ontem num desastre de automóvel, perto de Congonhas do Campo, na antiga BR-3. Ele vinha de sua fazenda, no município de Joaquim Murtinho, quando bateu com seu Opala numa camioneta do DNER.

O desastre foi às 12h25min, no km 374, e Arigó morreu na hora, com fratura de crânio. Segundo amigos, Arigó tinha viagem marcada para os Estados Unidos e estava prevendo sua morte. Chegou a dizer para alguns que ia morrer num desastre de automóvel antes de fevereiro.

Em Congonhas, após a notícia de sua morte, grande número de pessoas foi para as ruas.

Apesar da morte de Arigó, o Dr. Fritz vai continuar operando. Isto foi o que explicou Múzio, um famoso médium de Belo Horizonte. Múzio, que foi para Congonhas ver o amigo, disse que o Dr. Fritz vai continuar operando com o Dr. Pierre, que faz suas curas através dele.

— Nunca me apresentei como santo ou sábio. Tenho apenas uma missão. Nunca curei ninguém, assim como o dr. Fritz, que também cumpre uma tarefa em nome de Deus. As curas ou "maravilhas" são resultados da fé e do merecimento dos que as recebem.

Operando com uma faca de cozinha, José Pedro de Freitas, conhecido como Zé Arigó, transformou sua cidade. Para ele seguiam milhares de pessoas em busca de cura. Cobrando apenas o dinheiro dos remédios, Arigó operava câncer ou seio, cegos e paralíticos. Sem anestesia, pontos e nem um ninguém sentisse dor. Condenado por atividades médicas e curandeirismo, visitado por médicos norte-americanos e europeus, continuou em Congonhas operando em transe, dirigido pelo espírito do dr. Fritz, médico alemão morto pelo nazismo.

— Não sei o que faço quando entro em transe. Sinto uma dormência nos pés e perco os sentidos. Sou um médium sincero. Diziam que eu já havia operado pulmões, cortado ossos cancerosos sem provocar dores, sem usar anestesia e sem deixar o sangue correr. Confesso que não acreditava nisso e só vi que era mesmo verdade quando assistia a um filme que documentava meu trabalho mediúnico.

Primeira operação

O primeiro caso de Arigó foi uma operação no fazendeiro Lucas de Matos, que sofria de dores no estômago e depois de procurar vários médicos ainda não tinha conseguido ficar bom.

Arigó pediu uma tesoura e uma lata de marmelada. Abriu a barriga do velho fazendeiro e tirou pedaços de carne cheios de fibras, tratando e ferindo-o com um crucifixo. Lucas de Matos foi operado com sessenta e cinco anos e vivia até oitenta e sete. Seu pai, que foi vereador de Congonhas durante depois anos, pediu que naquele momento tenso que Zé fosse parar na cadeia, pois não acreditava que o fazendeiro Lucas continuasse vivo.

Depois que casou com dona Arlete, Arigó abriu um bar que teve seu apelido: Bar do Arigó, onde se fregueses, principalmente os que não tinham dinheiro, comiam e bebiam sem pagar. Pouco tempo depois estava falido e seu pai teve que liquidar a conta com o

fornecedores. Vendendo imóveis, gado e terras, conseguiu estabilizar-se financeiramente.

Foi trabalhando na Siderúrgica Nacional que reviveu seus dotes espirituais. Nesta véspera, sóbrio do sindicato da Siderúrgica, levou a Arigó sua filha recém-nascida, que não conseguia clarear por ter a língua presa. Arigó levou a criança a um médico conhecido, que convidou a mãe a ir a Belo Horizonte, porque era necessária uma operação. Arigó pediu à mãe da menina que ressasse e no dia seguinte ela foi até sua casa dizendo que ao acordar e ver a criança teria saído de sangue e tinha procurado o médico, que lhe explicou que a menina havia sido operada e estava curada.

— Via coisas terríveis à noite. Ficava tão desesperado que chegava a sair de casa destinado. Saltava pela janela e ficava andando pela rua. Não sei bem o que sentia, mas desde que agora una estava servindo de instrumento a forças mais fortes do que eu. Depois entendi que uma dessas forças — a mais poderosa — era o espírito do dr. Fritz, o médico que me orienta em todas as receitas e em todas as operações.

Trabalhando de segunda a sexta-feira, das 6 ao meio-dia e das 16 às 19 horas, passava uma receita atrás da outra, enquanto os doentes faziam fila em frente. As operações eram feitas com faca ou canivete, sem anestesia. Nestes momentos Arigó ficava completamente concentrado. Se o doente se agitava, passava a mão na testa, dizendo ou no rei do médico alemão. Quando acabava, a pessoa pagava os remédios e ia embora. E muitos afirmam que foram curados com suas operações.

Curandeiro

Acusado de curandeiro e prática ilegal de medicina, foi condenado e preso. Em 1959 o Supremo Tribunal Federal confirmou a sentença do juiz, condenando Arigó a 16 meses de prisão, por atividades mediúnicas e curandeirismo. Dez meses depois, um indulto assinado por Juscelino Kubitschek conseguiu libertar Arigó, que foi recebido com festa em sua cidade. Em 1963 um novo juiz reabriu o processo. Este processo coincidiu com a condenação do Conselheiro Lafaiete, que o condeu-

nava novamente à prisão. Só não foi preso graças à interferência do Supremo Tribunal Federal, mas continuou vítima da perseguição, sempre afirmando que não era médico, nunca pretendeu ser, e quem fazia as operações era o dr. Fritz.

Motivo de curiosidade e estudo, Arigó foi filmado por médicos americanos em 1968. Esta equipe americana acompanhou durante três dias os processos de cura e operações de Arigó, tomando o pulso dos pacientes, ouvindo as batidas do coração, medindo a pressão arterial e o estado emocional. Realizaram testes com o médium antes e depois de cada operação, isto depois de submeter Arigó a um check-up. Fizeram exames nos pacientes antes e depois de cada operação, compararam os medicamentos com os sintomas, fizeram fichas individuais.

Fraude

Arigó foi acusado de fraude pelo padre jesuíta Quevedo Gonzales, professor de Parapsicologia. Afirmou que o dr. Fritz nunca existiu, pois era apenas mão obra nos seus males médicos da Primeira Guerra. Afirmou inclusive que Arigó havia matado muita gente com suas operações e que suas curas e operações passavam da mais erram de suas manifestações da mão existir de sua influência do espírito do médico alemão.

O padre Quevedo concluiu sua acusação dizendo que todos os homens têm poderes parapsicológicos, que tornam possíveis a telepatia, a percepção cega, a levitação e até a realização de operações médicas sem instrumentos cirúrgicos e à distância.

Maravilha

Os cientistas americanos, entretanto, chegaram a classificar Arigó como a "oitava maravilha do mundo", atestando seus poderes mediúnicos. Os americanos estudaram os fenômenos de Arigó durante cinco anos, tentando encontrar uma resposta científica para as curas que ele fazia. Fizeram cinco viagens, sempre trazendo instrumentos diferentes, e examinaram cerca de quatro mil pacientes, verificando que o diagnóstico estava de acordo com o que Arigó dizia.

E ficaram surpresos ao ver diagnósticos feitos por Arigó, que só poderiam ser revelados com Raios-X. Lamentaram

o desprezo dos médicos, reconhecendo o poder espiritual de Arigó.

A pintora russa

Em 1969 Arigó curou uma pintora russa, Olga Tuszarewsky, que vendo uma fotografia sua num jornal americano resolveu vir ao Brasil para curar uma série de doenças que a atacavam e já começavam a impedir suas viagens. Arigó lhe receitou um quilos de remédio, entre injeções, drogas e pílulas, que lhe custaram Cr$ 600,00. A pintora foi embora de Congonhas em novembro se dizendo totalmente curada e que tinha vindo ao Brasil somente para conhecer "o mago de Congonhas, que tinha o maior respeito por sua obra humana".

Nem santo nem sábio

O próprio Arigó explicou suas curas não como milagres, mas como resultado da força dos doentes em relação à cura. Para ele, uma mente perturbada causa moléstias graves para o corpo. Afastando-se desta perturbação de ordem espiritual pode curar o corpo sem milagres.

— As curas são resultado da fé e do merecimento dos que as recebem. Não acredito que as pessoas venham aqui sem crença, sem religião, sem acreditar na bondade divina. Todos têm Deus no fundo do coração. A verdade é que os tempos são chegados e tentar conhecer e realizade com a capa da parapsicologia, apenas porque não a querem enfrentar, é um caso, um expediente do avestruz. Não adianta nada.

O diagnóstico não era feito por Arigó e sim pelo dr. Fritz, que realizava um trabalho acompanhado de Raios-X. Enquanto o médium alemão fazia a operação, uma chapa de radiografia aparecia na mesa. Arigó explicou que ele verdade havia uma equipe de quatro médicos da qual ele estava em quarto lugar.

— Não me considero perseguido, com tôda a certeza me faltam méritos para tanto, pois a verdade histórica é que foram perseguidos todos aqueles que ousaram pregar a verdade e verdade em contraposição aos conceitos de suas épocas. É isto é válido para a religião, a moral ou a ciência. Citações seriam odiosas. O próprio Cristo não fugia à regra.

Page 1 of a Rio de Janeiro paper, January 12, 1971, the day after Arigo was killed. His death was front page news all over Brazil.

Tarcesio, Arigo's son, at his father's grave two years after his death.

Arlete de Freitas, Arigo's widow, in center of family group, including three of his sons.

the reality of Ze Arigo's healings, but told t
major investigation was necessary to verify t
stories that were emanating from the village
has. He had insisted that Arigo had to be
believed, that no amount of description could
power and force of the man.

They had also encountered John Laurance in Rio, a
systems engineer in RCA's space program, and an
executive who had served on the advisory committee in
setting up NASA. Laurance had been discovering that not
only Arigo was worthy of a full-scale investigation, but
the entire Brazilian healing scene, with its unorthodox
use of the paranormal in both surgery and medicine.

These leads, among others, tempered the exhaustion
from the long drive and held the promise of an
illuminating discovery, if indeed the facts did check out.
When the microbus finally did limp into the narrow,
twisting streets of Congonhas late on the night of August
21, 1963, the search for bed and shelter overrode any
thought of scientific discovery. In the dark, the
surpassing beauty of the little plateau town was nowhere
evident; all they could find was a small, scrubby *pension*
on a cobbled street. But at least there was a cubicle and
bed for each, and the anticipation of encountering a
strange unknown quantity on the following day.

Congonhas do Campo sits in a crease of the plateau
mountains of the state of Minas Gerais. Except when the
towering thunderheads split open and release a cascade
of water, when rivers become swollen and angry, the
climate is fresh and stimulating. Nearly half of the
world's gold came from Minas Gerais in colonial times;
diamonds and semiprecious stones match the lure of its
rich iron ore today. With the mountains rimming
Congonhas, the sun comes up later and goes down
earlier, leaving ample room for the atmosphere of
mysticism that abounds all through Minas Gerais.

Out of this mysticism grew the works of sculpture

iich today draw visitors to Congonhas from over the world—the twelve Biblical prophets of Aleijadinho. Exquisitely carved from soapstone in the eighteenth century, they stand like life-size sentinels surrounding the high terrace of the Church of Bom Jesus, overlooking the village and gazing outward over sweeping distant vistas. Aleijadinho had been crippled with leprosy, but he had chipped away at the stone with tools strapped to his withered stumps of arms. Yet the precision of his works is magnificent and emotionally overpowering. Some call them minor miracles. Over sixty life-size figures of Christ and the Crucifixion, carved from cedar, are housed in small chapels in the hilly garden of the church. Both the wooden and stone statues are so vivid and lifelike that they have a profound effect on villagers and tourists.

On the bright, newly washed morning that followed their long trip, Belk and Puharich and their interpreters rose with the sun and prepared to find the strange peasant that had brought them so many miles. Reports had been that Arigo began work early. They were directed to the narrow cobblestone street called Rua Marechal Floriano, barely wide enough for a car to squeeze by. The town was just beginning to stir. A gaucho passed them on horseback, a riderless mule behind him. The man nodded in a friendly Brazilian way and continued on with only a casual backward glance at the two Americans.

They found Arigo's small "clinic" on a corner, a modest, undistinguished one-story cement building. Already over fifty people were waiting expectantly in the street, although the clinic had not opened yet. The town was bisected by a small, muddy river, where swarms of vultures were feasting on some undiscernible carrion. Beside it, the visitors found an open restaurant, not particularly appetizing, but serviceable in the face of morning hunger.

Having reached their destination after so long and arduous a trip, Belk and Puharich were less than elated; doubts continued to set in. They were to be joined that afternoon by Jorge Rizzini, a journalist and documentary film producer from São Paulo, who had been among the first to bring Arigo to the attention of the country. Rizzini, who was convinced of the validity of Arigo's work from his former visits to Congonhas, was most eager to establish objective scientific verification.

He had color motion pictures of several of the major operations Arigo had performed. These films were of extreme importance to Belk and Puharich's investigation, because they had learned on arrival in Brazil that both the Brazilian medical society and the Catholic Church were pressing a lawsuit against Arigo—not only for the illegal practice of medicine but for witchcraft as well. Reports were that Arigo was being extremely cautious about major surgery in the face of the legal charges. Rizzini, who was highly recommended to the Americans as a stable and level-headed journalist, had another qualification of major interest: his wife had been cured of crippling arthritis by Arigo; his daughter of leukemia. He would, they learned, be able to document this in great detail.

By seven in the morning there were nearly two hundred people in the streets as the doors to the strange clinic—a dilapidated former church—were opened. An old blind man, propping himself up with his cane; a slender, aristocratic woman of about forty, in a flowered print dress; a pale, thin man with an enormous goiter; a wan child in a wheelchair; a stout, busty black woman, holding her eyes with a handkerchief. They and the multitude behind them stood mutely in the line that now wound around the corner and all along the cobblestones of Rua Marechal Floriano. Most were from other parts of Brazil or South America, having come by bus or train or auto.

The word had obviously gone around the village that the research team had arrived, although the Americans had not announced their visit in advance. As the four men approached the door, they were unceremoniously waved ahead of the patients into the clinic by a soft-spoken black man named Altimiro. Inside was a powerful, barrel-chested man in a dark sport shirt and slacks, and muddy shoes. He had a thick black mustache, a generous crop of equally black hair, a bronzed face, and striking, penetrating eyes. He appeared unshaven and rustic. There was little need to ask who this was; it was Arigo. He greeted them warmly, as if he already knew where they were from and why they were there.

Far from mystical in appearance, he looked like a cross between a congenial truck driver and a local politician—which Puharich later learned was one of Arigo's consummate ambitions. In this Arigo was hampered, however. He had never gone beyond third grade.

They could stay and observe as long as they wished, he told Belk and Puharich through the interpreters, and were free to interview any of the patients and to ask any questions. In his early forties, Arigo seemed so burly, normal, and friendly that the Americans were taken slightly aback. After the initial shock, they leaned against the rough plaster wall and watched the patients move hesitatingly into the building, single file.

Inside the door was a large, barnlike room with pale lime-green plaster walls and a tile floor of geometric black and white design. There were rough wooden benches around the walls, and several rows in the center of the room, arranged like church pews. Lonely and despondent, the group moved silently to the wormy benches, then lined themselves against the wall when the benches were filled. The room, dark and musty, and now crowded, was framed by several doorways. One led to a room with two or three cots in it; it was unoccupied. Another led to the cubicle where Arigo worked. It held only a chair and a crude wooden table. Behind them was a picture of Christ, with a crucifix on the wall nearby.

On the walls also were several crude, hand-printed signs. A large one, stroked with black crayon letters on a crumpled piece of brown paper, read:

THINK AND OBSERVE THE OTHERS'
SILENCE, FAITH, AND DEVOTION

Smaller signs beneath it read:

DON'T LEAN AGAINST THE WALL

THINK OF JESUS

WAIT IN AN ORDERLY MANNER

To Puharich, there was something strange and unreal
about the atmosphere, almost as if he were watching a
scene from *Twilight Zone*. There seemed to be a mood of
quiet chaos in the rooms, an air of both expectancy and
despair. By now, the interpreters had passed along the
news that the gossip in the line had been all about the
"Americano doctor" who was here to watch. Several
patients glanced uneasily in Puharich's and Belk's
direction.

In a few moments, Arigo stepped to the center of the
room. He spoke Portuguese in a rough, peasant accent.
Softly, the interpreters translated what he said.

It was not he, Arigo told the gathering, but Jesus who
brought about the cures. He said that he knew the
anguish of the paralytics and the despair of the ill. He
pointed out that each man has his own religion and that
he did not want to know the conviction of any man.

"All religions are good," he said. "Is this not true?"

There was a murmur of agreement. Then he went on to
denounce the fetishes and incantations of Quimbanda,
one of Brazil's primitive ritualistic sects. This was not a
true religion, he told them, and could never be
considered as such. Whatever he was, the husky, dark-
haired Arigo was firm and positive in his convictions,
with a unique magnetism.

In the next moment, he was off on a sustained tirade
against smoking and alcohol. There was no ambiguity in

his disdain of these practices. He spoke gruffly, angrily, revealing several quirks and prejudices as he did so. Drinking and gambling, he was saying, were the curse of men, along with lying and cheating. But for women, smoking was the heinous crime—sufficient, perhaps, to justify a husband taking another woman.

Then, in his strange, mercurial way, he joked with the people for a moment; abruptly he became serious again as he led them in a recital of the Lord's prayer.

As he did so, the conviction that they had come to Congonhas on a wild goose chase grew in the minds of both Belk and Puharich. As moving and poignant as the scene was up to this moment, it was hardly a jump-off point for a scientific investigation. Arigo, his hands clasped and head lifted as he said the prayer, seemed more a small-town preacher at a tent meeting in the Bible belt than a phenomenon that had excited so much interest in all of Brazil and most of South America.

The prayer finished, Arigo turned quickly and went into his cubicle, closing the door after him. Some of the patients shifted uneasily on the benches; others went into whispered conversations. Two assistants, youthful dark-skinned girls, moved about the room quietly checking the order in which the patients would line up along the wall, facing them toward the small barren room where Arigo would begin his consultations at his table.

In a corner of the large outside room, a soft-spoken male assistant with soft, sad eyes sat at an ancient typewriter, waiting for the morning's activities to start. His function was not yet clear to the Americans. Nor did they know what quite to expect as far as Arigo was concerned. He had entered the small room alone. But in moments, he came back out of it, briskly.

He seemed to be totally a different person. He held his head high, almost arrogantly. His eyes, very burning and penetrating before he entered the room, were now radiantly piercing, but at the same time withdrawn, almost as if they were out of focus. They glistened in the dim light of the room. Now he spoke sharply, like a Prussian officer. The interpreters noted a thick German accent in his Portuguese, harsh and guttural.

Arigo pointed to another sign on the wall, which read: NO ONE WILL BE TAKEN CARE OF TODAY WHO HAS TAKEN ANY ALCOHOLIC DRINK. COME BACK TOMORROW WITHOUT ANYTHING TO DRINK.

Then, imperiously, he walked over to Puharich and Belk. "Come," he said, and led them through the now-open door of his treatment room. The attendants moved the line of patients up, along the wall of the big room and into the smaller one, where the first dozen patients took their positions. Arigo summarily ordered the two Americans to stand by the table. "There is nothing to hide here," he said. "I am happy to have you watch. I must assure you that what I do is safe—and that the people who are ill become well." He said this with the great confidence of a Prussian general, quite out of character with his former rural bearing.

Suddenly and without ceremony, he roughly took the first man in line—an elderly, well-dressed gentleman in an impeccable gray sharkskin suit, firmly grasped his shoulders, and held him against the wall, directly under the sign THINK OF JESUS. Puharich, standing next to the man, was startled by the action, wondered what to expect next. Then, without a word, Arigo picked up a four-inch stainless steel paring knife with a cocobolo-wood handle, and literally plunged it into the man's left eye, under the lid and deep up into the eye socket.

In spite of his years of medical practice and experience, Puharich was shocked and stunned. He was even more so when Arigo began violently scraping the knife between the ocular globe and the inside of the lid, pressing up into the sinus area with uninhibited force. The man was wide awake, fully conscious, and showed no fear whatever. He did not move or flinch. A woman in the background screamed. Another fainted. Then Arigo levered the eye so that it extruded from the socket. The patient, still utterly calm, seemed bothered by only one thing: a fly that had landed on his cheek. At the moment his eye was literally tilted out of its socket, he calmly brushed the fly away from his cheek.

As he made these motions, Arigo hardly looked at his subject, and at one point turned away to address an assistant while his hand continued to scrape and plunge without letup. In another moment, he turned away from the patient completely, letting the knife dangle half out of the eye.

Then he turned abruptly to Puharich and asked him to place his finger on the eyelid, so that he could feel the point of the knife under the skin. By this time, Puharich was almost in a state of shock, but he did so, clearly feeling the point of the knife through the skin. Quickly, Puharich asked one of the interpreters to ask the patient what he felt. The patient spoke calmly and without excitement, merely stating that although he was well aware of the knife, he felt no pain or discomfort.

Arigo, still speaking in a harsh German accent, told them that he often used this technique as either a diagnostic tool or for eye operations. To Puharich, this violated every medical technique he had known in his twenty years of experience since studying medicine at Northwestern. For Belk, who had studied psychology at Duke, the procedure was simply inconceivable. He felt limp and slightly nauseated.

Within a few moments, Arigo withdrew the paring knife from the eye, bringing out with it a smear of pus on the point. He noted it with satisfaction, then unceremoniously wiped the knife on his sport shirt and dismissed the patient. "You will be well, my friend," he said. Then he called the next patient. The entire "examination" had taken less than a minute.

The scene began moving so swiftly that neither Puharich nor Belk had time to collect his thoughts. Puharich was at least able to think fast enough to stop the first patient and make a quick examination of his eye.

There was no laceration, no redness, no sign of irritation. The patient explained through the interpreter that he felt altogether normal, that he had had no anesthesia beforehand, and that he had complete faith in Arigo. By now the second patient had been passed through Arigo and was headed toward the assistant and his typewriter in the corner of the larger room, carrying a slip of paper with some sort of prescription scrawled on it.

Puharich and Belk watched incredulously as the people moved up in line to the table, rich and poor, of all ages. Arigo would barely glance at them. For most, his hand began almost automatically scribbling a prescription at incredible speed, as if his pen were slipping across a sheet of ice. Occasionally he would rise, place a patient against the wall, wipe the paring knife on his shirt again, drive it brutally into a tumor or cyst or another eye or ear, and remove whatever the offending tissue was, in a matter of seconds.

There was no anesthesia, no hypnotic suggestion, no antisepsis—and practically no bleeding beyond a trickle. They did not observe Arigo's reported ability to make blood stop on verbal command. But they noted that he rarely asked a question of a patient; his diagnosis was wordless and immediate. In the speed and confusion of the first scores of patients on that morning, Puharich was content simply to watch and observe.

Obviously, there was much checking to be done. These prescriptions—what were they? How could Arigo write them so fast, barely looking at the paper, never taking time to analyze either the prescription or the patient? How could he possibly get the alleged miraculous results, when he spent so little time with each patient? How could the assistant read the hopeless scrawl on the plain sheet of paper to translate it for the pharmacist? Where had Arigo learned his pharmacology? How could he expect to arrive at a rational therapy without an examination of the patient or without even asking questions? How could a patient feel no pain when a paring knife was brutally pushed into one of the most sensitive and painful areas of the body—the eye? These questions would have to be suspended until full and incisive study could be made.

It seemed that Arigo averaged less than a minute for each patient. Arigo, obviously with tongue in cheek, insisted that whatever surgical work he would be doing at this time was merely an examination. He was actually under court injunction not to operate.

Recalling the scene later, Puharich said: "It was the first time in my life when I've seen a scene like this. Where, one minute from the time a patient steps up, until the time he leaves, he either receives a prescription or an actual operation, and walks out without any pain or disablement. Arigo never said much of anything. It was like a nightmare. Belk and I were looking at each other, speechless. We really felt we were in a science fiction atmosphere. Belk, who wasn't a medical man, finally had to walk out of the room. I continued watching. It sort of piles in on you. These people step up—they're all sick. One had a big goiter. Arigo just picked up the paring knife, cut it open, popped the goiter out, slapped it in her hand, wiped the opening with a piece of dirty cotton, and off she went. It hardly bled at all.

"But there was no opportunity to follow up anything at this time. He was working so fast that it was impossible to catch a patient before they stepped up. You were afraid to talk to any of them immediately afterward, because you didn't want to miss anything coming up. This first exposure to this man was almost too much to comprehend."

By eleven that morning, Arigo had treated some two hundred patients. A dozen or so he sent away, summarily, gruffly telling them that any ordinary doctor could handle their complaints. Others he scolded or chided. There had already been about ten eye and ear surgery cases. Each operation averaged only half a minute.

The surgery routine was almost always the same. The swift, almost brutal plunge of the paring knife. The violent and apparently careless maneuvering of the blade under the eyelid, or whatever part of the body he was working on, the casual wiping of the blade on his shirt.

In no case was there any preoperative procedure—no anesthesia, no sterile precautions, no hypnotic suggestion whatever. The patients stood by the wall, fully conscious, and walked out of the room without assistance. Puharich was watching carefully for hypnosis; it could at least explain part of the procedure. But there was no evidence of it. If anything, Arigo himself seemed to be in a trance state. This, Puharich and Belk later surmised, might account for the strange explanation they had heard in their earlier inquiries about Arigo, before they left Rio. It was alleged that Arigo claimed he incorporated the spirit of a deceased German doctor, whom he identified as Dr. Adolpho Fritz. It was Dr. Fritz, Arigo claimed, who did the operating and the prescribing of the complex pharmaceutical agents he wrote so swiftly. It was Dr. Fritz, a German physician who had died in 1918, who provided the instantaneous diagnoses.

Both Belk and Puharich, with their interest and experience in exploring the paranormal, were at least willing to examine this bizarre explanation with an open mind. On this day, not even the incredible objective evidence of Arigo's prowess could be adequately assessed. The facts that were piling up in chaotic profusion revealed one certainty: that Arigo was violating every rational procedure of medicine and surgery. And it was becoming evident that only the most extensive, lengthy study and technical evaluation could create an intelligent appraisal of that. The exotic and ephemeral concept of some sort of benign possession by a deceased German physician was too incredible to even consider at this time.

Promptly at eleven, Arigo rose from his small chair by the wooden table and declared the session at an end. He would be returning, he explained in his rough German accent, at two until six that afternoon. For those patients he was unable to see at that time, he would start again at eight in the evening and continue until all patients were taken care of, regardless of the time.

He invited the two Americans and their interpreters to accompany him as he strode across the large room, washed his hands in a small basin, and put on a jacket. He would be going to his regular job, he explained, a job with the government and social-security office, known by the acronym IAPETC. If the Americans wished, he indicated, they could go there with him, and he'd be glad to give them further information.

Without ceremony, he led them around the corner and down the cobblestone street toward the state welfare office. It was an omnibus health-and-welfare installation. There were pension records, small medical and dental offices, a line of people waiting for unemployment compensation, and the musty atmosphere of bureaucratic confusion. His jacket was unpressed and well-worn. He was still rough and unshaven, yet he carried himself with what seemed to be enormous energy and dignity. But now the German accent had left him. He spoke with the hearty, gusty crudeness of a First Avenue bus driver who affectionately cajoles, curses, and jokes with his passengers on his daily run.

Arigo was the receptionist. He directed the people to the various departments of the office, verbally whipping them at one moment, comforting them in another. His paramedical self had left him completely, but he still remained an imposing man. The people in line, poor and subdued, seemed to find affection and warmth in him, in spite of his gruffness. To the Americans, he was more of a riddle than ever. His personality change, from the moment he had left the clinic and gone to his job, was startling. His Prussian stiffness had given way to an earthy amiability. His eyes had lost some of the strange luster that had marked him as he worked with the patients in his clinic. He invited the Americans and their interpreters to go through the welfare office, make themselves at home.

They did so. Puharich was particularly interested in getting a playback from the dentist and doctor on duty there. Certainly, these professional men would have to have some sort of concrete opinions about this strange phenomenon who was in fact invading their professional field, and apparently attracting an avalanche of people into the village in direct competition with them.

The government dentist was most amiable about Arigo. He commented on how well liked he was around the town, how well he did his job for the welfare office, how much the people who came there enjoyed his kindness and jokes and good humor. He seemed indifferent to Arigo's separate medical activity, shrugging it off with a gesture of puzzlement. The pension-department physician was not much more eloquent. He also shrugged, and indicated that Arigo did his thing, and he did his own. He did acknowledge that he knew of no one who had been harmed by Arigo, and that the number of people from all over South America who came to see him was phenomenal.

His office hours at the welfare office were strange in North American terms. He worked from eleven in the morning until one. Then he began again at four, and continued until six. Arigo invited all four of his visitors to have lunch with his family, an invitation quickly accepted. His house, on the Rua Marechal Floriano, reflected a state of near-poverty, but in spite of flaking plaster and shoddy furniture, it was clean and neat. Arlete, his wife, was slim and smiling, rustling her five boys about the house, handsome boys all of them, with the same striking, deep-brown eyes of their father. She was wearing hair rollers, unselfconsciously.

Arigo kissed her affectionately, and they all sat down at a rough table, Arlete squeezing four extra places among the boys. The lunch was simple—beans and rice and some stringy chicken—but there was plenty of it. Arigo ate heartily, laughing, joking with the boys, clearing his plate in moments. Almost automatically, Arlete refilled it, and pressed more food on the visitors.

Studying the scene, Puharich could find nothing to suggest anything extraordinary about the man or his family. The wife was devoted, the boys lively, intelligent, well-mannered. The atmosphere was confused, but congenial and affectionate. Arigo had shelved whatever mystical qualities he had demonstrated with his patients. Puharich's thoughts kept going back to the inexplicable events of the morning: the surgery without anesthesia, bleeding, or pain; the incredible speed with which the man worked; the lack of fear in the patient as a sharp knife went into his eye. Somehow, he was thinking, he would have to find a way to prove to both himself and his medical colleagues back in the States that the whole thing was not a hallucination.

When Jorge Rizzini, the journalist, arrived that evening, part of the problem would be solved, because he was bringing a motion picture camera. Belk was already preparing his own still camera equipment, a step he had postponed during the morning session until he got more used to the bizarre events that occurred in such swift succession.

But would film be enough to convince the skeptics? Still pictures could of course be easily rigged; they would not be able to persuade a hard-core skeptic. Motion pictures are almost impossible to fake convincingly, therefore they were most important. Puharich would have to count on Rizzini for that part of the process; he hoped he would do well.

After lunch Arigo rested, but by two in the afternoon he was back in his barren little room at the clinic, where the line had formed again. Some of the new patients had arrived by chartered bus from Argentina. Again, the unbelievable procedure began and continued. Arigo was back in his trancelike state, with the strange glowing look in his eyes and the same thick German accent that had been shed during the routine of his regular job and at home. He continued to use his dirty knife, continued to wipe the wounds with dirty cotton, continued to airily dismiss the patient with no sutures, continued to write his prescriptions with astounding speed.

The interpreters were interviewing as many patients as possible. But this procedure was too slap-dash to make an intelligent assessment. The irrationality of the scene continued to be overpowering to both Puharich and Belk.

"There was one patient I remember," Puharich recalls, "who was hanging around all day. He was barefoot and had been in a wheelchair, and it seemed that he had a job as an auto mechanic. He simply came there and hung around, although he no longer needed the wheelchair.

"We asked him through the interpreters just why he was doing this, and he explained that he had been in the Brazilian brigade in the Allied army in Italy during World War II. He had been wounded, and received injuries to both knees. He couldn't describe technically what happened, but his knees had locked up, frozen on him. He had had something like thirteen operations since the war. He said he had heard about Arigo and came to him.

"Arigo had looked at him, and very roughly said: 'What the hell are you doing in the wheelchair, you bum?' Arigo was never reluctant to swear at people when the occasion seemed to demand it. The man had said: 'I can't walk. My knees are locked.' Arigo answered: 'You're a rotten, lazy bum. Get up and walk!' The man protested that he couldn't. Arigo repeated his demand. The guy had no choice. He got up and started walking across the room. Arigo never touched him. The man couldn't believe it had happened. But he was scared to death the condition might return, so he continued hanging around, just to play it safe.

"I examined the knees, although this is the kind of case that would need intensive study to verify completely.

They were still a little stiff, and you could see the multiple scars from the many operations he had had. But he was able to move with considerable freedom. This was the kind of case I would be looking for when we returned with full diagnostic equipment and personnel. But at the moment, it was convincing enough to indicate the need for further study."

By the time Jorge Rizzini, the intense, thirty-five-year-old Brazilian journalist, arrived from São Paulo, Puharich had plotted the best possible way for shooting both stills and motion pictures the next day. Unlikely as it was, there was still the possibility of fakery or of simply an unconventional and indiscernible hypnotic technique that might have brought temporary relief to the hundreds of patients that were filing by Arigo each day.

Rizzini, however, was not inclined to go along with this theory. He had experienced two very definitive cases close to home: his wife, who had suffered hopeless arthritis and had been given up by medical doctors; and his daughter, who had been medically assessed as having incurable leukemia. Both had come to Arigo; both had been cured, and the cure confirmed by the same doctors who had given them up. He also told about the daughter of past Brazilian President Juscelino Kubitschek, who had been successfully treated by Arigo for a kidney disorder that had defied conventional treatment in both Europe and the United States.

Rizzini's 8mm Kodak did not have a zoom lens, but it would be adequate to record some of the operations. Puharich and Belk were still concerned about getting enough raw evidence to persuade a representative group of other American doctors to join them in making a thorough study of Arigo. Even with motion pictures of the unconventional operations, there could be enough doubts left to make persuasion difficult. It seemed to be something that had to be seen directly on location to be believed.

All through the next day, they took pictures. Puharich

began to follow specific cases, noting the symptoms before Arigo examined a patient and then recording the prescription or operation. If he were able to organize a new study, he concluded, it would be necessary to involve at least three doctors and several technicians to do the job right. Medical histories would have to be taken in detail, and before the patient got in line, a thorough examination by a qualified physician would have to be made. Some patients brought their past medical records. These would have to be examined and recorded. Another doctor would have to observe the treatment of the patient by Arigo, recording this in full detail while it was being filmed. Another doctor would have to follow up the case immediately afterward. Then, to be complete, consultations would have to be made weeks or months later with the patient's own doctor as to the permanence of any cure and the effectiveness of the prescriptions or operations.

That day, Arigo again stuck to his promise that no one would leave the treatment center uncared for. For the second time in a row, he closed the clinic after one in the morning, but showed little sign of fatigue. Meanwhile, Rizzini had shot considerable color footage; though his lens equipment was skimpy, the film would be sufficient to establish some of the extraordinary qualities of Arigo's surgical prowess.

After the second long night of observation, the two Americans went back to their small *pension* more baffled than ever. Rizzini was more convinced than Puharich or Belk, because he had previous films—made before Arigo was placed under court injunction—of Arigo performing major operations, including the removal of a cancerous uterus. Further, he had his own two cases involving his wife and daughter, which he swore had been medically confirmed.

From what Belk had learned from his wanderings about town, the consensus of the local doctors was, oddly enough, that they generally approved of Arigo even though he put a dent in their practices to some extent.

The priests of two Catholic seminaries in town seemed to have mixed reactions. They more or less tolerated Arigo, who had once, at least, been a strong Catholic. But one priest told Belk that he thought Arigo was in league with the devil and that he hoped the new trial coming up in the near future would forever end his heresies.

Belk could find no evidence whatever that Arigo ever charged anyone for his services, and the word was that if he did charge, he would immediately lose the strange powers endowed by "Dr. Fritz." Belk was also unable to collect any evidence that anyone had been harmed by Arigo's unconventional practices. Both the Brazilian Medical Association and the Roman Catholic Church were pressing hard against Arigo in the court case, and apparently had been scrambling unsuccessfully to find a single case where Arigo had injured someone.

On his iron cot that night in the tiny hotel room, Puharich lay awake, trying to come up with the best way to make a conclusive test of Arigo's ability—one that would be irrefutable as far as modern clinical opinion was concerned. It was obvious that Arigo, as cooperative and unsecretive as he was, would spend little time doing test sequences for the camera or any sort of pure showmanship demonstration, although there was much of the showman in him. Arigo was intent on treating the ill, and seemed to want nothing to interfere.

If Arigo were to be documented properly, there would be a need not only for considerable funding, but for arousing the professional interest of qualified doctors. They would have to be willing to admit the possibility that there was something strange going on here in the field of medicine that was well worth finding out about. Naturally, there would be resistance to such an idea. Puharich had felt it himself on arriving in the village. He still had doubts, but they were fading in the light of Arigo's indefatigable dedication to his patients, most of whom had come miles to see him.

It was during these thoughts that he absentmindedly

scratched his arm—perhaps for a mosquito or flea bite. As he did so, he was reminded of a large and rather annoying but benign tumor on the inside of his right elbow, known as a lipoma. It was not dangerous, and he had had it checked within the last two years by his own doctor, Sidney Krebs, M.D., of New York City.

Medically, a lipoma is a fatty tumor that rolls around freely under the skin when it is examined. While they do not tend to become malignant, lipomas can often be rather large and unsightly. What causes them is really not known. Puharich's tumor had been there for seven years, and measured about half an inch high, half an inch wide, and one and a half inches in length. His doctor had suggested he might have it surgically removed, which, while seldom risky, is rarely an office procedure. Full sterilization is necessary in an operating room, and the usual scrubbing, painting, and draping of the tumor area is practiced.

The surgical procedure involves incision over the fatty tissue, the spreading of the incision with two retractors, and the use of hemostats and cauterizing the blood vessels to check the flow of blood for clear visibility. Usually, another clamp is placed over the tumor itself, and the tumor is cut free with a scalpel. The opening is then sewn up with sutures. Antiseptics and antibiotics, of course, are utilized to prevent infection. Without these, septicemia—blood poisoning—could result.

The average surgeon requires about fifteen to twenty minutes to complete the job. In Puharich's case, the tumor was directly over the ulnar nerve, which controls the movement of the hand. Also, the brachial artery lay nearby, another possible complication. It was for these reasons that Puharich had been hesitant about having the tumor removed, and since it was not incapacitating, he had learned to live with it.

But an inept operation could be incapacitating— permanently. The movement in the fingers could be restricted or totally disabled by damage to the ulnar nerve. A slip that would sever the brachial artery would bring obvious danger.

In other words, the tumor was nothing to take lightly, in spite of its benignity. Speaking of the experience later, Puharich said: "When I felt the lipoma on my arm, lying there in bed, I said to myself: Well, here is a legitimate thing that Arigo could work on. Because I could see by now that you couldn't just play games with him. If he was going to do something, you had to be sick or have something real. I said to myself: This is a good idea. I'll see if he will operate on this, and I'll see what happens. I know what the condition is; I'll see if these people are faking the lack of pain. I'll find out if he really hurts or not. I'll find out firsthand how the process works. If I get infected, I can always be flown down to Rio. I simply could not believe what I was seeing and experiencing with Arigo. Here was one way I could prove to myself and my colleagues that we were not hallucinating."

The decision did not come easily. But it was the one sure way to put Arigo's skills to the test. Puharich would be able to discover just what the lack of anesthesia, antisepsis, and sutures meant firsthand—and whether indeed Arigo was capable of preventing the major flow of blood.

The decision made, he turned over on his side on the shaky iron cot and went to sleep.

2

In São Paulo a group of highly trained physicians and surgeons from the city's largest hospital—some of them graduates of the best medical schools in the United States —meets regularly to consult mediums. These mediums, they believe, draw on the skills and knowledge of doctors no longer living to bring them diagnostic and treatment information they could get nowhere else. The doctors claim that the clinical and therapeutic results are amazingly effective, and far beyond what modern medical techniques alone could produce.

These sessions are conducted *not* in an aura of mysticism, but in an atmosphere of pragmatism. The doctors of Kardecist persuasion do not believe that the use of trained mediums replaces skilled medical training; they believe it supplements it. Their rationale for the use of these methods springs from the theory that the swift advance of medical science left large pockets of unexplored truths in its wake. More specifically, the feeling is that the primitive witch doctor or medicine man, in spite of his wild gyrations and mysterious herbs, exercised some highly effective techniques that were discarded by materialistic science only because they were surrounded by such a large envelope of superstition and hideous black-magic rituals.

There is much evidence to support this theory. Many

great modern tranquilizers such as reserpine (sold under many trade names) long lay dormant in modern pharmacology; the Indian snakeroot plant, from which reserpine derives, known as *Rauwolfia serpentina*, had been used effectively in India and Nigeria for centuries. Curare, one of the most effective adjuncts in modern anesthesia, is a resinous poison derived from several varieties of tropical plants. The Brazilian Indians used the poison on the tips of arrows. Scientists at the University of Ibadan in Nigeria have recently crystallized an herb concoction from a witch doctor that seems to have an amazing capacity to bring about remission in malignant tumors. Initial tests now being conducted at the university have shown it to bring 100 percent remission of such tumors in laboratory mice. For the first time in history, the ancient techniques of acupuncture are being taken seriously by science.

But most interesting are the recent studies at the same university regarding the methods that the Nigerian witch doctors have been using in psychosis. The new studies have uncovered considerable validity in this primitive tribal psychiatry, some of which seems destined to find its way into modern therapeutic use. A critical aspect of witch-doctor psychotherapy lies in the acceptance of the once-scorned concept of "possession," the taking over of the psyche of a living individual by an alleged deceased personality.

In Brazil, the picture is slightly different. The Kardec movement was brought there from France by intellectuals. Its first adherents in the mid-1800s were attorneys, doctors, army officers, scientists, engineers, people from the creative arts, and educators. The movement was paralleled among the less educated bulk of the population by the strange mixture of African religious culture and enforced Catholicism, which ranged from the primitive rites of Quimbanda in macumba clearings to the less primitive mixture of Catholicism and Yoruba tribal beliefs called Umbanda. Both grew out of the early days of Brazilian slavery, both embraced the belief in spirit possession and magical rites. Umbanda, however, more softened by the Christian ethic and embracing both Catholic and tribal saints, rejected black magic as part of its creed. Quimbanda did not. Both forms were "spiritist" in character.

The result of all this has left modern Brazil with three strata of spiritist belief, from the primitive Quimbanda through the more refined Umbanda to the intellectually elegant Kardecists. And although Catholicism claims an enormous percentage of all these groups, the reality is that it has had to compromise and look the other way as far as their spiritist practices are concerned.

This was the ambience that Puharich and Belk faced in their expedition to Congonhas do Campo. Neither knew exactly what to expect, but Puharich remained firm the next morning in his resolve to let Arigo operate on him.

At breakfast Puharich told the others about his decision. They were surprised, and there was considerable concern. Belk, who had a pinched-nerve condition in the small of his back, said he was willing to try some of Arigo's medication—but surgery, that was a different thing. Puharich, however, was determined, and the group made their way to Arigo's clinic for the third straight day.

The preparations for filming had already been made. Belk had a Polaroid camera with black-and-white film. One of the interpreters had a Minox B camera with the same type of film. Rizzini was prepared with his 8mm Kodak motion picture camera, loaded with Kodak II color film. The other interpreter would handle the lighting.

Puharich had also decided to ask Arigo to perform on him the eye "examination" with the kitchen knife, which seemed to be one of his specialties. With Puharich's two tests recorded on film, the capacities of Arigo would be clearly confirmed—either for better or for worse.

They approached Arigo, and Puharich asked through the interpreter if he would be willing to undertake the surgery on the arm and the eye probe. The request, overheard in the crowded room, brought silence to the patients gathered there, and an air of expectancy. The "Americano" doctor was now about to become one of them. Arigo threw back his head and laughed, and said of course he would do so. Then he turned abruptly to the crowd, and said, "Has anybody here got a good Brazilian pocketknife to use on this Americano?"

This brought Puharich up short, but he could not turn back now. Half a dozen pocketknives were offered almost immediately from among the patients. The atmosphere was almost carnival-like. Belk found it hard to continue looking at the scene. He fingered his Polaroid nervously.

Arigo studied the knives critically. They were a variegated collection, some of them looking dull and rusty. He rejected several, then finally selected a Brazilian version of a Swiss army knife.

As the interpreter translated, Arigo spoke in his bluff and hearty way. "The American scientist has courage," he said good-naturedly. "He deserves an audience. I am going to demonstrate to this materialist what a spirit can produce. But he is right, my brothers. A scientist has to take all kinds of chances. Pasteur—didn't he take a chance with microbes? That is what a good scientist does. Not the scientists who are afraid to come here to Congonhas. But now we'll demonstrate something he has never seen in the United States."

The preamble was characteristic of Arigo's rough rural style, but was hardly reassuring.

"We'll do the arm first," Arigo said. "Just roll up your sleeve, Doctor." The action was moving so fast now that Puharich turned quickly to check the camera setup. Rizzini was already lining up his motion picture camera; Belk and the one interpreter seemed to be set with their still cameras. All three were now considerably tense and nervous. The operation was a one-shot take. There could be no such thing as a retake, and Puharich was as apprehensive about this as he was about the operation. He instructed the other interpreter to bounce the battery light off the ceiling, to prevent burning the image in the lens. Then he turned back and prepared to watch Arigo make the incision.

But Arigo instructed him to look the other way, and, it had become obvious, when Arigo commanded, it was useless to argue with him. Puharich obliged, again checking and directing the cameras and lighting.

In considerably less than thirty seconds—some of the others said it was less than ten—Puharich felt something wet slapped in his hand, along with the pocketknife itself. He looked down and saw the bloody form of the lipoma and the knife Arigo had used to extract it. On his arm, where the tumor had been, there was a small slit, with a trickle of blood dripping down from it, but very little, considerably less than two inches. The skin area was flat; there was no longer the bulge of the tumor.

Puharich was stunned. There had been no pain whatever in the arm. He had felt only a slight, vague sensation. The others had watched with incredulity. Just before the operation, Rizzini had started his camera rolling. It continued to roll all through the process and afterward. Arigo had taken the knife, seemed to scrape it over the skin, and within seconds, had pulled out the lipoma with his hands. It was totally alien to any surgical procedure.

Arigo smiled, and said to Puharich that Dr. Fritz had told him to say: "This is a demonstration only—so that people will believe. I think every doctor in Brazil should come here and do what you have done. After the legal process against me, you must come back, Dr. Puharich, and I will do major surgery for you."

Puharich, in one sense, felt vaguely unsatisfied. "I experienced absolutely zero. I couldn't believe this had happened, yet it had, and there was no mistake about it," he said later. He immediately asked for the knife-in-the-eye procedure, but Arigo told him he had enough for the day. "Besides, you have nothing wrong with your eye," he added.

Belk, in the meantime, was taking the Polaroid film out of the camera, the shot he had made at the moment of the incision. But it was badly overexposed. The interpreter with the Minox camera had frozen in fear at that moment, and had forgotten to snap the picture. Only Rizzini's motion pictures would be able to supply the urgently needed documentation of the incision—and it would be impossible to know until these were developed on his return to São Paulo. Both "before and after" still and motion pictures of the area of the forearm had been taken in profusion, so at least these steps in the procedure would be well documented.

There was another test factor in prospect that would be of major significance. Arigo had not washed or disinfected either the skin or the knife. The entire area was dirty and unsanitary. Septicemia was a distinct possibility under these circumstances unless strong antibiotic treatment was commenced immediately. If, without this, the wound healed cleanly, a further proof of Arigo's powers would be provided. Puharich determined to avoid any use of antiseptics on the wound, and to shun any antibiotics unless the wound became critically infected later. He permitted Altimiro, Arigo's soft-spoken assistant who typed the prescriptions and did sundry dressings of wounds, to tape an unsterile gauze square over the wound.

Puharich now felt that he had gotten over the big hump. He could confirm at least that this was no twilight zone, that it was something very real and valid. With only a pocketknife and a few other instruments, which were kept in what appeared to be a cookie tin, a beat-up fountain pen, and a plain paper tablet, the Brazilian peasant was treating more patients in a day than a great university medical center saw in a week. Whatever he was, Arigo was some kind of undefined medical genius.

Puharich and his interpreter finally cornered Arigo for a serious talk. He asked if any doctors had come to Congonhas and made a serious study of his work. Arigo said that very few had come, and although some had supported his work, the Brazilian Medical Association was dead set against him, as well as the Roman Catholic Church. Arigo deeply regretted the latter, he said, because he had considered himself a devout Catholic, and he still put all his faith in Christ. He took no personal credit whatever for what he did. He added that he wasn't supposed to be doing any operations, that in the past he had done major ones with no reports whatever of death or injury resulting. These he had done publicly. He confessed that if a patient really needed an operation now, he might do it privately, regardless of the legal risk.

When Puharich asked Arigo if it would bother him if he came back with a medical team for some extensive research, Arigo replied that if it were done right, it would help him immeasurably, since no one had ever really validated his work scientifically. Some of his patients had actually been doctors, he said, but they didn't tell anyone out of fear of professional reprisals. He added that he had bishops and nuns and priests who had come to Congonhas for treatment, but that the Church itself remained against him. The government was of course technically against him. It was the public prosecutor for the state of Minas Gerais who was formalizing the charges against him. The lawyers, the judges, the legislators—many of whom came to him for treatment— all were sympathetic, but unable to do much if anything about it because of the Penal Code.

He went on to tell Puharich that he needed public support, and that a formal scientific confirmation of his work might help considerably. With Arigo's cooperation assured, Puharich made a firm resolve to come back to Congonhas as soon as practically possible.

Before they left Arigo, Belk requested and received a prescription for his back condition. To make the "diagnosis," Arigo simply glanced at Belk casually, while his right hand automatically scribbled out a prescription. Altimiro typed it out for him, a task he performed at machine-gun speed.

Puharich found Belk's prescription grossly absurd for a

back condition, and completely irrational from a medical point of view. Further, it called for massive doses which seemed totally out of line. In addition to vitamin B12 capsules, the prescription included Novazolon and Livisym, two digestive enzymes, and Pankreon, a pancreas enzyme. The drugs were trade-name pharmaceutical preparations of Brazilian manufacture, and in normal therapeutic use in the ethical drug field. But the combination simply did not make sense. Belk, however, was willing to take a chance and to give them a try, just as Puharich had done with his surgery. The back condition had not responded to any of the intensive medical treatment Belk had undergone over several years. X rays in the United States had shown a compression of a vertebra in the lumbar area. It would obviously take considerable time before the unconventional prescription could prove itself out—if at all. He was skeptical about possible results.

Whatever explanations there were about Arigo's extraordinary and baffling prescriptions were vague. Patients had reported that the prescriptions worked when they came from Arigo where they would work for no one else. Puharich had made copies of several of them; he would give them thorough study later. No doctor he knew of would offer the prescription Arigo had given Belk for a compressed vertebra. By stretching the imagination, a rationale might be found in the idea that there could be some benefit to the blood and digestive system arising out of the medicines, and therefore the condition in the back might improve with general bettering of the system. But this was a wide stretch of the imagination. The enzyme preparations were not chemical, but natural ferments, and were supposed to give the digestive juices a boost. There was no doubt about it, Arigo's pharmacology was as mysterious as his surgery.

As he packed, Puharich went back over the operation in his mind. Rizzini, whom they were going to meet later in São Paulo to screen the film, had convinced him that removal of the lipoma had taken less than ten seconds. Against the conventional surgery time of fifteen or twenty minutes, this alone was incredible. The film would confirm this—if it came out well. The botching of the still photographs was rankling, but understandable. There had been considerable tension at the time, and several of the patients looking on had actually cried. Anything that Arigo did obviously had the capacity to arouse emotions. Perhaps that was part of his secret.

On reflection, Puharich could recall that the only sensation he had felt was equivalent to a slight pinprick. The incision, he noted, was actually smaller than the lipoma. This was also contrary to surgical routine. Both Belk and Rizzini were able to tell him that it was removed by hand, without any instrument. Belk seemed to think the tumor almost popped out. Beyond the lack of pain and major bleeding was Arigo's method in itself. It would be a rare surgeon who could work at that speed and not do damage to the nerve localized in the area. Arigo seemed to work in blatant defiance of medical precautions—but then again, Arigo had made it plain that he couldn't take any credit for anything. It was all in the lap of Dr. Adolpho Fritz—a deceased German doctor who must have learned a lot of pharmacology and surgical techniques since he died in 1918. It was all too bizarre. Yet the material evidence was there to see; and that fact was irrefutable: Puharich had preserved the tumor, intact, in a glass bottle.

It was also a clear fact that they had been unable to gather any evidence that Arigo received any money or gifts whatever for his services. "He won't even accept a cup of coffee," the mayor of Congonhas had told Belk when he inquired earlier. The mayor, José Theodoria da Cunha, confirmed to Belk what he had heard from some of the local doctors: that nearly everyone in town had nothing but praise for Arigo, including most of the doctors themselves. Mayor Cunha's brother was a physician practicing in Belo Horizonte, the nearest large city, some eighty kilometers away. He had studied in the United States, completing his training at St. Luke's Hospital in Kansas City in 1952. He was baffled by Arigo, but confirmed his work without hesitation.

Musing over the experience with Arigo in his notes, Belk wrote: "Without doubt, he is the busiest and quickest 'doctor' I have ever seen. He outdoes Henry Ford's production line in Detroit. All patients are serious. Some are brought in on stretchers. Lourdes in France would run a poor second, if that. Competition is going to be tremendous in the healing business if Arigo wins his lawsuit . . .

"When Arigo comes to trial for practicing medicine without a license, he will no doubt be guilty, because he has healed thousands. He is permitted to write prescriptions for one and all without control, which amazed us. When Arigo pushed the knife blade in the eye of the first patient, and plunged it behind the eyeball, I was afraid it would pop out completely, aside from the risk of infection, using a kitchen knife.

"I'm leaving my address with Arigo, and have offered to send him a ticket to the United States. To me, he has proved a case. As a taxi driver at the depot told me: 'Sure I know Arigo. I drive down from Belo with them sick, and return with them well.' I believe this hack driver."

On the way to Belo Horizonte that afternoon, skirting over the precipitous roads of Minas Gerais, Belk and Puharich agreed that physicians from America and Europe should come to Congonhas, study the phenomena, and try to explain the process. Just how was another question. Arigo was apparently beyond the accepted limits of parapsychology, to say nothing of medicine. As the tall, white buildings of Belo Horizonte suddenly broke into view over the soft green mountains, both men knew that there was an enormous job to be done, and they would need all the help they could get to persuade, cajole, and convince other researchers that it was worth doing.

At Belo Horizonte, Belk got his strange prescription filled. It cost about fifteen dollars in American money. He felt a little sheepish in taking the medication, and was not able to muster much confidence that it would do any good. On the other hand, the thousands of reports that had been recorded about Arigo's patients suggested that the Brazilian's mystique was much more important than the drugs involved. Was it, then, some rare and undefined placebo effect?

In spite of his wonderment concerning Arigo's painless skill with the pocketknife, Puharich could not help feeling that he was bound to get blood poisoning. He found himself feeling his arm constantly for signs of septicemia, looking for the telltale red streaks, or for any signs of tetanus. But by the next day, the wound was already starting to heal cleanly, with the complete absence of infection. He couldn't pull the wound apart, no pus whatever appeared. He continued to refrain from using any antiseptics on the wound, satisfying himself with changing the bandage.

Neither Puharich nor Belk had the luxury of much free time for setting up the major study they wanted to do. Although the Belk Research Foundation had been founded to unite such fields as biology, medicine, physics, chemistry, and other disciplines in the study of the paranormal, Henry Belk still had his hands full as one of the chief executives of the chain of 350-odd department stores that bore his name all throughout the South. His merchandising work with the Belk stores was demanding, but his consuming interest in parapsychology, which had begun in his studies at Duke, was reflected in his setting up the foundation.

Belk, an alert and outspoken man who speaks with a Southern drawl, had been restless for some years about the lack of progress made in understanding the depth of the human mind and in exploring its full potential. He was intrigued by the new signs beginning to show up in the field of experimental psychology, and the scientific attention just beginning to turn toward the accomplishments of the Eastern mystics who had for centuries demonstrated that they could control involuntary processes of the body, which had previously elicited hardly a glance on the part of modern science. There were vast unexplored areas here, and Belk was impatient to get on with what he felt was a long-neglected job.

He was not by any means inclined to be taken in by pretenders. In fact, in any research program he had sponsored or participated in, he went for the jugular vein in looking for fakery.

He had been looking for trickery in watching Arigo, but had to admit that he could not find it. Puharich had done likewise. In any study of parapsychology, an experienced researcher will as a matter of course check thoroughly on the possibility of fraud. There are too many charlatans in the field to take chances. Any physician who shows even the slightest interest in parapsychology or psychic healing is automatically subject to criticism, a fact that Puharich was well aware of. He had already been subject to his share of it, but was willing to take that for granted, as long as he was sure in his own mind that he couldn't be taken in by trickery or charlatanism.

Puharich was confident that his own scientific training enabled him to make considered judgments on this score. After earning his medical degree at Northwestern, he had done research in physiology in the graduate school there, completed his internship and residency in Oakland, California, and had received a General Foods Corporation research fellowship for experimental electrobiology. He was licensed for the practice of medicine in California, Maine, and New York, with a specialty in internal medicine.

The object of his current medical research was the development of what are called transdermal hearing devices, designed to enable a person suffering from total deafness to receive electric signals transmitted through the skin, which are in turn translated into "words." This and other research in the field of bioengineering expanded his interest in blending this technical work with such fields as telepathy and extrasensory perception. He was frequently asked to present papers to various government and scientific organizations that were making cautious probes into the paranormal, covering such subjects as the biochemical basis for extrasensory perception and the problems of instrumentation and control in this field. His audiences included the Department of Defense, the Medical Research Laboratory of the Army Chemical Corps, the Institute of Radio Engineers, and the Sixth Naval District. To the last group, he had presented a demonstration by Peter Hurkos involving telepathy and clairvoyance.

In addition, he was assisting a cardiovascular research team at New York University in the bioengineering development of electronic and mechanical systems for a ventricular assist program. Both this and the hearing-device project were extremely demanding. But, like Belk, he was convinced that the extraordinary recent developments in the exploration of the mind warranted important study and the sacrifice of personal time to try to advance it.

When Belk and Puharich arrived in São Paulo, the first news they received from Rizzini was that the film had come through with flying colors. The operation, Rizzini told them over the phone, showed up clearly in spite of the skimpy 8mm camera and the unsophisticated lens. In addition, Rizzini had available the previous films he had taken of Arigo, before the legal proceedings had begun against him. During these times, Arigo had done more complex surgery.

The Americans lost no time in going to Rizzini's apartment, where his projector was set up and waiting. They reran Puharich's operation several times.

Puharich studied it intently. If anything, Rizzini had overestimated the length of time from Arigo's incision to the removal of the tumor: it was closer to five seconds, not ten. Instead of a direct surgical incision, Arigo seemed to scrape the blade across the surface of the arm, moving the knife so fast that it was almost impossible to discern exactly how he did it. If the tumor had not completely disappeared from his arm, and if Puharich did not have the lipoma in a bottle, he would almost think it had been sleight of hand—a device that some charlatans in the Philippines had used. Within the brief seconds involved, the lipoma was out, and a thin trickle of blood rolled down the arm.

The film was effective as proof of the event, and it was enough to rule out any possibility of unconscious hallucination, which, of course, had been practically ruled out earlier. What's more, the wound had continued to heal cleanly; no pus formed, no systemic poisoning was evident. Two wildly improbable medical events had taken place: the removal of the tumor and the total absence of infection. There was little doubt that Arigo was involved in an unidentified compartment of medicine that could have profound effects world-wide. The film sequences that followed confirmed this.

In the sequences involving the eye operations, there was no question, as they had also noted in person, that the blade of a sharp knife was scraped down over the open eye, was plunged deeply up into the sinuses, was manipulated with force, was used as a lever to extrude the eyeball partly out of the socket, and that no injury or damage resulted, after careful examination. Under normal conditions, the pain involved would have been literally unbearable. In the film sequences that Rizzini had taken earlier, a cataract was removed in a matter of seconds from a fully conscious, unflinching patient. A later medical examination by a qualified ophthalmologist confirmed the success, Rizzini told them.

Another fully conscious patient was filmed with a large

hydrocele—the painful and alarming condition where a testicle becomes swollen enormously, often doubling, tripling, or to an even greater extent surpassing its normal size. Arigo was seen plunging an enormous syringe into it and draining the fluid into an empty Orange Crush bottle. The fluid quickly overflowed this container, and a large Coke bottle was substituted. All through the process, which is agonizingly painful normally, the patient stood calmly, and even smiled at the camera. When the process was completed, with quarts of fluid removed, Arigo had told the man: "Now you can get married."

Another unusual sequence followed. Arigo operated on a large but relatively uncomplicated abscess on a patient's back. As usual, he plunged the knife in brutally, cut deeply into the flesh of the small of the back—a sector heavily served with blood vessels and therefore inclined to bleed profusely. Very little blood flowed out, but the abscess was drained, and Arigo turned the patient over to Altimiro to complete the draining and extract the remaining matter. Although the patient was totally calm and without pain during the time Arigo was operating, he screamed in pain as soon as Altimiro touched him. In other words, whatever power it was that permitted Arigo to cut painlessly into one of the most sensitive areas of the body, it was apparently not transferable to his assistant.

In spite of the clear evidence in the films, in spite of the preliminary data collected, and in spite of direct observation of literally hundreds of cases by the two Americans, there was still bound to be an uphill battle in soliciting support for the needed future research. The very fact that Arigo claimed to be "incorporated" by the spirit of a deceased German physician was enough to turn off most of the scientists who might be otherwise interested. This bothered Puharich and Belk too, and strained their own credulity. It was incredible enough to accept the documented empirical evidence, without having to consider a concept so foreign to the practical mind that it might shut off intelligent inquiry before it started. And yet this strange claim of spirit "possession" could not be ignored or buried, since Arigo insisted it was not only an integral part of his work, but was the entire essence of his skills and powers. Far from enhancing an explanation of what Arigo did and how he was able to do it, this was a stumbling block. A scientist who stood up before a meeting of a professional organization and began with a statement about Arigo and "Dr. Fritz" would be likely to be laughed off the podium.

Nor was this all. There were reports that other "spirits" entered into establishing Arigo's prowess as a miracle healer. These were even more far-fetched than "Dr. Fritz," and included the spirits of several other deceased surgeons and doctors of various nationalities, along with a thirteenth-century monk. Belk had picked up this information in his research around the town of Congonhas, and he was not at all happy about it. It clouded the main issue: Was Arigo capable of bringing about cures by medicine and surgery that defied the concepts of modern medical science? And if so, how and why? Both he and Puharich were now ready to concede on the first question, but the how and why was obscured, by what appeared to be folklore and mythology, which would not be easily susceptible to current methods of inquiry. Both were willing to concede the potential of paranormal phenomena from their previous study of the subject; but both were wary of the possibility of fakery.

Even more disconcerting had been a discussion with Altimiro concerning another "explanation" for the phenomena. Belk wrote in his notes:

"Now the most interesting point Altimiro said was that Fre Fabiano de Christo (the thirteenth-century monk who was supposed to be one of Arigo's sources of assistance) had a green ray which was the source of the effectiveness of the operations. This negated pain, the necessity for antisepsis, controlled the flow of blood in the operations, etc. This ray was invisible to Puharich and me. For certain, Arigo and his helpers can't explain it and after five years, they take the whole thing for granted. Maybe I need smoked glasses."

Puharich was inclined to table the whole strange concept of Dr. Fritz and his alleged colleagues in favor of concentrating on the empirical medical facts about Arigo. This was a big enough job in itself, without this imponderable complication that seemed to grow out of the Brazilian tradition entrenched in the Kardec philosophy.

When they left São Paulo for Rio, the two American researchers encountered some of the background of this intellectualized form of spiritism. Spiritism differs from spiritualism, in that it emphasizes healing. Spiritualism had been so much in currency in England and the United States in the time of William James, and still continues with less intensity. Adherents of both forms believe that legitimate mediums, or "sensitives," can document cases of telepathy, clairvoyance, and precognition, and, in some cases, communication with the deceased. Further, the spiritists point out, studies of mediums by such responsible researchers as William James, Sir William Crookes, and other scientists of the era had shown that evidence of automatic writing, where the medium becomes an instrument of an alleged deceased spirit, pointed inescapably to their being in communication with what they called the spirit world. The Kardecists of Brazil, including doctors and scientists, were going beyond this. They felt that this paranormal power could be harnessed for medical use, and claimed to have enough real evidence of its effectiveness to bring important medical results in patients that modern medicine could not help.

In Rio, Belk and Puharich explored this prevalent attitude in greater depth, both with John Laurance, the RCA and NASA executive engineer, and Luis Rodriguez, a retired pharmaceutical manufacturer who had turned almost all his time and attention to trying to consolidate modern psychiatry with the best nuggets of truth and technique culled from a careful sifting of primitive psychiatry and medicine. He felt that Freud, Jung, Adler, and the other pioneers had stopped far short of getting at the roots of the real causes of psychosis and neurosis. He would only concede that the theories of Freud's era were valid up to a point.

Rodriguez agreed with Puharich and Belk that ESP and other aspects of mediumship unquestionably exist, but that the vast majority of those calling themselves mediums were either outright frauds or entertaining magicians. The three also agreed that psychic healing existed in various forms, from the time of Jesus and before to the modern psychiatrist in his treatment of psychosomatic disorders. They also agreed on other, more esoteric aspects of parapsychology, but Rodriguez's main point was that this sort of phenomenon was prevalent all throughout Brazil, and that Arigo was only one of many who had displayed similar powers. The others were not quite as dramatic surgically, but nonetheless showed strong evidence of bringing about almost impossible cures in patients given up by doctors.

John Laurance concurred in the assessment of Arigo's near-miraculous surgery. He was also convinced that there was no fakery involved, as had been found in the Philippine healers. But he felt that Arigo should be considered in context with the entire psychic-healing scene that had historically grown up in the ambience of Brazil. After careful study, Laurance had found that it was not possible to deny the reality of results obtained by Kardecist doctors, who, despite their impressive conventional medical training, called on mediums to buttress their diagnoses and treatment.

As a cautious student of psychic phenomena, Laurance was finding that as he learned more about the field, the fanatical, superstitious, and noisy elements became less important, provided that the same cold light of reason he applied in his scientific work was used as a tough screen to filter out the static. His background and experience was highly technical and exacting. Working with advanced space-vehicle systems and the NASA satellite programs allows little room for error, and he brought the same discipline to his investigations of the paranormal.

Laurance was impressed by the fact that the Kardecists in Brazil had established two large hospitals associated with medical schools that enrolled over two thousand students for a four-year course. They combined the study of traditional medicine with the practical use of mediums as an adjunct that could supply therapy that simply was not available in the channels of orthodox medicine. In this way, they found cures that could be obtained in no other way.

One of the techniques employed here was a form of psychic surgery considered more sophisticated than that of Arigo. It employed mediums who claimed they were instruments of a group of deceased doctors and surgeons, just as Arigo claimed. Both, therefore, were following one of the tenets of Allan Kardec which said: *The spiritual world is in constant contact with the material world, each reacting constantly on the other.* Kardec, aware of how difficult this premise would be for the skeptical world to swallow, added: *This is what the spirits themselves have dictated. If your reason says "no," then reject it.*

There were obviously many who did reject it, but in Brazil there were many who did not. They included the educated Kardecists and the untutored masses of Umbandists and Quimbandists. And it was among these adherents, and others willing to experiment when everything else in medicine failed, that the Kardec-trained psychic mediums worked.

Their technique involved surgery on what the Kardecists call the spiritual, or etheric, body. The trained mediums use actual surgical instruments, and the patient is placed on an operating table. All the motions of regular surgical procedure are followed, but no incision is made, because the motions are conducted a few inches from the body of the patient. The scene becomes an exacting pantomime of an operation in a modern hospital. The theory is that the mediums are operating on the spiritual body, which they consider to be very real, and the results will follow in the physical body. An enormous number of successful cases have been verified by responsible doctors, but the concept of psychic surgery is so alien to the average person that the process remains largely unknown in the Western world.

From the North American point of view, the radical nature of the concept is so remote and strange that qualified scientists would quite naturally have dismissed it out of hand. Evidence that the scope of future research would go far beyond Arigo was indicated by the fact that Brazilian Air Force medical doctors were studying another medium in northern Brazil who was performing operations very similar to those of Arigo.

Puharich and Belk were intrigued, but the documentation of Arigo was a massive enough job in itself. Studying Arigo would at least be dealing with actual surgery, even if the underlying cause spun out into the remote unknown. Arigo also provided a clear, single focus for clinical study, as strange as it was. And even here, the problems were monumental. Simply delimiting the extent of the research would be a demanding job. While it would be tempting to extend the research because of what was happening elsewhere in Brazil, it would be simply impractical.

Rodriguez propounded some interesting theories that went beyond the study of Arigo. He felt that the Kardecist concepts, which were basically beyond the mystic-religious beliefs of the past, could be organized and presented in an objective, matter-of-fact manner that would solicit science to assist in making breakthroughs in the nature and mechanics of these esoteric phenomena. As a result, equally new breakthroughs might follow in medicine, electronics, and even economics and politics. As a further result, the basic nature of man might be developed and brought up to the level of his runaway materialistic progress.

Rodriguez was strong on the theory that modern psychiatry had bypassed many truths by ignoring the primitive medicine man's inclusion of the so-called spirit world as far as psychosis and neurosis were concerned. Arigo, by demonstrating what a simple, uneducated peasant could do, symbolized this vacuum in modern research. Rodriguez encouraged Belk and Puharich to follow up strongly, and offered any help he could give them when they returned to Brazil.

The whole complex phenomenon was in the wind almost everywhere in Brazil, and some of it filtering to Europe and North America. But harnessing that wind was another problem. By the time Belk and Puharich were preparing to leave Rio, the press had seized on Arigo's operation on Puharich, and the story was spread across the country in blazing headlines. Arigo, in fact, seemed to rival Pele, the great soccer star, as far as Brazilian press coverage was concerned.

The story of Puharich's operation caused a sensation. It disturbed Puharich and Belk because such sensationalism might turn off the responsible support they needed. It also foreshadowed the problems they might have in returning for more depth research. It wasn't the kind of thing that could be done in a glass cage. A wide press would also be damaging if some of the publicity filtered up to the United States before the facts had been assessed and put in proper perspective.

To harness the research properly, Puharich would have to begin with the concrete and medically recognizable. From there, the exploration would naturally have to travel out of conventional orbit, simply by the nature of what Arigo did. But first things had to come first. One of the basic facts at hand was that when Arigo used a knife on a patient, there was overwhelming evidence, if not proof, that the knife did not hurt. The second basic was that when he cut into the patient's body, the wound did not bleed, or at least stopped bleeding on Arigo's verbal command. The third basic was that the wound from the unsterile knife did not become infected. These were the things that would have to be examined medically from every possible angle. Where the research trail would lead from there was impossible to tell.

In reviewing his notes of both his direct observations and the film sequences, Puharich tried to justify what he saw in line with his medical training. He was thinking specifically of the cataract operations Arigo had performed with such ease and speed, a matter of seconds. In conventional surgery, the patient is completely immobilized under deep anesthesia. Complete scrubbing and sterilization is imperative. The operation—to remove the clouded lens of the eye—under these conditions varies from ten to thirty minutes. Arigo, whose hands and knife worked so fast, seemed to carelessly plunge a blade into the cornea of the eye of a fully conscious patient standing against the wall, and the lens seemed to pop out almost magically. Yet there was no magic or sleight of hand here, because Puharich had examined the patient before, during, and after the process, and verified that the lens of the eye had been removed. The more he reflected on it, the more incredible it was.

Or the hydrocele drainage, which he had seen clearly in the film. Some hydroceles are classified as elephantiasis. This is a chronic condition where the tissues of the scrotum become enormously enlarged as the lymphatic fluid builds up in the sac and doesn't drain away. In some exaggerated cases a wheelbarrow must be used to support the enlarged organ. It is most often caused by a nematode worm called *Wuchereria bancrofti.*

The usual medical practice is to drain the sac with a needle for temporary relief, after anesthetizing the area completely. This is repeated, along with antibiotic medication, as the condition demands. But it does not get rid of the blockage of the lymphatic tubes that caused the condition. In some cases, the testicle must be amputated.

But Arigo drained his cases without anesthesia, and was reported to have brought about permanent cures.

It was this sort of thing, along with the myriad other treatments Arigo used, that would have to be examined and analyzed. By the time Belk and Puharich returned to the United States, Puharich was already blocking out the areas they needed to explore. The entire personal history of Arigo would have to be gathered and studied.

What were the roots of this capacity that enabled Arigo to do what he did? How was his psychological background formed, and what influenced it? What about his early boyhood? What triggered him into launching this unusual career? How could he possibly work so indefatigably, handling hundreds of patients a day? Where did he learn his pharmacology? The "Dr. Fritz" theory was so incredible, it was hard to consider. While Arigo's handwriting was crude, the spelling of the most complex modern pharmaceuticals was correct, from antibiotics to cortisones, from the leading drug manufacturers of the world. And they were written at lightning speed. It was essential that answers to all these questions be found in order to understand the phenomenon.

Belk had his reflections, too. What was most difficult for him was to put what he had observed into the disciplines of parapsychology. But one very real piece of evidence was foremost in his mind: within three weeks after he had started taking the medically irrational prescription Arigo had given him, his backache had disappeared.

3

In 1950, thirteen years before Puharich and Belk came to Congonhas do Campo on their research expedition, Brazilian Senator Lucio Bittencourt lay on his bed in his room at the Hotel Financial in Belo Horizonte. There were many conflicting thoughts going through his mind. The campaign for the national and state elections of that year was tough and vigorous. He was not only running for reelection as senator, but had taken on the added chore of stomping through the mountain expanse of the state of Minas Gerais on behalf of Getúlio Vargas, the quixotic presidential candidate who had dominated Brazil's political life for many years. Vargas was now in the process of staging a comeback, after a five-year hiatus forced on him by a military junta. With two campaigns to run, one for Vargas and one for himself, Senator Bittencourt had his hands full.

But there was another complication, a serious one. He had been told by his doctor in Rio de Janeiro that laboratory tests showed he was suffering from lung cancer, and that his only hope was an immediate operation. Otherwise, there was little chance he would survive. His doctor had recommended an operation in the United States, where some of the surgical techniques for this particular type of operation were more advanced.

Senator Bittencourt fully intended following his

physician's advice. But he felt so intensely about the political struggle he was involved in that he postponed the decision until after his campaign sweep through Minas Gerais. Dedicated to the cause of the Partido Trabalhista Brasileiro—the Brazilian workers' party—he felt that only Vargas would be able to continue pushing for more benevolent treatment for labor and more progressive steps in agriculture and education.

The senator had recently stopped in Congonhas do Campo. Although it was a small village, it was politically important because it was deep in the heart of the iron-mining district, and the miners faced an uphill struggle against poverty and deplorable working conditions.

He had been impressed with the dynamic, thirty-two-year-old former union president who greeted him on his arrival in the town. His name was José Pedro de Freitas, and he was obviously strong as an ox, extremely vital, and a natural leader dedicated to the cause of the workers. It took little time to discover that José was known everywhere as Arigo, a word in Brazil that translates roughly as "jovial country bumpkin," but was well loved in spite of it.

The senator was quick to recognize Arigo's considerable magnetism and crude good nature. Arigo, in turn, rankling under the dismal working conditions of the miners, assured Senator Bittencourt of the support of his union. Welcoming the assistance, the senator invited Arigo to bring a group of his miners into Belo Horizonte for a rally to be held the next day.

After they arrived in the city, they found that the rally had been postponed for a day. The senator invited Arigo to stay overnight at the Hotel Financial, a towering, modern hotel on the Avenida Afonso Pena in the bright, new, growing city. Arigo, although he had a great fear of elevators, agreed to stay and registered in a room down the hall from the senator. He insisted, however, on walking up three flights to do so. That evening they joined other campaign workers at a *churrasco* at the

Churrascaria Campones, where barbecued meats were piled high along with *feijao*, black beans seasoned with onions, garlic, and spices, and *arroz de Galinha*, rice blended with chicken, boiled eggs, and olives. It was a festive evening, and there was a bountiful supply of *chopp*, the frothy Brazilian beer. Arigo had a glass or two of wine, although he seldom drank.

The festivities carried through until late in the night. Although the worries about his health hung heavily over the senator, he joined in with the others, quaffing a considerable number of mugs of his favorite dark beer.

Sometime after midnight, the senator and Arigo returned to the Hotel Financial, walking through the wide, deserted *avenidas* of the city. Senator Bittencourt had trouble getting to sleep. The combination of the stress of the political campaign and the worry about his physical condition did not lead to quietude.

The senator did not recall just how long he lay tossing in his bed. He was aware, though, that just when he felt he might doze off, the door to his room opened. In the half-light from the hallway spilling through the door, he could not clearly tell who it was. The shape of the man was similar to the burly contours of Arigo, and as the light switch was snapped on, he saw that it was.

Arigo was holding a razor in his hand. His eyes were glazed, with a far-off look, as if he saw nothing in front of him. He crossed to Senator Bittencourt's bed, as the senator gaped in wordless amazement. He recalled feeling very faint, as his vision blurred and the figure of Arigo dissolved into an undiscernible form. But for some reason, he felt no fear whatever. Perhaps he was hallucinating, he thought. He did not cry out, did not try to address Arigo. He remembered hearing Arigo's voice, in a very thick German accent. The voice said there was an emergency and that there would have to be an operation.

At that point, Senator Bittencourt blacked out. When he came to again, the light was still on and his watch showed that it was five in the morning. There was no one in the room. He felt very weak and faint, but he sat up quickly as the memory of Arigo's entry into the room flooded back to him. The recollection was hazy at first, but it began putting itself together in his mind. He remembered clearly Arigo coming into the room, razor in hand. He remembered Arigo approaching his bed and speaking to him in a thick guttural accent about the need for an emergency operation. He remembered having no fear. His memory could not, however, penetrate beyond the moment at which he blacked out.

He quickly took off his pajama top and looked at it. There was a fairly large bloodstain on it, and part of it had been slashed. He got up shakily and went to the mirror. Turning his back to it, he saw a clean, neat incision in the dorsal area of the rib cage. The blood had already clotted.

Moving slowly, because of his faintness, he dressed. He was now shaken and frightened, if not panicked. His calmness, so inexplicable at the time Arigo came toward his bed with the razor, was shattered. Leaving the blood-stained pajamas on his bed, he walked down the hall to Arigo's room. His legs were still weak. He knocked on the door, and Arigo, half-asleep, opened it.

The senator said that he desperately needed a cup of tea, and wanted Arigo to go to a *farmacia* with him at once. He would explain everything later. Puzzled and confused, Arigo quickly dressed and joined him. In silence they walked down the Avenida Afonso Pena to a sleepy pharmacy.

They entered the establishment, and Bittencourt asked for a cup of tea, explaining that he did not feel well. Then his knees buckled under him and he collapsed on the floor. Arigo attended to him while the clerk rushed to the street to find a policeman. He was back in moments with one. By this time, Bittencourt was beginning to revive. Arigo, by now assuming that the senator had had too much to drink, explained the situation in those terms.

After Bittencourt gulped down the cup of tea, he said he was feeling better, and felt strong enough to return to the hotel.

Walking slowly back, he told Arigo that the reason he had fainted was that Arigo had come into his room and operated on his back. Arigo was shocked. He accused the senator of having drunk too much beer, but Bittencourt held to his story. He admitted that at first he thought he was hallucinating, but now the memory was clear in his mind. The bloodstain on his pajamas and the incision on his back would prove it.

Arigo protested that he had done no such thing. Back in the senator's room, however, he studied the slashed pajamas, the bloodstain, and the incision. There was no question that Bittencourt had been operated on. The wound was fresh, the blood still moist. But he insisted he had had nothing to do with it. Senator Bittencourt, worried and distraught, said he was leaving immediately for the airport to catch the first plane to Rio to see his doctor.

Arigo was almost in a state of shock. Although he had no memory whatever of going to the senator's room, a series of strange spells had been plaguing him for a long period of time. He helped Senator Bittencourt into a taxi, mumbling almost incoherently that if he had done anything like this, he had no memory whatever of doing so.

With the senator on his way to the airport, Arigo got into his jeep. He was tense and nervous. Whatever had happened, he knew himself well enough to know that he would never do anything out of malice or foolhardiness. Yet *if* he had done this incredible thing, he obviously must be bordering on insanity. He prayed that Senator Bittencourt's doctor would find that he had done no harm —if, indeed, he had done anything at all.

The hour and a half it takes to drive from Belo Horizonte to Congonhas do Campo allowed Arigo considerable time for reflection. From what had been happening to him over the past several years, he was convinced that what Senator Bittencourt had described might very well have taken place—even though Arigo had no memory of it.

It was hard to define when it all started. Arigo had been born on his father's farm on October 18, 1918, and his early boyhood varied little from the norm. He was one of eight brothers, all of them healthy and robust, and none of them suffering from any real deprivation. The father, Antonio de Freitas Sobrinho, owned several parcels of land and farmed them diligently. He was also one of the town fathers of Congonhas do Campo. He had, in fact, been chairman of the town council, and continued to sit on the board. Some of Arigo's relatives were even considered wealthy, including an aunt who had large ranch holdings and an uncle who was to become mayor of the town.

Although most of his brothers went on to higher education, including one who had a law degree and another who was a priest, Arigo was not a good student and dropped out after struggling through the first three years of school. He contented himself with working in the fields of his father's farm, living an unstructured boyhood that allowed him time to spend with the many friends that collected around him. He was very popular. He was garrulous and congenial, sinewy and strong from his earliest years. His formal name of José Pedro de Freitas was dropped early in favor of Arigo, which, in spite of its suggestion of hillbilly qualities, was used affectionately by his friends. Arigo did not mind it; he actually enjoyed it.

Even in his brief school years, he was bothered by what he described as "a bright, round light, so brilliant that it nearly blinded me." He also experienced moderately persistent audio-hallucinations, describing them as "a voice that spoke in a strange language." These were infrequent enough to brush off, and he learned to put up with them. He also refrained from discussing them at length with anyone, including his family.

The entire de Freitas family was devoutly Catholic, and Arigo grew up in that tradition. The Church of Bom Jesus do Matosinho, high on the steep hill overlooking the red tile roofs of the village, and guarded by the almost breathtaking statues of Aleijadinho, fostered reverence and devotion, even for non-Catholics. Arigo worshiped and believed in his faith with the intensity that marked everything he did.

He was outspoken, with little regard for subtleties or niceties. He often used barnyard language, but he did so with a certain charm that nullified criticism. He spoke his mind bluntly, spontaneously. He was at times grossly flamboyant. Yet he was sensitive. He was often moved to tears, even as a man. He was affectionate, embracing his friends "with fire," as a friend put it. He was compassionate. He loved people, especially children. He was obstinate and unyielding, often to his own disadvantage.

Congonhas do Campo was a Catholic town. There were two monasteries on the nearby mountaintops, at times reachable only by jeep. Arigo's family, in their religious devotion, were disproportionately lavish in their contributions to both the Church and the monasteries. While Catholicism in Brazil is more relaxed and less dominant than it is in the Spanish-speaking Latin republics, it is still a powerful force, and 90 percent of the population professes to be part of it. However, as Pedro McGregor points out in his illuminating book *The Moon and Two Mountains*, the spiritist groups, frowned on by the Catholics, had 71 orphanages against 73 for the Catholics and 25 for the Protestants. As for social assistance shelters, the spiritists, with their emphasis on charity, had 125, compared to 81 for the Catholics and 25 for the Protestants. The Catholics in Congonhas do Campo were especially uneasy about intrusion by the spiritists, whether Umbanda, Quimbanda, or Kardecist, and fidgeted uneasily when there were any but minor stirrings along these lines.

Arigo began to notice his fourth cousin, Arlete Andre, in the early part of 1943, and fell in love with her. When they were married later that year, there was great rejoicing in his family, because Arlete was also an intensely devout Catholic, as well as being a graceful and intelligent girl. By this time Arigo, at the age of twenty-five, had left the confinement of his father's farm in favor of working in a local iron mine, where his strength and muscles could serve him well.

Arigo would rise in the chill of the plateau mornings at three, for the mines where he worked were a dozen kilometers away—about seven and a half miles. He and most of his fellow miners would walk this distance each day, both going to and coming back from work. For their efforts, they would receive a meager wage and massive calluses on their hands from swinging a pick all day.

Working conditions were brutal. Most of the miners could not make ends meet. Some of them, Arigo told a friend, would bring empty lunch pails to work so they could disguise the fact that they were without money to buy food. Arigo burned with a strong sense of justice, and his indignation grew until, as the newly elected president of the union local, he sparked the workers into action. The result was a strike, led by Arigo.

Even though Brazil's 1946 Constitution protected the right of workers to strike, both the federal and state governments reserved the right to declare strikes illegal, without the inconvenience of observing due process. The common theory behind such action was that anyone who stirred up a strike was likely to be a communist. Whether he was a communist or not, he was likely to be declared so.

Arigo was not, but the police moved in anyway. He was fired, but he resolved that he would continue to fight the injustices he and his fellow miners had suffered. His wife Arlete stood by him firmly and took in work as a seamstress. His father also came to his support, and was able to set Arigo up in a tavern-restaurant combination in the village which became known as Bar do Arigo.

In a way, it flourished. Arigo's popularity drew a brisk trade. But his generosity worked against him. He could not resist lending money to a friend, or giving food to a stranger. He extended credit liberally, and nòt at all wisely. All the money he borrowed from his father went into the restaurant-bar. Very little was left for living, but he and Arlete and their growing family managed to survive in the little old house on the Rua Marechal Floriano.

Arigo kept afloat, his business buttressed by the considerable number of tourists who came to see the dramatic statues of Aleijadinho. But as his children continued to arrive in quick succession, he began having persistent and disturbing dreams. In them, the same guttural voice kept talking to him, in a language that sounded like German, which he had heard spoken at times but could not understand. His dreams were sometimes accompanied by blinding headaches, which woke him up and from which he could find no relief. As his fears increased, he came to dread the nighttime.

He wanted to keep his anguish to himself, but finally had to confide in Arlete that he could not sleep at night. At times he would have to cry out in agony. Rather than disturb Arlete, he would dress and walk the streets of the town until the pain subsided. Other nights, Arlete would wake to find him crying beside her in the bed.

One night an unusually vivid dream came to him, so vivid that he could not get it out of his mind. The scene was an operating room. There was a group of doctors and nurses gathered around a patient on the table, all dressed in surgical gowns. They seemed to be working with surgical instruments on the patient, meticulously, endlessly. Directing the procedure was a rather stout, bald man who was speaking to the others in the same accent and tone as the voice that had been plaguing him for so long. What disturbed Arigo so much was not the scene itself, but its utter reality. He could not separate it from the actual. And night after night, the same dream returned.

In spite of this, he was able to block the dream from his thoughts when daylight came. His business was taking a turn for the better. He was able to buy some real estate, and dabbled in the used-car business with moderate success. Whenever the constantly repeating dream and the blinding headaches reached a crescendo, he would climb the cobblestone hill to the Church of Bom Jesus and pray.

It wasn't long until a night came when the dream shifted from a nightmare to a full-scale hallucination. The fat, bald-headed doctor identified himself as Dr. Adolpho Fritz. In the hallucination, he told Arigo that he had died during the First World War and that his work on earth had never been completed. He had observed Arigo for a long time and knew of his generosity and love for his fellow man. He had chosen Arigo as the living vessel to carry on his work, with the help of other spirits who were doctors before they died. If Arigo was to find any peace, he would have to begin serving the sick and disturbed people who needed him. Arigo was to take a crucifix he had found on his father's farm some time before and hold it in his hand. In this way, he would cure the sick.

The doctor standing before him was so real, the instructions so far-fetched, and the fear so great within Arigo that he leaped up from the bed and went screaming, naked, through the streets of the village. Within moments a crowd had gathered, and Arlete ran out of the house after him. He was led gently back toward his house by several friends who had been brought to the street by his cries. He was sobbing and barely coherent.

The situation was obviously serious. Back in his house, Arigo grew calmer, while Dr. Venceslau de Souza Coimbra, the family doctor, was summoned. The doctor could find nothing wrong physically and prescribed a sedative. He felt, however, that Arigo should receive immediate psychiatric attention. Arigo agreed completely. He was now convinced that he was having delusions and that he was utterly unable to combat them by himself. Father Penido, a parish priest, was also summoned, and prayed with him.

The priest listened attentively as Arigo described his strange dreams and hallucinations. If Father Penido was more than attentive to the substance of that night's dream and to the advice given to Arigo by the strange German doctor to go out and heal the sick, there was good reason for it. The Catholic Church, in Congonhas as elsewhere, was touchy about the whole idea of spiritism making any inroads among the people, whether it involved the crudities of Quimbanda or the intellectualism of the Kardecists. So far, Congonhas had remained mostly free of this disturbing influence, a condition devoutly wished for by the Catholic clergy.

What Arigo was telling Father Penido about the dreams and hallucinations was alarming because it was indicative of what many spiritist healers had claimed was a sign of the development of a medium. Arigo was a solid Catholic. He knew little or nothing about Kardec. With his peculiar, untutored charisma he could become dangerous to the Church establishment if he leaned toward the work of a healer or a medium. Father Penido warned Arigo of this danger, and told him that he would immediately arrange for both medical and psychiatric examinations in Belo Horizonte.

Arigo was more than willing. He went the next day for a complete physical examination, including X rays and blood tests, in the nearby city. He had a long consultation with a psychiatrist. Neither doctor could find anything particularly disturbing. His physical health seemed excellent; his psychiatric examination showed no signs of manifest psychosis, or even neurosis. Follow-up examinations confirmed the original conclusions.

But the headaches, dreams, and hallucinations continued. In spite of the anguish and distraction they brought, Arigo continued building his business and even started to dabble in local politics. He was still smarting from the injustices he had found as a miner, and felt the only way he could combat these was to support the cause of labor both nationally and locally. He continued consulting with Father Penido and other members of the clergy, and continued seeing a doctor. No evident physical symptoms showed up. Occasionally, during the day, he would have a brief fainting spell, blacking out and remembering nothing afterward. He became convinced he was going insane, and pleaded with both the priests and the doctor to help him further.

At length, because the nature of the hallucinations suggested the possibility of possession, Father Penido decided on the need for the exorcising ritual of the Church. It was carried out with all the ancient and elaborate ceremony that had characterized the process back through the history of the Catholic Church: the burning of incense, the chanting of litanies and adjurations, the blessing of the house to free the sufferer from evil spirits.

Apparently the spirits were not listening, because the ritual did not work. On the other hand, the dreams and hallucinations did not seem to involve evil spirits. If anything, the attitude of the alleged Dr. Fritz was benevolent. But Arigo was literally exhausted from resisting the German doctor of the spirit world. Whatever anyone else thought, the events that were plaguing Arigo were inescapably real to him.

Almost out of desperation, he wondered what might happen if he gave in to the intransigent demands of the so-called Dr. Fritz. He had a chance to try shortly later. He encountered a friend of his who was a cripple, who walked on crutches and received much sympathy from the citizens of the town. Hardly thinking before he spoke, Arigo found himself blurting out in his rough-hewn way:

"It's about time you got rid of those crutches." He grabbed them from the man and told him to walk. The man did so, and continued to remain able to do so.

Far from relieving his mind, the incident filled Arigo with more fear. If all this were true, he was being shouldered with an enormous responsibility which he had no rational way of carrying out. In addition, he had been warned by Father Penido about spiritism and the Kardecist philosophy, and had no desire to go against the tenets of the Church. In spite of his fear, and very tentatively, he tried again with some other friends who were sick with varied complaints, simply by using verbal commands to them. They reported back that whatever he had done, it had worked. But at times, he had to be told that he had issued these commands. He had no memory of them. But strangely enough, his headaches and hallucinations had stopped altogether during the few weeks he had given in to the impulse prescribed by Dr. Fritz.

It wasn't long before word spread around the town, and it brought Father Penido on the run. The priest spoke sharply. Arigo had placed himself in direct conflict with the Church. He was already being spoken of as a *curandeiro*, the Portuguese word for quack or charlatan. Arigo listened to the priest intently. He was anything but a rebel as far as the Church was concerned. Further, he was repelled by what the priests had told him about spiritism: it was a heresy of the first order, and should be avoided at all costs. He confessed to his weakness in giving in to the instructions of Dr. Fritz, and agreed to stop.

One of the first steps he took was to put up a prominent sign on his door: IN THIS HOUSE, WE ARE ALL CATHOLICS. SPIRITISM IS A THING OF THE DEVIL. Arlete, whose concern had been growing even more than Arigo's, was pleased with this action. Perhaps now they would have some peace. But this had no sooner been done when Arigo's dreams, hallucinations, and headaches returned with a fury, along with the daytime blackouts, in which his memory was wiped out for the duration. There were more visits to Belo Horizonte, this time to several doctors and psychiatrists, but the image of Dr. Fritz became more insistent.

While all this turmoil did not at first affect the business at his restaurant, Arigo was very concerned about what it would mean to his political aspirations. He knew enough about his own motives to know that his political hopes were not slanted for personal gain, but arose from a real and almost irresistible impulse to help his fellow man. This was no casual idealistic impulse. In fact, he found it a distinct liability at times, and he worried about it. He had many friends who worked in a local factory that was experiencing shaky financial times. Many of them were worried about the plant closing, and Arigo offered them almost unlimited credit. He did the same for many others, and could not resist lending money to almost anyone who asked for it. He was not a good businessman, and after a short period of burgeoning prosperity, he was alarmed to discover that he was heading for financial disaster. In spite of this, he gathered and bought clothing for the poor and their children on dozens of occasions.

Now he was faced with this new and unsought thrust from "Dr. Fritz," and his conscience was caught in a squeeze between an obsessional drive of unknown dimensions and the Catholic Church, which would look on him as a heretic if he yielded to this undefined impetus. He was in this state of confusion in 1950, at the age of thirty-two, when Senator Bittencourt had arrived in town to solicit his political support.

The memory of all these chaotic scenes was in his mind as he drove his jeep back toward Congonhas. However deep his concern for his fellow man, Arigo always drove with utter disregard for life and limb. In Brazil, as in nearly all developing countries, awareness of the deadliness of the motor vehicle has not yet set in, in spite of the frequent bloody and harrowing accidents that strew the roads. His tension and worry from the incident in the hotel room with Senator Bittencourt were terrifying, and he was again tormented by the fear that he was on the verge of insanity.

As he screeched around the hairpin turns of the road to Congonhas, he searched his mind trying to remember if he actually *had* gone into the senator's room with his razor and done what the senator said he had done. He could remember none of it. His razor was in its regular place when he packed to leave. There was no evidence of blood on it. He had had only two glasses of wine to drink, and had clearly remembered going to bed and starting to go to sleep. His next memory was of the senator pounding on the door and asking him to go with him to get a cup of tea.

What might happen after Senator Bittencourt's plane reached Rio brought Arigo more terror. Suppose the senator brought charges against him? What if the "operation" caused him to die? What would Bittencourt's doctor say when he saw what had happened? That the operation had taken place could not be denied. And, with the long history of his *curandeiro* impulses recorded among the villagers and in the files of the Church and the Belo Horizonte doctors, it would be logical for them to assume that Arigo had done the operation, even though he didn't recall it at all. The whole problem had reached a new intensity, and he did not know how to cope with it.

It was a confused and disarrayed Arigo who arrived in Congonhas do Campo later that morning. His most pressing decision was whether he should tell anyone about what had happened. Both Arlete and Father Penido would be totally distraught if he told them, and the town would be in an uproar. There was already too much talk around the town about the puzzling cures that had resulted from his previous actions. He struggled with the decision to tell or not to tell, but could not bring himself to make it.

In a very short time, the decision was made for him. Incredible news arrived from Senator Bittencourt. He had gone immediately from the airport to his doctor in Rio. He had been examined, the wound probed, and X rays taken. Because of the strangeness of what had happened in the hotel room in Belo Horizonte, he had shrunk at first from telling his doctor anything until the examination was complete. He merely had mentioned that he had been operated on.

The Rio doctor, assuming that the operation had been done in the United States, as he had instructed, glowed with satisfaction about the results of the X rays. He explained to the senator that the tumor had been cleanly removed by a very unusual surgical technique that did not seem to be known in Brazil. As far as he could tell, the prognosis should be excellent. Yet before the operation, he had been very pessimistic, and frankly did not think that Senator Bittencourt had much longer to live. He would follow up with further tests, but the picture had changed from one of complete despair to unqualified optimism.

It was then that the senator told the doctor what had happened. The doctor listened, incredulous. He found it impossible to believe. But Senator Bittencourt insisted, and the doctor was forced to accept the explanation. If this was true—and the doctor had confidence in the senator's veracity—there would have to be some sort of study to verify the medical skills of this rare *curandeiro*. Either that or the Brazilian Medical Association would have to take action against him. In the meantime, the fact remained that Senator Lucio Bittencourt was a well man, and if the future tests turned out to be as favorable as the doctor was confident they would be, the senator would remain in good health indefinitely.

The additional tests *were* favorable, and Bittencourt was not one to keep a good thing quiet. After dispatching the incredible news to Congonhas do Campo, he told the story to everyone who would listen. Within days, it spread across the press in all of Brazil. In Congonhas do

Campo, Arigo became a folk hero overnight—to the consternation and distress of both the Church and his family. Arigo protested that he was not at all sure he had done such an operation, that the incident, if it happened, was just one more of a long string that was bringing him nothing but anxiety and apprehension.

The immoderate exuberance of Senator Bittencourt was matched by the towering disapproval of the Church. Father Penido took Arigo in hand and reminded him of his promise to stop such behavior. Things had now gone too far. Arigo protested that it was impossible to stop what he never remembered doing, or what he was not conscious of doing. He had not knowingly, he assured the priest, done anything whatever to violate his promise. The situation presented a baffling point of order, and strained the competence of Father Penido in trying to come up with a viable answer. The problem was almost imponderable and raised the specter of spiritism where it was least welcome.

Disturbed as she was, Arlete comforted, supported, and ministered to her disquieted husband. His life seemed to be piling up with a series of crises, involving his business, his political hopes, and his psychological stability.

Meanwhile, the hallucinations featuring Dr. Fritz would not let up, and they gave him no surcease. Because of Arigo's basic honesty and charisma, the villagers for the most part stood behind him as loyally as his wife. Senator Bittencourt returned to the town with lavish praise for Arigo's inconceivable surgical prowess, which encouraged the small spiritist group in town to become more vocal and conspicuous. They felt that spiritism was the only possible explanation of the seeming miracle that Arigo had performed. They claimed that Arigo was a bona fide medium who had not yet realized his potential.

The spiritists went even further. They claimed that during some of their mediumistic sessions—carried on in the intellectualized Kardec tradition, and strictly without

Umbanda rituals of any kind—Dr. Adolpho Fritz had made himself known to them. He told them that he had spent sixteen years preparing Arigo to carry on the work of healing. The discarnate German doctor, allegedly speaking through the medium, said that he had been working on a medium up north in Bahia, but that the man did not have Arigo's selfless qualities and would be likely to turn his talents to self-aggrandizement, to say nothing of commercial advantage. Since one of the strict rules of the Kardec philosophy is that no healer can accept any money for his work, Dr. Fritz had turned to Arigo, whom he was sure would not violate that principle.

When told of this theory, Arigo dismissed it. The little he knew about mediums came from the pungent warnings of Father Penido, and he would have none of it. Still distressed, he tried to continue his ordinary routine in the face of the fast-moving events that were overrunning his life.

He tried to assume a posture of normalcy, difficult as it was. Not all the Catholic clergy were as severe as the official position of the Church itself. Padre Pascoal, who had taught Arigo his first catechism, was particularly fond of him, and felt that he had spiritual qualities of great depth and beauty. The padre had been a chaplain in World War II and had observed many strange things on the battlefield that could not be explained. As a result, he had studied hypnotism and parapsychology. He was convinced that Arigo was undergoing some kind of parapsychologic experience that was worthy of extensive study. He comforted Arigo, asked him to have faith and courage. "God puts things in the right place at the right time," he told Arigo. "He writes straight things in curved lines."

The consternation that swept the streets of the village when Senator Bittencourt brought his astounding medical news reverberated everywhere. José da Cunha, mayor of Congonhas, had grown up with Arigo in the village. He tried to piece together the background of his friend to explain the phenomenon that seemed to be growing into a modern legend. But he could find little to explain the roots of Arigo's mysterious powers. Arigo had always held his friends spellbound with stories and anecdotes, always seemed to have a fresh viewpoint on everything. He was always bursting with great good humor, and constantly joking with his friends. The mayor couldn't resist the temptation of wondering whether all the recent happenings were not just one of Arigo's jokes. Whatever it was, the mayor was convinced of Arigo's basic goodness and his unqualified affection for other people. What would follow next in this strange series of events neither he nor anyone else in the village could know.

What did happen next came with such suddenness that it brought one of the biggest shock waves that Congonhas do Campo had ever experienced.

The woman was very sick. She suffered from cancer of the uterus. There was no hope at all, and death was expected at any minute. She lay on her bed, surrounded by close relatives and a few friends. Candles were lit in the quiet room, and the priest arrived to administer extreme unction, the last rites of the Church. The family were good friends of Arigo, and he and Arlete called at the house to pay their last respects to the dying woman. It was a solemn scene, and a sad one. The priest completed the ritual, and quietly left.

In the silence that followed, Arigo bowed his head with the others in silent prayer. Then he began to experience a feeling which had become familiar to him: a tingling that began in his head and slowly moved down through his legs. He started to tremble and his eyes became clouded.

Then, without warning, he burst into the kitchen and ran back into the room in a matter of moments. There was a large kitchen knife in his hands. With a sharp, commanding voice, he ordered everyone to stand back. The gathering was frozen with terror, and didn't dare move. Pulling down the sheets, he spread the woman's legs and plunged the knife directly into the vagina, probing violently, twisting the blade, slicing the flesh to widen the opening.

A woman relative screamed and ran out of the room. The others stood transfixed. The dying woman lay quietly, unperturbed, as he continued to plunge and jab the blade mercilessly. Then he removed the blade, forced his hand into the opening, savagely twisting his wrist as he did so. In a matter of seconds he withdrew his hand, yanking out an enormous bloody uterine tumor, the size of a small grapefruit. He crossed to the kitchen, dropped the knife and the ugly flesh into the sink, and then sank down on a chair beside it.

It had all happened so fast that the onlookers simply could not believe what they were seeing. There was little bleeding, beyond that on the blood-soaked tumor. One relative muttered that he was going for a doctor, and ran out. Others looked mutely, helplessly toward Arigo, who was now holding his head in his hand and sobbing. A sister of the dying woman shook herself free from her paralysis, ran to the kitchen, and returned with a basin of warm water and a washcloth. Arlete moved almost as if in a dream, and knelt beside her husband. There were tears in her eyes.

Arigo seemed to be in another world. He could hardly respond to Arlete's questions. When he seemed to have gained more control of himself, she took him by the arm and led him out of the house, still sobbing.

The doctor arrived shortly afterward, and quickly examined the dying woman. He looked first for hemorrhaging, but there was none. The patient was conscious, had felt no pain, and was not at all sure what had happened to her. Her pulse and heartbeat were satisfactory. She felt no discomfort whatever, either during or after the experience. She felt only relief now. The doctor turned to the others and asked them to describe what had happened. They did so, in meticulous detail.

The doctor then examined the tumor. There was no question that this was a uterine tumor. What's more, it was a growth that was considered to be inoperable. He wrapped it to take with him for further tests. Then he rechecked his patient. This was unquestionably the strangest medical case he had ever encountered—if not in medical history. Just what the prognosis would be for his patient, he had no possible way to determine.

But the information that finally did emerge a few days later was that the patient was getting better. On the heels of Senator Bittencourt's case, this news literally rocked the town. Within days, people began lining up outside Arigo's house, imploring him to treat them. Knowing the new turmoil that was now seizing the Catholic clergy, he turned to them for help and looked to the Church for refuge from the clamoring demands of the sick. The Church authorities pleaded, cajoled, and demanded that Arigo not give in to the supplications. He tried to resist, but the impulse spurred by Dr. Fritz would give him no rest. And when the dying woman he had operated on rallied and was able to return to normal life, the pressure to help those who were begging for treatment became irresistible. One morning, when nearly a hundred people gathered outside his door, Arigo opened it and let them come in, one by one.

But when he finished seeing them that day, he remembered little or nothing about what he had done. He was told that he had either written complicated prescriptions in all the proper pharmacological terms or had taken a kitchen knife or household scissors and had operated. He had asked questions of none of the patients. His diagnosis was instant, the minute the patient came up to him. He either wrote out the prescription or took hold of the knife. Again, there was no pain, no bleeding, no sterile precautions. Most puzzling to many was that he often spoke in a German accent.

Arigo continued letting the sick in, day after day. His household turned into total chaos. He continued to have little or no memory of what took place—an amnesic veil descended on him from the time he met the first patient until the last was gone. But out of the chaos came two very clear results: his hallucinations and headaches stopped, and patient after patient reported complete cures —including some that had an unqualified medical prognosis of death.

It was obvious that this could not keep up. Arlete was thrown into total confusion. The Church had now hardened in its posture: Arigo *must* stop this, or find himself unwelcome in the faith. The command stopped just short of the threat of excommunication. Arigo, his headaches and hallucinations gone, toughened in his own way. He still accepted the Church wholeheartedly. He was faithful to it. He went to Mass regularly and received Holy Communion. He did not want to give up the Church, but he felt that he was inexorably compelled to continue his healing work. He was needed—why else did the people jam the streets in front of his house from daybreak on?

He was soon visited by a man named Orlandino Ferreira, who was the nominal leader of the Kardecist group in Congonhas do Campo. By now there was no question in this gentleman's mind that the previous communication with Dr. Fritz, through their own medium, was valid. He talked soberly and at great length to Arigo, explaining what was happening in terms of the Kardec philosophy.

Ferreira told Arigo that according to Kardecist belief, the spirit of Dr. Adolpho Fritz was "incorporated" in him —a case of benign possession, as opposed to the black-magic practice of conjuring up evil spirits. When Dr. Fritz entered into Arigo, he literally took him over, supplying any diagnostic or surgical knowledge necessary for the case at hand. In other words, it was not Arigo's fingers or hands doing the operations, nor was it Arigo's mind prescribing the complicated pharmaceuticals which Arigo consciously knew little or nothing about.

But there was more involved than Dr. Fritz, Ferreira went on to say. There was a complete spirit band that worked together in this cause, which he would explain later. He wanted Arigo to know some of this background so that he would have more peace of mind to carry out his important work. And Ferreira assured Arigo that by accepting this Kardecist phenomenon that had arrived in such an unwelcome way, he would have no need of forswearing the Catholic Church. Further, his faith in Christ would be more profound than ever. He knew the terrible conflicts that must be going on in Arigo's mind, and assured him they would be eased rather than aggravated if he followed his new calling.

There certainly would be no conflict in basic belief, Ferreira continued. Kardec taught that science and religion were not even remotely in conflict with each other. Science merely was revealing the laws of nature, and in doing so was glorifying God. But science had much more to learn—especially in the areas of the paranormal, which had not even been scratched yet. The Kardec spiritists believed that the spirit world is simply less condensed than the material world, the world known to science. But it is the primary world of reality, and the material world is subservient to it. Thoughts and emotions create very real and traceable electrical energy patterns in the physical body, as a polygraph or an EEG will easily record. So much more so does the human will, or the soul, according to the Kardecists. The biggest job of science is to explore this relationship between the spirit sphere and the material world, he added.

Arigo was in no position to absorb this type of philosophy at the moment. But it opened his mind to new vistas and encouraged him to go on with his healing work. He was persuaded by Ferreira to recognize the possibility that he was a medium, and as such, a channel to this strange new world he was not only learning about, but experiencing.

Arigo also recognized that he was now in the position

of an acrobat split between two tightropes—the Church on one side and Kardec spiritism on the other. It was not a comfortable position, yet he was unable to fall either way. The continuing complication was that he was usually unable to remember anything he did after he felt the strange tingling sensation that marked the takeover, or "incorporation," by Dr. Fritz.

And there were the mundane problems that were plaguing him. In addition to the condemnation of his behavior by the Church establishment, his family life was suffering acutely. His restaurant was faltering now, on the edge of bankruptcy.

And in the distance were ominous rumbles signaling that the Brazilian Medical Association, along with the Catholic Church, was preparing legal action through the police of the state of Minas Gerais, Division of Robbery and Falsification.

4

The stress on Arigo was not eased by Senator Bittencourt. The senator continued to relate his miraculous surgical experience with Arigo wherever he spoke, and the more the senator talked, the more the Brazilian press picked up the story and repeated it. As a result, people began coming from great distances to line up early in the morning outside Arigo's little house. The crowds became more cosmopolitan. They were no longer confined to the poor and beseeching. The tailored suits that marked the prosperous businessman, the chic lines of a Dior dress, mingled occasionally with the dusty work clothes of the farmer or miner. Cars with out-of-state license plates began to appear in profusion.

Arigo worked with his patients indefatigably, continuing to mutter German words, a language he never knew or studied, issuing loud and blustery commands, seizing a knife and lunging at the passive patients, who, for reasons unknown, never flinched or resisted. The local pharmacist found himself hard put to stock up on many strange new drugs he had never heard of before. A heavy preponderance of the drugs, he discovered from the detail men, were of German origin. Some were so new that they had barely arrived in the pharmaceutical warehouses of Rio or São Paulo. Others were old and hadn't been generally prescribed in years. All, however, were part of the modern pharmacopeia. Arigo's hands wrote the prescriptions in a matter of seconds, his pen moving so fast that the prescription was ready almost before the patient could reach for it.

Tourists who came to see the statues of Aleijadinho often stayed on to see Arigo about a chronic ailment. They returned to their homes with glowing stories about what they had seen and experienced. Some felt there was a metaphysical connection between the miraculous statuary of the little crippled leper centuries before and the miraculous cures that Arigo seemed to be perpetrating. The spiritists in town had already accepted this theory.

In spite of the growing reverence he inspired, Arigo was no saint and never pretended to be. He stoutly maintained that it was not he who was curing, it was the teamwork of Dr. Fritz and Jesus. He denounced "low spiritism," carefully avoiding, however, any condemnation of the Kardec intellectuals, who were now creating a heavy influence on his outlook. He would announce at the beginning of each session that no one would be allowed to pay anything, not even the smallest gift. "Jesus never charged for what he did," he would tell the gathering. "Neither will I. But I am a sinner like you."

Though her household was now a shambles, Arlete continued to be mutely patient, torn and puzzled by this inexorable tide that had gathered. At the end of the long day and evening, there would be vomit and some—very little—blood to clean up. And Arigo might inexplicably vomit himself, as if he had absorbed some of the ills of his patients, his eyes watering and clear fluid uncontrollably flooding from his mouth.

The sheer foot-traffic problem became onerous. Arigo had no one to help him. Arlete had all she could do to handle the growing family and the sewing she took in to buttress their diminishing income. Ferreira, watching the incredible tide that was growing each day, talked with Arigo about establishing a spiritist center where the burden would be eased from his family. Plans were made to shift the clinic to the empty church across the street from Arigo's house, no longer in use, and better adapted to handling the crowds.

It was during this time that a gentle, soft-spoken man in his late forties named José Nilo de Oliveiro began having trouble with his left eye. Better known as Altimiro the Black, because of his dark skin, he worked as a compositor for the publications of the Catholic Church, having retired from a clerical job with the state welfare and pension office. Since his livelihood depended on his sight, his worry increased over the days. His doctor told him he had a cataract, and that it was inoperable at the time. He held out no hope for corrective surgery in the foreseeable future.

Altimiro, along with the entire village and country, in fact, had heard of Arigo. He was aware of the growing hostility of the Church against Arigo, and dismissed the brash idea of visiting this living legend. He was also inclined to think that the reports coming out about the healer could not possibly be true. But when he learned that several priests and other officials of the Church had quietly gone to Arigo and reported cures where conventional medicine had failed, he mustered up his courage and stood in line.

What he saw as he moved up toward the front of the line both frightened and fascinated him. The giant, bull-sized man was explosively speaking his guttural Portuguese, sprinkled with words that must have been German, ordering the line to move along, scolding some, putting his arm around others, alternately writing prescriptions and slicing his kitchen knife into a patient without any preamble. Altimiro found himself transfixed by the man, by his skill and sureness and confidence. By the time he reached the front of the line, his apprehension suddenly left him.

Before he knew what was happening, Arigo had pushed him almost roughly against the wall, asking him no questions. He reached for a knife on the small table in front of him. For some inexplicable reason, Altimiro felt no fear whatever. He mutely watched Arigo's hand, the knife blade coming toward his eye. Then he felt a very slight pain, less than a pinprick. In seconds, he felt Arigo press into his hand a tiny gelatinous piece of membrane. Then he heard Arigo say: "Go with God."

Altimiro moved off numbly, and by the next morning his eye could see clearly, without the thick-lensed glasses used for cataract cases. When he sheepishly visited his doctor later for an examination, the doctor was at a total loss for an explanation. If the lens of an eye is removed, it is considered impossible for the eye to accommodate and focus properly. His defective eye now did so. Altimiro was content to let the question ride. His brief exposure to Arigo made him determine that he wanted to work for this man, regardless of the circumstances.

His resolve was buttressed when he took his uncle to Arigo. The uncle was suffering from stomach cancer, and his doctor held out no hope. But Altimiro watched in suspended disbelief as Arigo took a large kitchen knife, plunged it into the viscera, reached in his hand, and pulled out a tumorous mass. When some bleeding began, he saw Arigo lift his eyes toward the ceiling and say: "Jesus does not want you to bleed." Miraculously, the bleeding stopped. Then Arigo spoke again: "Dr. Fritz, please close the wound." He then ran a piece of cotton over the gaping cut, wiping it lightly. The wound joined neatly, without stitches. Altimiro was almost in shock by the time it was over, but he told Arigo that he wanted to work for him, without pay. Arigo, as if the whole thing were preordained, accepted immediately and without comment.

In spite of his twinges of conscience about the conflict between the Church and Arigo, Altimiro became an invaluable adjunct to Arigo. It wasn't too long before he was able to type up the illegible scrawl that Arigo scribbled as prescriptions. In addition, Altimiro devised a system where he would issue numbered cards to the people standing in line, on a first-come, first-served basis.

Arigo had not yet brought the entire Church thundering down on him, but it seemed to be only a question of time. A sympathetic pocket of priests, including Padre Pascoal, were in charge of the Church radio station that sat high on the hill next to the Church of Bom Jesus, under the shadows of the guardian statuary of Aleijadin- ho. They had become convinced through quiet investiga- tion that Arigo was achieving unheard-of results. Intense scientific study was needed, rather than censure, they felt. They were inclined to look at the phenomenon as parapsychology rather than spiritism. In this way, Arigo would stand a better chance of being accepted by the Church.

In fact, a young aggressive priest, Bonaventure Kloppenberg, who had been vigorously attacking spiri- tism throughout the country, had recently written: "The Catholic Church does not prohibit the study of parapsychology or the phenomenon of the medium. The Catholic is permitted to study either metaphysics or parapsychology. In fact, Catholic scientists in universities should study these fields."

It was this sort of loophole that Arigo's friends in the Church establishment clung to, for they liked Arigo and wanted him to stay with the Church.

But there were others of the hierarchy less charitable. They were already in contact with the medical society of Minas Gerais to see just how they might go about bringing down the law on Arigo. In spite of what amounted to an open practice of illegal medicine, they would have to tread very carefully to push a trial. It would most certainly be held in Congonhas do Campo, and there was no telling what the citizenry would do if their folk hero were thus treated.

Arigo was widely popular, had been so even before his mystique in miracle cures had developed. He was known as a champion of the downtrodden and for his dedication to the cause of the miners. His sudden blooming into a healer now made him revered as well as popular. Brazilian authorities everywhere in the country were always forced to look the other way when it came to the primitive forms of spiritism in the Quimbanda and Umbanda traditions. There would not be enough prisons to hold all the followers of these ritualistic Afro-Brazilian religions. The Kardec spiritists were less conspicuous and more respected. Further, Arigo had now attracted as patients some of the leading statesmen and political figures in Brazil, so far had his fame spread. For the time being, it was more prudent for the police to look the other way—but it couldn't be certain how long that would last.

After finally having to sell his restaurant, Arigo concentrated on real estate and the used-car business to support his family. He also decided to campaign vigorously for the post of mayor of the town. No one quite understood where he got all the energy to add this burden to his already overloaded schedule. He continued, however, to place his healing work ahead of all other commitments.

A portrait of Arigo began to be pieced together from many points of view. Slowly, a tapestry emerged as his fame—or notoriety, depending on the observer—spread across the country. The tapestry was as confused and variegated as a Picasso print, but there was truth rising out of the paradoxes. Arigo was in fact many personalities, involving grossly contradictory traits. Adding to the confusion were the subjective projections of those who shaped the portrait.

Some related to his coarseness. Some saw him as saintly, and endowed him with this quality above all others. Some saw only his sensuality, because he was a sensual man, and many stories were spread about his real or supposed infidelities. Many would not believe he was so selfless that he refused money or gifts, although no real evidence was ever presented that would refute this.

Before he started each daily session, he publicly declared that no one would be permitted to pay. He would not even accept a cup of coffee. He repeated this so often that any under-the-table dealings would have sprung into public currency like a brush fire, fanned by his enemies.

The cross section of observers who tried to dissect and analyze Arigo was widely diversified. Aside from the blatantly curious, the people who gathered before his door each day were motivated by one essential problem: modern medical science had gone as far as it could go with them, and had given up. The problem might be minor and chronic, or major and lethal. Wasn't it worth the chance, they thought, to *try* something else, even if it seemed patently absurd?

One point of view came from an intelligent, attractive press officer of the United States Information Agency in Belo Horizonte. She was a devout Brazilian Catholic, and therefore was ostensibly not supposed to have any faith in the Kardec healing philosophy. She had a nine-year-old boy who suffered painfully and persistently from acute asthma. The family doctor had prescribed allergy medications and injections, but these were almost totally ineffective. The attacks continued and worsened. As a last resort, she made a timid decision to take her boy to Arigo.

She arrived early in the morning, but there were already more than a hundred people in line, mostly working people of modest means. She was impressed by watching Arigo as she waited her turn, and, though rather frightened by his rude, blustering manner, she sensed a deep kindness underneath. His treatment of the boy followed what was now his usual procedure. In a matter of seconds, Arigo's beefy hand had scrawled out a prescription. He said practically nothing, asked no questions. She was directed to take the paper to Altimiro, who quickly typed it out, and the session was over.

She had an impulse to donate some money, but was sharply told this was not permitted. Later, she had many second thoughts about filling the prescription, but her desperation overcame her fear. With considerable trepidation, she took the prescription to the drugstore and had it filled. She followed the instructions carefully, worried about whether the medicines would do any harm. She was very pessimistic because the long courses of other drugs that her regular physician had been administering over several years had been next to useless. How could the prescription from the untutored Arigo possibly be any better?

She watched anxiously over several weeks, relieved to notice that at least there were no side effects or adverse reactions. But the weeks extended into months, and the frightening asthma attacks never came back again.

As an intelligent woman and a Catholic, she was at a loss to explain the dramatic change. All she could say was that she no longer doubted Arigo and was enormously grateful to him. But she remained puzzled and unenlightened about what had really taken place.

Not long after Arigo's fame began radiating out of his little mining village, H. V. Walter, the British consul in Belo Horizonte, got wind of his prowess. Being a man of intense curiosity and erudition, Walter was fascinated by the stories that were filtering down from Congonhas do Campo.

Not the least of these stories came from his close friend Carlos Paranhos da Costa Cruz, a dentist whose office was in the same building as the British consulate. Cruz, a graduate of the University of Brazil, appeared in the consulate office one day visibly shaken. Walter offered him a stiff pink gin and asked what the story was. Dr. Cruz told him that he had just returned from Congonhas do Campo with his father-in-law and sister-in-law, and didn't know how to describe what had happened.

Sonja, his sister-in-law, and a woman of means and education, had been suffering acutely for six months from pains in her back. In addition, there was a suspicious lump growing in her midsection, and she was losing weight rapidly. The condition was diagnosed by her

93

doctors—including her own father, who was a doctor—to be cancer of the liver. There was little hope, because the condition was considered inoperable. Out of desperation, Cruz went with her and her father to Arigo.

Arigo asked no questions, and didn't even examine the patient. He abruptly took Cruz and his father-in-law aside and told them that she had a tumor on the liver. She would have to be operated on immediately. Both were reluctant, but Arigo insisted there was no other choice.

Within minutes, Sonja was placed on newspapers on the floor of Arigo's small room. Arigo brought some cotton and several instruments, including scissors and knives. He selected a penknife and made an incision. Both Cruz and his father-in-law knew that it was impossible to cut into the liver without massive hemorrhaging, and neither could explain why they permitted this to be done, or why they stood by passively as Arigo cut into the patient with an unsterilized knife and no anesthesia. Perhaps, they thought later, it was because this was the last chance: all else had been given up.

They watched for the blood to spurt out, but only a thin trickle slid from the sides of the wound. Then, Cruz claimed, an even stranger thing happened. Arigo inserted the scissors deep into the wound, removed his hand, and the scissors seemed to move by themselves. Cruz turned to look at his father-in-law, who nodded and exchanged glances. Later, they were to compare notes and confirm, at least to themselves, what they had seen. In moments, Arigo removed the scissors, reached into the wound, and pulled out a tumorous growth. With a showmanlike flourish, he slapped the tumor into Cruz's hand. Then he took the cotton and wiped it along the incision. When he was finished, the edges of the wound adhered together without stitches and Arigo momentarily placed a crucifix on it. Then he told Sonja to rise, which she was able to do. She was weak and shaky, but felt no pain.

The trio left Congonhas stunned and speechless. Cruz

and his father-in-law, both being professional men, found themselves faced with believing what was unbelievable and accepting something that was scientifically impossible to accept. To them, the experience was more incredible than any in Lourdes, if only because this operation was real, tangible, verifiable—and yet it was a miracle.

The British consul listened intently to Cruz's story. He had been at his post in Brazil for over a decade and was prepared for almost anything. He followed the case with interest. Although the biopsy confirmed cancer, the liver regenerated itself—and Sonja gained back all her lost weight and was completely restored to normal health. Carlos Cruz, determined to find just how such an event could happen, returned to Congonhas do Campo several times, taking H. V. Walter with him. Although he was a layman, the consul had broad interest in medical science, and watched in astonishment as Arigo went through his daily routine.

Cruz, finding that his further observations of Arigo confirmed the unbelievable capacity of the man, was forced to come to the conclusion that there simply was no scientific explanation for it. Even Arigo's use of the German language was startling enough. Cruz was hoping to gather enough data to persuade several different professional societies to make a special study, and perhaps even the Ministry of Health. It was obvious that the law could not permit Arigo to continue his practice, and the authorities were certain to clamp down on him. This made good sense. But if some way could be found to bring Arigo into a carefully controlled scientific study, medicine might be able to make some entirely new advances that would carry it into a new era.

H. V. Walter was astounded and impressed with Arigo's work, but not at all impressed with the religious aura that Arigo surrounded it with. The consul was a hard-core realist who frankly felt that all religion was poppycock, and was convinced that Arigo's piety was simply window dressing. Yet his world travels had taught him that primitive man's instinct was often more sophisticated than modern man's. Carlos Cruz was not so sure, but he was not concerned about the religious aspect. The scientific study under legal conditions was to him the most important thing, and he was hoping to get this set up before the inevitable happened, when Arigo would be clamped down on by the police.

In spite of the threat hanging over Arigo, the ground swell continued unabated. It was estimated that a thousand Argentinians a month were arriving. In one instance a chartered planeload flew into Belo Horizonte, the passengers taking a special bus from there to Congonhas do Campo. Bus transportation from Rio and São Paulo was scheduled around Arigo's workdays, with special sections added at times. The invasion of outsiders into the little town created a mixed blessing. The economy was of course booming, but the accommodations were inadequate, and many townsmen claimed that they were being exposed to diseases that might be contagious.

On one occasion, Arigo rose from his bed after midnight and drove to a remote clearing several kilometers out of town to meet by prearrangement a truckload of lepers. They had slipped out of their hospital and made the surreptitious pilgrimage to see him after learning about several former lepers who claimed to have been cured by Arigo. Arigo arrived in the predawn darkness in his jeep to find them hiding behind the truck in the light of campfires and flickering candles. There were more than a score of them.

They rushed to embrace him. He accepted their embraces without fear, and began treating them individually with an improvised "laying on of hands" method. Daylight was just beginning to suggest itself over the mountains when he had finished with the last leper. Arigo hauled his heavy, bulky frame into the jeep and started back to the village. He wept openly all the way back. Only Altimiro knew of these clandestine excursions; if they came to light, the repercussions in the village would be overwhelming.

The varieties of patients swarming into Congonhas do Campo continued to be a cross section of the entire spectrum of society. An admiral arrived with his wife to seek treatment for her cataracts; the operation was instant and verified, as Dr. Cruz and the British consul watched. The daughter of one of Brazil's leading social families was brought to Arigo in a wheelchair. Specialists in Rio had given up on her leg injury, the result of an equestrian accident. Arigo yanked the leg forcefully. On her return to Rio, she was walking normally, and her cure was confirmed by the same specialists who had given her up.

Estimates of the number of patients Arigo was treating each day ranged from the wildly exaggerated to the timidly cautious. Television news programs, which frequently interrupted regular programs with special news bulletins on Arigo, insisted that the crowds were as high as a thousand each day. Whatever the exact number was, the crowds were impressive; the most conservative estimate was three hundred a day, excluding the families and friends who accompanied the patients on the trip.

Some tourists, arriving to see the Aleijadinho statuary, were completely caught by surprise on learning about Arigo. Armin Bauer, from Germany, was so taken aback on encountering this utterly incredible phenomenon that he wrote up his experience for *Die Zeit* when he returned home. He was a well-traveled man, his journeys having taken him on several safaris in Africa and all through Asia and around the world. Not knowing Portuguese, he had some trouble making himself as informed as he wanted to be about Brazil, a country which he and other tourists found easy to fall in love with.

He had arrived to visit a friend, an executive with the Volkswagen company, in São Paulo. Learning about the staggering elegance and artistry of the Aleijadinho sculptures, he set off for Minas Gerais to see them, and the countryside as well. In the streets of Congonhas do Campo, he was delighted to find another German, accompanied by his adult daughter. They were the only ones he had encountered on his trip who spoke his language, always a welcome event when one is traveling alone. He was startled when they told him that the reason they had come to Congonhas was to seek a cure for the daughter, who was suffering from leukemia. Her illness had been diagnosed by doctors in Germany as terminal, and they had come here as a last resort. Why on earth, Bauer asked, would they come to this little mountain town? They told him about Arigo and asked him if he'd like to come with them.

Bauer felt embarrassed and uncomfortable, but accepted their invitation. He also felt it was tragic that these fellow Germans were putting their trust in a village faith healer of dubious qualifications at best. Although he felt a little foolish, he went with them to the Centro Spirito de Bom Jesus de Nazarene, the new location, named by the spiritists, where Arigo was now practicing.

Bauer was impressed by the cathedral silence of the large room and the wide spectrum of social classes waiting to see Arigo. He managed to look over Altimiro's shoulder as he typed up one of the prescriptions, expecting to find it nothing more than a list of black-magic potions and herbs. Instead, he saw pharmaceuticals listed from Schering, Bayer, Squibb, Upjohn, and other famous houses. He was also surprised to notice the number of people who waited for hours in line simply to tell Arigo they had come back to Congonhas to give him their devout thanks for curing them in the past. And as Arigo took a pair of nail scissors and hacked at a pterygium—a winglike growth that fixes itself immovably across the eye from the conjunctiva to the cornea—he noticed several people in line fainting or collapsing, including a foreign journalist. But the patient stood calmly, unperturbed, and fully conscious.

On his return to Germany, Bauer wrote for *Die Zeit*: "I really don't think this can be explained by spiritism, as some of the Brazilians say. Arigo has none of the atmosphere of mysticism surrounding him. This should be urgently looked into—it needs special study. Scientists are going to have their doubts—nothing like this has happened before. It has to be seen to be experienced."

Arigo was swamped by requests for appointments from prominent people, Brazilian and otherwise. The Peruvian consul in Rio telegraphed for an appointment, but like the others, he had to come on a first-come, first-served basis.

Of the constant stream of journalists that came into Congonhas do Campo, several were inspired to write books about him. Among them were Reinaldo Comenale, who flatly called Arigo the eighth wonder of the world. Geraldo Serrano wrote that Arigo was far from a saint, but that scientists would be afraid of the challenge presented by Arigo, since they would be quickly convinced they would lose the battle with rationality. Jorge Rizzini eventually published a book about Arigo, recounting his own direct experiences with him, and backed up by his documentary film footage. A highly regarded professor of philosophy named J. Herculano Pires produced a carefully documented book, perhaps the most profound one written about the phenomenon. The problem that all the authors faced was one of restraint. After observing Arigo over weeks or months or years, they simply could not refrain from going overboard in adulation and wonderment.

Under the circumstances, this was understandable. As Arigo's fame grew, a large segment of the medical profession began to get interested, both favorable and unfavorable in attitude. They would soon be facing the same problem: maintaining objectivity in the face of utterly incredible empirical facts. The problem would be in separating the subjective from the objective. Obviously the most important phase for study would be the objective evidence, because it could be measured and grasped.

As the public clamor and confusion grew throughout

Brazil, Arigo continued to grapple with his down-to-earth problems as well as those of his healing powers. He was still determined to run for office in Congonhas do Campo as the only means of trying to correct injustices he had found as a miner and as a friend of the underprivileged. In some quarters, his political hopes were considered as censurable as his healing work. Arigo found himself running against his own uncle, Lamartine de Freitas, for mayor.

Lamartine de Freitas was establishment to the core. He was a staunch Catholic, unadulterated by the alleged heresies Arigo was committing daily. He was also a landholder of considerable stature, and a heavy favorite of the conservative voters in town. Arigo was of course just the opposite. Under normal conditions, this would have made him the favorite, and carried the tide as far as mass votes were concerned. However, the official Church had it noised about the town that Arigo was a man who wasn't going along with the mandates of the Church.

Further, Arigo's political enemies spread the word that the only reason Arigo was conducting his bizarre clinic for the poor and sick was to gather votes for his political career. Many other stories were circulated about him: Arigo was a brawler (he had had a fight with an unruly patron of his bar, and had thrown him out); Arigo collected money from his patients surreptitiously; Arigo arranged for kickbacks from the druggists and pharmaceutical companies; Arigo had a mistress and an illegitimate daughter in Belo Horizonte or Rio. There was no evidence for any of these charges, but the opposition made sure the stories were spread.

Arigo lost the election by some two hundred votes, but his supporters charged that the ballots had been tampered with when they were held for the night at the local post office instead of being forwarded to the town of Lafaiete, where they were legally required to be sent for a nonpartisan count. By the time his uncle assumed the office of mayor, the cards were down. Lamartine de

Freitas called Arigo to his office and summarily demanded that he either give up his clinic or leave town.

Arigo bluntly refused. The two forces of the establishment and the maverick now moved into more clearly defined battle positions. The attempt was obviously to make Arigo an outcast, but the tides of people that swept into Congonhas to see him increased. Eventually, his uncle backed down, and Arigo went on with his healing work with greater vitality than ever. This function seemed to be an entirely separate compartment of his life. Some speculated that the reason for his being able to suspend his mundane functions when treating the sick was that he literally was not conscious of what he was doing when he performed surgical operations or wrote prescriptions. For the confirmed spiritist, the answer was easy: he wasn't Arigo when he worked at his clinic. He was Dr. Adolpho Fritz, and Arigo's body was only a shell, a functionary that carried out the benificent urges of the deceased German doctor, who took on far greater skills in his afterlife than he had possessed on earth. This was such a far-fetched concept that few others could grasp it. All that was really obvious was that Arigo was clearly suspending the laws of physics, and even the most caustic skeptic had to admit this, if he took the time to observe the man in action. Most critics did not bother to investigate, however. They dismissed the stories they heard about Arigo as impossibilities—an attitude hardly to be faulted in the face of such incredible events.

Interesting evidence on Arigo's lack of awareness of his own work showed up when Jorge Rizzini asked Arigo to look at some of the color motion picture films he had taken of Arigo performing an operation. Rizzini set up his projector in the clinic after the last patient had left. The film began rolling, and the first scene depicted Arigo stabbing a penknife into a patient's eye. Arigo, no longer in the trance state that seemed to characterize his working hours in the clinic, watched the scene with growing horror. Within moments, his head dropped down on his chest, and he fainted. When he came to, he rushed from the room yelling in a loud voice that this was too terrible to look at.

But it was apparent that Arigo could not stop the work in the clinic even if he wanted to. It was a compulsion of overwhelming magnitude.

He was able at times to get away from it, and stoutly refused to treat anyone on Saturdays and Sundays, when he would retreat with his family to a house on his wealthy aunt's farm. She was the only member of the family who was a spiritist, and she encouraged him to keep on. Here Arigo enjoyed his only hobby: the growing of roses. Like everything else he attacked in life, he was obsessive about the literally thousands of rosebushes he nourished and grew. With the financial help of his aunt, he sent them out by the carton to hospitals all over the state of Minas Gerais and elsewhere. They came to be a trademark of his. When he was entreated by a patient on a weekend, he would become surly and tough, and say: "Do you think I'm made of steel? Don't you know I have a family?"

As the praises for Arigo grew across the country in both the press and television, his detractors gathered their forces. The Catholic clergy was of course the spearhead, along with the bulk of the members of the medical association of the state of Minas Gerais. But individuals too bore resentment against Arigo, among them his political enemies. Antonio Maia Seabra, a resident of Congonhas, was one of these. He accused Arigo of being a rank opportunist who was looking out after his own interests. He spread stories that Arigo's operations were all tricks. He also passed rumors along that Altimiro, in handing out the cards that designated the position of the people in line, charged fifteen cruzeiros for each card, which he split with Arigo. He also saw to it that stories circulated to the effect that any patient Arigo treated would have to sign a card indicating he would vote for Arigo in any forthcoming election. He insisted that Arigo swilled one or two bottles of wine with each meal.

Seabra was joined in his attack by two doctors in town, each of whom quite understandably resented the intrusion into their bailiwick. Dr. Coimbra, Arigo's family doctor for years, could no longer tolerate the fact that Arigo was blatantly practicing illegal medicine, and made his feelings widely known on the subject. He went beyond this legitimate criticism to ascribe motives that Arigo's friends staunchly claimed were untrue. Dr. Coimbra accused Arigo of practicing black magic, and said that the sole reason Arigo continued his illegal practice was simply to become famous so he could gain political power.

But most of Arigo's detractors admitted that Arigo was a hard worker, a good father, and a good family man—in spite of rumors of occasional extramarital excursions. Altimiro, who was now facing the same censorship from the Church as Arigo, was also highly thought of in the community. Obviously, any defense against the practice of illegal medicine was impossible, even by the most passionate advocate of Arigo. The sinister part was the attempt of many, principally for political reasons, to look for devious motives that did not exist in the man.

Resentment also followed in the wake of the number of distinguished visitors who made the long trip to Congonhas for the sole purpose of seeing Arigo—and, in the process, ignored the local politicians. Rumors stirred that Juscelino Kubitschek, freshly elected President of the country, had arranged for his daughter to see Arigo to be cured of massive inoperable kidney stones that had resisted several specialists' care in Europe and North America. Later, this was to be confirmed. But even the rumor of it at this time intensified the resentment of Arigo's enemies. Kubitschek was overwhelmingly popular throughout the country, and was already embarking on the construction of Brasília, the fantastic new capital that was to rise out of the wilderness in the geographic center of the country.

Other patients at the time included President Kubitschek's personal pilot, the head of the President's security police, a prominent judge, the captain of the Minas Gerais state police, and several generals of the Brazilian army. These and others amounted to a formidable array facing down Arigo's critics, and undoubtedly slowed the impetus of the court proceedings that had not yet struck.

Further, a group of doctors in the neighboring town of Lafaiete, aroused by the flood of rumors that was swamping the entire country, began an informal investigation of Arigo. They included Dr. José Demasio, Dr. Antonio Castanheira, and a Dr. Viterino. They were joined by Dr. João Ranulf de Melo, of Congonhas. Together, they observed two cataract operations and two ovarian-cyst operations, one by way of the abdomen, the other through the vagina. On careful examination before and after the surgery, they agreed that the operations were completely valid, that the tissues involved were skillfully removed, and that practically no scar was left. As usual, there were no anesthesia, no antisepsis, practically no bleeding, no pain, and no stitching. As for the crucifix that Arigo later placed over the surgical areas, the doctors had no comment. They agreed, however, that there was no natural explanation for what they had observed, that no ordinary doctor could possibly do this, and that an intensive scientific study on Arigo should immediately be set up, if they could gather the necessary funds.

The initial ignition for all these staggering phenomena had of course been Senator Lucio Bittencourt, and his continuous praise carried the momentum along. His health was excellent, and he was a prominent living testimonial to Arigo's inexplicable powers. One day after a particularly long line of patients, Arigo was joined by his friend Gabriel Khater, a newspaperman who served in Minas Gerais as a stringer for several Brazilian journals. Arigo was disturbed and uneasy. Khater probed him about this, and Arigo finally told him that he had seen in his mind's eye that day a black crucifix that disturbed him greatly. Pressed for the reason, Arigo said that each time this had happened, someone close to him had died. Khater tried to cheer him up, to get his mind off the somber symbol. But it was little use. Arigo went home as distressed as he was before.

The next morning, Khater was about to go through his usual routine of scanning several newspapers of the day when he was stopped short by the first paper he picked up. The lead headline read: SENATOR LUCIO BITTENCOURT KILLED IN AUTO CRASH.

Arigo was crushed by the loss of his friend, but he was further upset by the ominous proclivity he had of seeing ahead when a tragedy was about to happen. It left him depressed and worried. But he went on with his overwhelming routine in spite of it.

It was only a few days before he received another jolt. He was going about the usual treatment of his patients when a sudden sharp reaction went through him. He stopped his pen in midair and put it down.

Sitting by his typewriter, Altimiro noticed the unusual action. He watched Arigo leave his table, cross into the big room, and confront a man in the line.

"Are you a policeman?" Arigo asked.

The man said that he was.

"Come with me," Arigo said.

He marched the man into his small office and abruptly sent the waiting patients there out into the big room. He told Altimiro to stay with him, then closed the door. Arigo's eyes were blazing. Altimiro had never seen them that way before.

"You came down here," Arigo said to the policeman, "to ask me for a prescription because you want to take that prescription to the judge, is that correct?"

The policeman nodded.

"In this way you will get evidence to bring a court proceeding against me, is that not right?"

The policeman looked frightened, but he nodded again.

"First," said Arigo, "you have to take care of your family. You have not seen them for a long time. You have neglected them. Is that not true?"

The policeman muttered something, but eventually said yes.

"It is your duty to take care of them first," Arigo said. "And then you can take care of your judge and your courts. So I will write you a prescription. Do you agree to follow it?"

The policeman said that he would.

Arigo took a sheet of paper, and wrote on it swiftly: READ THE BIBLE. EARLY IN THE MORNING. IN THE AFTERNOON. AT NIGHT TIME. 3 TIMES A DAY WITHOUT FAIL.

He handed it to the man, whose face was flushed. The policeman studied the sheet of paper, nodded, and left the room. Arigo went on with his work.

5

In these days of the early and mid-fifties, there were
many preoccupations throughout the world, not the least
of which was the Korean War, as far as the United States
was concerned, and the development of the hydrogen
bomb, as far as the world was concerned. While the latter
was the major fruit of midcentury physics, the biological
explosion was just shaping up, to result in reaching the
threshold of living matter with James Watson's and
Francis Crick's discovery of the critical function of RNA
and DNA.

Medicine was continuing to make giant strides with the
development of cortisone, of Max Theiler's vaccine to
combat yellow fever, of streptomycin, of Jonas Salk's
polio vaccine, of other new broad-spectrum miracle
drugs.

Advances in physics were coming so fast that it looked
as if the study of elementary particles might reach a dead
end, a point where science began to blend with
metaphysics. Not the least interesting was the discovery
of the antiproton at the University of California,
suggesting the almost absurd concept of antimatter.

This concept clearly brought the pragmatic physicist to
the threshold of the paranormal. It even suggested the
possibility that there were stars or whole galaxies in the
universe made of antimatter. No science fiction writer

could invent a more far-out idea, yet the discovery of antimatter, identical to normal matter except that its protons and electrons are charged in opposite directions, was being routinely verified from MIT to Cal Tech. On colliding with normal protons and electrons, antimatter causes the total destruction of both.

Explaining the new phenomenon, physicist Leon Lederman of the Brookhaven National Laboratory said bluntly: "A new and deeper world and anti-world symmetry is now believed to hold, in which the anti-world does not only have anti-particles replace particles, but also is a mirror image of our world." He went on to add: "It is not possible now to disprove the grand speculation that these anti-worlds could be populated by thinking creatures."

Such revolutionary concepts were shaking the conventional views of science, and this inspired some scientists to set up, in the early fifties, organized studies in fields that science had neglected or overlooked. The scientists involved knew nothing of what was going on with Arigo in the town of Congonhas at the time. They did, as a group, feel that research on paranormal events and energy-transfer phenomena was being grossly neglected in the light of the major advances in physics and medical science.

One of the groups consisted of a generous handful of physicians, engineers, surgeons, neurologists, executives, and professors. They were working in varied fields, including universities, hospitals, government, and industry, in addition to those in private practice. There was a senior research scientist in surgery, a manager of an astroelectronics division of a large corporation, a chief research psychiatrist, a professor of surgery, a professor of philosophy, a neurologist, and others. They worked in a variety of highly respected institutions, among them Stanford University, New York University, Massachusetts General Hospital, the University of Pittsburgh, and Radio Corporation of America. Eventually they formed themselves into a loose organization known as Essentia Research Associates, based in New York.

At about the same time that Arigo was burgeoning with his healing work in Brazil, some of this group began a tentative exploration of telepathy for divisions of the United States government, including NASA and the U.S. Air Force. But for the most part, progress was fitful and public funds were hard to come by; the Essentia Research group could make only tentative probes into the paranormal, including nonsensory transfer of information.

Dr. Henry Puharich, who later was to join Henry Belk in the encounter with Arigo in Brazil, was one of the Essentia Research group. He joined forces with John Laurance, who belonged to a similar group called Life Energies Research. This organization was centering its interest on the use of complex electronic sensors to locate and identify energy systems surrounding the human body. These ill-defined energies had been crudely studied in the past, but advanced study would have to wait on the development of sensitive instrumentation. There was definite interest in many quarters, from the Pentagon to NASA to the Atomic Energy Commission, and Puharich and others were invited to fill many speaking engagements. But interest was still too sluggish to generate the large amount of funds necessary to reach any comprehensive conclusions.

If, in the mid-fifties, the work that Arigo was doing had come to serious attention in the United States, greater strides in enlightenment might have been made. As it was, any scientific study would have to outrace the pressures being brought to bear by those who wanted the courts to clamp down on his practices forever.

Fortunately, there was a growing number of highly qualified physicians and surgeons in Brazil who were beginning to take Arigo seriously enough to examine the facts. Some of this interest was reflected in peculiar ways. One surgeon tried to use hypnosis to duplicate Arigo's bold use of a knife in a patient's eye. The surgeon used a small, dull, spatula-type instrument to minimize any damage, but even though he put the patient under deep hypnosis, the results were disastrous. He had barely touched the instrument to the eye when the patient backed off in terror. Whatever Arigo was doing, it apparently was not within the grasp of the ordinary surgeon.

The resentment of doctors against Arigo was certainly understandable, not only from the point of view of competition, but also of pride. The educational requirements for doctors in Brazil are as strenuous as they are in the United States, with pre-med, medical school, internship, and residency—all requiring a beefy investment of time and money. For a country bumpkin who never went beyond third grade to command such attention throughout the entire country and attract internationally prominent citizens naturally stung their professional pride. On the other hand, those doctors whose curiosity was greater than their resentment found themselves in considerable awe at what went on before their eyes.

One of these doctors was Dr. Ladeira Margues, of Rio de Janeiro, who was growing tired of hearing and reading about Arigo, and determined to go up to the provincial reaches of Minas Gerais to find out more about this legend. He took with him another doctor from Rio who preferred to remain anonymous, and they prepared themselves for the worst.

Several months before the two doctors had gathered their courage against what they were sure would be the scathing criticism of their colleagues, a woman by the name of Maria Silveiro went to her own doctor in the city of Vitória, the capital of Espírito Santo state. She had been suffering constant pain in her lower midsection, and her concern was growing.

Her fears were shared by her doctor, who immediately called in a specialist. It wasn't long before the diagnosis was definitely confirmed as ovarian cancer, and it was recommended that an operation be carried out immediately. With her husband, Ismenio Silveiro, a prominent local official in Vitória, they made arrangements for the operation to be done in the best hospital in the city.

The surgery was performed, but it was completely unsuccessful. The prognosis was shattering: she had only a few months to live. All the doctors concerned with the case had given her up.

Ismenio Silveiro confided in a friend of his, Virgilio Mendes Ferraz, about his wife's illness. Ferraz was one of the wealthiest men in the area, a prosperous landowner who was known throughout the state. On hearing Silveiro's plight, he told him about his own wife's similar experience. She had been pronounced a hopeless case of cancer by every specialist she had visited, and there were many. He had been told about Arigo, and as a last resort, he took his wife to Congonhas do Campo, with little hope or expectation. Arigo performed a startling operation on his fully conscious wife, and within weeks she was restored to full health.

Ferraz had been so overcome by the miraculous cure that he sent Arigo a check for $50,000. He had been surprised when Arigo promptly returned the check to him, stating that he could not accept money or gifts of any kind.

Ferraz urged Silveiro to take his wife to Arigo, stating that anything was worth the risk in the face of the prognosis the doctors had determined. The Silveiros arrived in Congonhas do Campo at precisely the same time that Dr. Ladeira Margues and his anonymous colleague arrived from Rio.

Feeling somewhat uncomfortable, the two doctors from Rio were ushered into the small back room of Arigo's clinic, beyond his own usual working area. This was the place reserved for the more serious operations. The room was sparsely furnished. An old door, stretched between two saw horses, was used as an operating table. There was also a shabby wooden bed for the minimal postoperative care that Arigo felt necessary at times—although it was rarely used. The Rio doctors were invited to stand by the operating area and observe as closely as they wished.

Arigo was his usual self—gruff, abrupt, almost arrogant. A largish window let in adequate light, and the Rio doctors steeled themselves to watch Arigo in action. Maria Silveiro was ushered in by her husband, and then Arigo took over. He half pushed, half guided the woman onto the flat door that served as the operating table, having spread some old newspapers on it beforehand. He called for Altimiro to bring his instruments, and as usual, they rested in a battered tin can. There were a pair of tweezers, a couple of scalpels, a paring knife, and some scissors. Arigo was in his trancelike state that characterized his personality change to that of Dr. Fritz, a change so vivid that reporters and even other doctors came to refer to him by that name instead of Arigo.

Speaking with his guttural German accent, Arigo turned to the husband, ignoring his distress and worry, and asked whether he preferred the operation to be done by incision in the abdominal wall or by way of the vagina. The husband preferred the latter. Without further ceremony, Arigo asked the husband to lift the dress of the patient. Then he immediately began the operation with extraordinary rapidity. The two doctors from Rio watched in disbelief.

In any operation of this type, a speculum is obligatory. This is a surgical instrument that spreads the tissues or openings in the body so that full inspection can be made and the instruments introduced into the area without impediment. Arigo's scanty armamentarium included no such refinements. They watched as he shoved three pairs of scissors and two scalpels into the vagina, each one with a single violent movement. The doctors immediately turned their observation to the patient. Surely, they felt, there would be agonizing pain from this crude procedure. However, she lay calm and motionless, with no response whatever. In describing what happened next, Dr. Margues said:

"Arigo was taking hold of one half of the scissors. Then we began to see the other side of the scissors start to move alone. It was as if another hand had taken hold of the free handle and was beginning to make clear motions, causing the scissors to snip and cut. The sound of metals and tissues being cut was obvious. In moments, 'Dr. Fritz' removed the scissors. When he saw bleeding begin, he ceased what he was doing, and said: 'Lord, let there be no more blood.' There was no further hemorrhage, as the operation went on.

"He reached then for the pair of tweezers. Calling this to our close attention, he pushed them into the vaginal opening and took out a piece of tissue some thirty-one inches long and fifteen inches in width. The patient was relaxed and unruffled during the whole process, which lasted only a few minutes. She reflected no pain at all. There was no anesthesia administered, nothing was sterilized, and no antisepsis was involved."

Later, she was to give birth to a healthy son, and regained her full health.

Both doctors found themselves in the position of having to accept what they had clearly seen, to be "a slave to the facts," as one of them put it. Yet they knew they would be exposing themselves to censure if they publicly acknowledged what had happened. Dr. Margues made no bones about it, and reported the experience in detail to his colleagues and others. The problem of course was credibility—and what reporting such an event might do to destroy the credibility of a doctor who had the courage of his convictions and spoke out.

It was not an easy decision for a professional man. The official position of the medical societies was clearly defined: Arigo was a *curandeiro* and a charlatan, if not a practitioner of witchcraft. It was an open-and-shut case, and the medical society of Minas Gerais was champing at the bit at the slowness of the police Division of Robbery and Falsification for not expediting the legal proceedings and bringing the whole thing to an end. They surmised, probably correctly, that there were high government officials whose lives or those of their relatives had been inexplicably saved by Arigo, and thus were not at all interested in pushing for the incarceration of a man they owed so much to.

And perhaps these people of influence were responsible for the pilgrimage of many more doctors to Congonhas do Campo who were willing to take the risk of professional censure.

Whatever day the visiting doctors arrived in the village was unimportant as far as representative cases were concerned. Each day Arigo faced such a broad spectrum of diseases and disorders that any doctor could find something of specific interest for any medical problem.

But some doctors came to Congonhas do Campo as the result of specific cases they had followed with interest. These were desperate patients who came to Arigo as a last resort after all else in medical science had failed. Dr. José Hortencia de Madeiros found himself observing Arigo for just such a reason. Dr. Madeiros, who was an X-ray specialist with the State Institute of Cardiology, was the friend of a young couple who were deeply concerned because of the illness of the wife. Although Dr. Madeiros had been practicing medicine for many years, and had been trained in his X-ray specialty in Sweden for two years, he could do little for the wife, a young Polish woman in her late twenties. The husband was Austrian.

She had been rushed to Pronto Socorro Clinic in São Paulo, where she arrived in desperate condition, with symptoms of an intestinal obstruction. She was examined and X-rayed, and it was apparent that an immediate operation was necessary. During the surgery, it was found that her transverse colon was blocked by a tumor, and this was removed. A colostomy was performed, in which an opening is cut in the abdomen and the colon is joined to it to permit defecation into a colostomy bag.

The tumor was rushed to the laboratory for a pathological examination, but the surgeons felt sure that the woman had cancer, and that there was little hope. The ganglia on her peritoneum were grossly enlarged, and a nodule on the liver had been noted during the operation. The laboratory test clearly confirmed carcinoma.

With the tests confirming malignancy, the case was hopeless. All the doctors consulted agreed to that. However, it was decided that one final attempt should be made, and she entered the Central Cancer Hospital in São Paulo for another operation. There was a sense of futility about it, but both the husband and Dr. Madeiros felt that nothing should be left undone.

The abdomen was opened again, and by now the condition was even more hopeless. The cancer had metastasized throughout the entire abdominal area; a new growth the size of a large egg was found in the left section. Meanwhile, the patient's weight had dropped mercurially. She was now slightly over seventy pounds. She had previously weighed nearly 130. The surgeon's report at the Central Cancer Hospital was even more pessimistic than that of the clinic. He reported the case to be totally incurable, and outside the resources of medical science.

Two independent checks were made on the metastasized tissue, one by the chief of anatomic pathology at the Central Cancer Hospital. The diagnosis was clearly reconfirmed as mucocellular metastasic carcinoma, and the two independent reports concurred without question on this. The patient was overwhelmed by a carcinogenic invasion. The prognosis in the reports stated a potential life expectancy of two months at best. Dr. Madeiros rechecked all the facts of the case, and found there was nothing else to do but agree.

With his wife little more than a living skeleton, the husband came to Dr. Madeiros with one last, and probably futile suggestion: he would like to take his wife to Congonhas do Campo to see Arigo. He realized how ridiculous this might be, but if Dr. Madeiros thought she could survive the trip, he would like to do it.

Madeiros had heard of Arigo, and his interest had been piqued by the reports coming down to São Paulo from Congonhas do Campo. He also knew of the attitude of the medical societies toward the healer, but, as a doctor of both curiosity and compassion, he saw no harm in making one last stab, even if it failed miserably. And because he was a close friend of the couple, he decided to accompany them. At least, he thought, he could try to keep the wife out of pain on the long trip.

It would be disastrous, the doctor knew, to attempt the trip by car or bus. Instead, a small plane was chartered to fly to the airport at Lafaiete, the closest air facility to Congonhas. The wife had now faded to sixty-five pounds.

The patient was carried by her husband to Arigo, accompanied by Dr. Madeiros. In the stillness of the musty clinic, Arigo's voice was booming with his German accent, sprinkled with occasional German phrases. The husband, being Austrian, gathered the courage to speak to Arigo in German, and was answered in that language. Arigo gave the desperately ill woman no special attention. She was simply one among the many hundreds who filed by his table on that day or any other day. He looked at her, his eyes glazed in the usual trance state he experienced every time he assumed the character of Dr. Fritz. His hand swiftly scrawled a prescription. He merely said to the wife: "You take this, and get well."

The trio were abruptly ushered to Altimiro, who instantly typed up the prescription. Within two hours they were headed back to São Paulo. On the plane, Dr. Madeiros studied the prescription. Though the medicines comprised up-to-date pharmaceuticals at that time, he considered the combination totally irrational. And the dosages prescribed were far in excess of any ordinary prescription. The drugs included Kanamicine, Olobintin, Neurorubin, and Dexteascine, all trade-marked drugs and available at almost any drugstore in Brazil.

Kanamicine was a drug of Japanese origin, manufactured under special license in Rio de Janeiro. It was basically an antibiotic, used mainly in intestinal infections. It had caused serious side effects at times. Olobintin was an ancient German formula manufactured in Rio, designed to increase the defensive forces of the organism, and supposedly had special effectiveness in fetid bronchitis and pulmonary gangrene. It was an injectable. Dr. Madeiros could find no real reason for this to be included, but he had heard from other doctors that Arigo's prescriptions had a strange way of working, regardless of their absurdity. He had also heard that when other doctors tried to imitate Arigo's unconventional combinations, the drugs were ineffective. Neurorubin was also produced in Brazil, and consisted of a vitamin B complex, with a heavy proportion of vitamin B_{12}. The rationale for Dexteascine was obscure.

In spite of his pessimism that the drugs would do any good, Dr. Madeiros agreed to take a chance, out of frustration and despair, if nothing else. When they arrived back in São Paulo, he administered the abnormal dosages and waited, feeling very nonprofessional in doing so.

Within a week, the fatally ill patient improved to the point where she could get out of bed and walk around her room. By the end of the second week, she had regained over twenty pounds of her lost weight. After six weeks of the treatment, she weighed nearly five pounds more than when she had first been stricken with the disease. Dr. Madeiros could hardly contain his surprise. He agreed to return to Congonhas do Campo with the patient and her husband for a recheck by Arigo.

He was now very anxious to follow up his observation on the healer, and especially interested in confirming the apparent cure. To the best of his knowledge, the patient appeared to be permanently on the road to recovery. She was still walking around with the awkward colostomy bag as a means of getting rid of waste matter. Arigo had said nothing about having it removed, and, for the time,

Madeiros saw no sense in challenging Arigo's advice, in the face of the unbelievable success achieved thus far.

Back in Congonhas do Campo, Arigo abruptly pronounced the patient out of danger and presented her with two more prescriptions, as unconventional as the first. One of the new medicines was an antibiotic used for urinary-tract infections. Dr. Madeiros found he could at least agree with this logic, since the colostomy and original intestinal obstruction had had an extremely damaging effect on the urinary system.

The patient returned to Arigo for a third time, with her mother. Arigo declared unequivocally that she was completely healed. He instructed her to "undo the operation," referring to the colostomy. She returned to São Paulo with the news, and arrangements were immediately made to surgically reverse the colostomy, closing up the surgical openings.

The new operation was performed in a large São Paulo hospital by one of Brazil's leading surgeons. Dr. Madeiros waited impatiently to find out just what would be discovered when his patient's abdomen was reopened for the first time since she had been given up for lost.

The search for the tumor was negative; all that remained was a harmless formation of fibrous tissue. The intestine was rejoined, and began to function normally. Eleven months later, the patient was without any sign of her previous devastating condition.

Because he had followed this case from start to finish and was familiar with every detail of it, Dr. Madeiros did not hesitate to publicly announce his findings. Many of his colleagues had had similar experiences with Arigo and their patients, but hesitated to report the cases in medical journals or to the public. In view of the pending lawsuit against Arigo, any such announcement was frowned on both by the Catholic Church and the medical associations. In spite of this, Madeiros returned several more times to Congonhas do Campo. In the operations he observed, he was startled and impressed by what appeared to be almost instant scar-forming of incisions, with no stitches being used at all. It was another inexplicable phenomenon that accompanied most of Arigo's healing work.

Another doctor of considerable stature who was willing to run against the tide of official opinion was Dr. Ary Lex. He was a lecturer at the Surgical Clinic of São Paulo University, a specialist in surgery of the stomach and digestive system, and practiced at the Hospital das Clinicas, the largest hospital in South America. What intrigued him was that although the Church and the medical societies were scouring the field to try to find someone—anyone—who had been harmed by Arigo and who would testify against him in the impending legal action, they had been totally unsuccessful.

If there were any such cases around, they were not making themselves known. By all logic, persons allegedly damaged by Arigo's crude surgery or prescriptions should certainly have been emerging on the scene by now. There were enough doctors and establishment priests out to get Arigo, in fact, destroy him, that it should have been easy for them to find someone who at least *felt* he had been harmed by Arigo. The fact that none had been uncovered was important supportive evidence for Arigo's validity, Dr. Lex felt.

As a former president of the surgical section of the São Paulo Medical Association, Lex was aware that he was treading on dangerous ground by making a study of Arigo. He was known for his fight against any sort of quackery or unethical practices. In the course of this work he had uncovered a number of frauds and trickery, and was successful in exposing them. It became quickly apparent to him that Arigo was an entirely different kettle of fish.

He went to Congonhas alone, without any colleagues, because he had too many doubts that he would uncover anything special about Arigo. He was surprised and pleased to find two other professors of medicine in

Congonhas do Campo who had the same idea in mind. When he watched what happened that day in Arigo's clinic, he was thankful to have the other professionals there.

Together, they watched four operations within the space of half an hour, scattered among some thirty nonsurgical cases. Since Dr. Lex had never found a mediumistic healer who survived his scrutiny under test conditions, he watched carefully as Arigo went to work. The only politeness Arigo showed to his three distinguished visitors was to invite them to come as close as possible to observe. Dr. Lex quickly discerned that while Arigo himself seemed to be in a trance state, he made no attempt to use any hypnotic techniques on his patients, nor did he use any type of passes with his hands or other means of suggestion. Dr. Lex was particularly interested in this, because he felt it might explain some part of Arigo's success, but he was now convinced that the patients were not even in a partial trance state.

The first operation was the drainage of a synovial cyst, without any surgical preparation or anesthesia, as usual. And, of course, no antisepsis. It was successfully completed in a matter of moments. For the second operation, Arigo asked Dr. Lex if he wanted to hold the patient's arm. He did so, enabling him to get an extremely close view of the removal of a lipoma. Arigo did this in less than half a minute. But what interested Dr. Lex most was the technique used. Instead of cutting the skin with the scalpel, Arigo massaged the back of the blade across the arm until it suddenly opened. Then with his hands, he pressed down on the flesh, and the fatty tumor came out as a unit.

In the third operation, Arigo faced the same problem and operated in the same way. For the fourth, Arigo permitted Dr. Lex to hold the patient's head as he prepared to operate on a pterygium. This winglike growth across the eye was firmly locked into the cornea. Arigo picked up a pair of unsterilized nail scissors, as Dr. Lex watched in disbelief. No patient, he was sure, could stand the direct cutting into the eyeball without full anesthesia. But as usual, the patient was wide awake as Arigo pushed the points of the scissors into the eye with unbelievable roughness, snipping freely at the eye tissue and talking in his German accent as he did so. The growth was removed cleanly, but the eye began to hemorrhage profusely, the blood starting to pour down the patient's cheek.

Arigo looked to the ceiling and ordered the blood to stop. Then he took a piece of questionably clean cotton and pressed it into the eye. After a moment or two of wiping, he removed the cotton. The bleeding had stopped altogether.

Questioned later by author J. Herculano Pires, Dr. Lex said: "The only possible adjectives I can find to define this are spectacular and astounding."

Then he went on to say: "During all these operations, I talked with the patients, asking them if they felt any pain. The patients were conscious, quiet, did not react and said that they did not feel anything. Arigo acted in a natural fashion, was confident of himself to the point that at one time he cleaned the scalpel violently on my colleague's head. He—the doctor—also did not feel anything, despite the violence of the act."

Dr. Lex observed several of Arigo's "pointed knife" examinations of a patient's eye, in which Arigo literally stirred the knife far up inside the orbital cavity, looking away from the patient and talking to others as he did so. "He sometimes made the eyeball to protrude as if it were going to come out of the eye socket," Dr. Lex told Pires. "All of this without asepsis or anesthesia and without signs of pain to the patients."

But as admiring as Dr. Lex was about Arigo's form of surgery, he was distressed with his prescriptions. "I was frightened by them," Dr. Lex said. "I consider them great absurdities. They do not seem to make any sense. Olobintin and Kanamicine are really obsolete drugs. They have dangerous side effects and adverse reactions."

Dr. Madeiros of course concurred with this. Yet he had seen the prescriptions work, and on inquiry had not found any harm coming from them as far as he could determine. This was hardly adequate research, he knew, and the problem was as puzzling as ever. Both Dr. Lex and Dr. Madeiros agreed completely on one thing: serious research should be done on Arigo—long, intensive, and complete, and under strict medical control.

"In spite of his faults," Dr. Lex said, "he is a remarkable phenomenon. I don't criticize Arigo alone. It seems to me he should merit greater attention from many scientific societies. The fact that there is no scientific control of the medium's activities does expose him and his patients to a series of dangerous situations. There is also the danger of misuse of his faculties. Scientific proof is lacking at the moment. It should be established, of course. But I can say without question that I have observed for the first time a case of authentic paranormal phenomenon in my own field of medicine."

Later, Dr. Lex was to return to see Arigo and observe a confirmed case of cancer of the liver in which Arigo removed the tumor with his hands, an unheard-of procedure. The biopsy reconfirmed a cancerous condition, and the patient's full recovery was likewise confirmed. He was a wealthy lawyer, a solid, pragmatic materialist. When he recovered, he became a spiritist.

There were other doctors, many of them, who came to Congonhas do Campo, either openly or covertly. Some came to scoff, but most went away completely convinced that here was one of the strangest cases in medical history. The consensus was that Arigo was unbelievable— yet the cold, empirical evidence of the success of his operations left them with no choice other than believing the unbelievable.

But there were not enough of them to mount any effective opposition in the face of the attitude of the medical societies. And even those who were convinced completely of Arigo's validity felt that he could not go on with his practice in an open, uncontrolled situation. Unscrupulous charlatans, inspired by Arigo, would proliferate throughout the country, with utterly disastrous results for the public. Medical anarchy could develop. Anyone who appears to suspend the laws of physics is faced with overwhelming and totally unique problems. Among Arigo's problems was the further complication of his being a blasphemer and heretic in the eyes of the Catholic Church.

Finally, after the long delay, the legal machinery of the court process came to a head. On August 1, 1956, an official named Helvecio Arantes, of the robbery and falsification division of the state police, sat down at his desk and wrote:

> Judicial Directive executing orders from the Secretary of Public Security of the State of Minas Gerais to verify the facts relating to the practice of illegal medicine by the individual known as José Arigo, whose real name is José Pedro de Freitas, to inquire concerning the practice of illegal medicine.
>
> Ze Arigo and all the persons having knowledge of these acts will be called. A prescription written by Arigo can be found at the drug store Farmacia Congonhas Limitada.

The first detectives of the *policia* to arrive in town were themselves immediately detected by the townspeople. Arigo had already smoked out one of their advance scouts. The villagers were no less observant. The detectives met with nothing but resistance from most of them. Even with the threat that the withholding of information was against the law, few would talk against Arigo. Most refused to give out names of those who had been treated by Arigo. But of course there were Arigo's enemies, and these came forward willingly to testify. But since none of them had visited Arigo's clinic as patients, there was little concrete they could say.

When word was noised about that Arigo's opponents were talking to the police, ground swell began among his supporters to testify in his favor: they would state publicly that no one had been harmed by Arigo's healing work and that thousands had been cured by him. What they didn't realize was that even if they praised Arigo to the skies in their testimony, they were digging his grave. Every testimonial that showed Arigo as an effective healer was condemnatory in the eyes of the law. The police were not interested in whether he healed or not. All that needed to be proved was that Arigo was practicing medicine.

Even with the police filtering into the town, Arigo continued his daily work. The long line in front of his clinic formed every morning with its cargo of sickness and despair, streaming in from Belo Horizonte, São Paulo, Rio, across the border in Argentina, and elsewhere.

One night, after a long day's work, Arigo climbed into bed next to Arlete, who was half asleep. Arigo did not speak to her, but in a few moments she heard him begin to talk.

He was praying for his enemies.

6

By sheer coincidence, it was in Congonhas do Campo that the idea for the extraordinary capital city of Brasília was born. The village was also the place where the paths of Arigo and President Juscelino Kubitschek crossed for the first time. It was an event that was to affect the lives of both.

Kubitschek, a tall, powerful, striking man with a thick shock of black hair and a charisma all his own, campaigned vigorously throughout Brazil in his bid for the presidency in the 1955 elections. He was immensely popular wherever he went. He had been a strong supporter of President Vargas' policies, and he eloquently pledged to the electorate that he would bring them fifty years of progress in five. More frequently than not, his enemies would give him credit that he meant what he said. But even before he was elected, there was a stockpile of complaints about the extravagance of his ideas.

Kubitschek's background was as impressive as his appearance. A qualified physician, he had specialized in surgery both in Paris and the Middle East, and for many years afterward had served as a medical officer in various government agencies in Brazil. But the lure of politics grew in him. He went successively from the post of a federal deputy, to mayor of Belo Horizonte, to governor of the state of Minas Gerais. A cosmopolite, he spoke French and English as well as Portuguese, and was at ease in many foreign capitals.

His pre-election campaign visit to Congonhas do Campo was marked by a speech in which he promised the crowd gathered in the Rua Marechal Floriano that if elected he would meticulously respect the Constitution. Only if this were done would there be peace in Brazil. "I will obey all the concepts of the Constitution," he told the crowd, "article, by article, by article."

One of the crowd called up to the platform to ask: "If you are of this disposition to obey the Constitution article by article, are you ready to obey the article that requires that a new capital be built in the middle of the country?"

The question took Kubitschek aback. He was silent for nearly half a minute. For years, Brazilian statesmen had been groping for a way to open up the vast interior of the country. Since it was founded, Brazil had been like a giant flywheel, without a hub in its vacant center. The weight of the population was clumped along the coast, like a heavy, unbalanced burden that left the rich interior resources inaccessible. Kubitschek felt that he could not now back down on the pledge of strict constitutional observance he had just made. But frankly he had overlooked the article that called for the building of an interior capital. He looked directly at the man who had asked the question, and said: "You are right. I had not thought about this subject. But you *are* right, and I will *build* Brasília!" Later, of course, the city was to rise up from the wilderness to the astonishment of the rest of the world. And in spite of the heavy accusations of waste and corruption leveled at Kubitschek, even the critics now agree that it has opened up Brazil.

Kubitschek had of course heard about Arigo before—hardly anyone in Brazil had not heard about him. But that day in Congonhas do Campo when he observed Arigo in action, he was dumbfounded.

"I don't understand," Kubitschek later said. "I knew about his fantastic prestige from many of the prominent people who told me what Arigo had done for them. But being a physician and surgeon myself, I found him so extraordinary that I cannot find words to express it. The people had faith in him. No one could fail to do so. He was a *god*."

Kubitschek was so impressed that he and his wife accepted Arigo's invitation to have lunch with him. Arlete, with her hair in curlers as it constantly seemed to be, served a modest meal, and Kubitschek and Arigo began a friendship that was to last for years. The friendship became critical to Kubitschek when one of his daughters had to be taken to the United States for a spinal operation because of a critical and massive deformation of the spine. The operation was so delicate that she had to remain completely immobilized for many months.

"Because of this," Kubitschek described the situation, "she developed two enormous kidney stones after she returned to Rio de Janeiro. My wife was very, very nervous, because this complication could lead to a serious and perhaps lethal condition. My wife said to me: Could we ask Arigo to come down to Rio and see what he could do for our daughter? I agreed. I reached Arigo by phone. I told him our daughter was critically ill, but did not tell him what her problem was.

"Congonhas do Campo is a six-hour drive, but he was here in Rio the next afternoon. He came in our home, and before I had a chance to tell him anything about my daughter's condition, he handed me a prescription written on a plain piece of paper. As a doctor, I recognized that it was a specific for eliminating kidney stones. But how could Arigo know her condition? Since I had not been practicing in recent times, I checked it with my own doctor. He indicated that he didn't feel it would do much good, but felt there would be no harm in trying it. Arigo's prescriptions were said to have an effect entirely beyond the bounds of the prescription itself. I gave her the medicine, and she became completely cured."

From that time on, President Kubitschek and his wife

would often go out of their way to stop in Congonhas do Campo for an informal visit with Arigo. They presented him with a solid-gold wrist watch, but Arigo bluntly refused it, explaining that he could not accept any gift or money.

Conditions in Congonhas do Campo had now become so jammed from the sick and the dying who clustered in the streets that Walter de Freitas, Arigo's brother, built a modest hotel next to the Spirit Center where Arigo worked. It was not a work of art, but something had to be done to increase the accommodations in the village, which had been strained to the limit. The hotel of course drew more attention to Arigo, who had now taken on his job as receptionist in the state welfare and pension office as a means of supporting his family. This, added to his work in the clinic, brought him to the brink of a sixteen-hour day, every day, with the exception of weekends, when he often worked at selling real estate or in his beloved rose garden.

Reporters continued to grind out miracle stories, which had proliferated to the point where they became commonplace. Roberto Freire, a journalist from *Realidad*, who was also a doctor, pressed Arigo hard on the reports that he must be making money from kickbacks on the prescriptions that he was writing, although no evidence could be found.

Arigo insisted this was not true. He admitted that his fame as a healer might help in some of the real estate sales, but that was the extent of it. He said that he was determined to give his children a good education in contrast to his own meager one, and that he welcomed the occasional financial help he received from the wealthy members of his family.

The reporter asked him: "Does your brother own the hotel, Arigo? They say you are partners and that you will not take care of anyone who doesn't stay there."

Arigo stood up angrily. "I used to treat my patients in my own home," he said. "One of the complaints against me was that I was contaminating all the boardinghouses and hotels of the city. My brother Walter alone built the hotel. I made no suggestions whatsoever. You saw— during the consultations I ask only that the patients have faith, pray, and take the medication. Let my enemies prove that my brother and I are partners. Let them examine my bank account. God would not help me to cure if I were dishonest."

As the reporter left, Arigo's anger had faded, and he asked: "You are a Catholic?"

"Yes," said the reporter.

"Good," Arigo answered. "Our Christ is the same. The rest doesn't matter."

At the office of the state police in Congonhas do Campo, Regional Inspector Helvecio Arantes was preparing for the interrogation of witnesses in the Arigo case. He was a little disturbed about the reports coming across his desk that the citizens of Congonhas do Campo were not particularly interested in talking to his interrogators. In spite of this, he had complete confidence that he would have a cut-and-dried case. Some of Arigo's enemies would be bound to talk. All that was needed was a handful of them, and the case would be as good as sewn up.

When Antonio Maia Seabra arrived in the police office on August 1, 1956, Inspector Arantes lost no time getting down to the questioning. After a few preliminary questions to determine that Seabra was a forty-two-year-old resident of the town and a citizen of good standing, he said: "Tell me what you know about Arigo."

Seabra said: "I knew him when he had his restaurant and bar. Several years ago. Now he's working for the pension office."

"What kind of person is he?"

"Well," said Seabra, "he's a very smart man. Always looking out for himself. Trying to get ahead in politics. He takes advantage of anything he can to do this."

"What about his trying to heal people. What do you know about that?"

"Well, I suddenly noticed he began this practice of illegal medicine some time ago. People began coming to his house all the time. He'd give them some kind of piece of paper with a prescription on it, then he'd promise them they'd get well."

"Did you notice anything else?" the inspector asked.

"Yes," Seabra said. "He started operating on people. People who were very, very sick. The ones that the doctors couldn't help."

"Did they get well?"

"I couldn't say that. I don't know."

"Did you actually see any of these operations?"

"No," Seabra answered. "I never really saw any."

"Just heard about them?"

"Yes. I just heard about them. There was all kinds of talk about them. All over the town."

"What did you hear about them?" the inspector asked.

"They all say they were just tricks. Tricks done with the guts of a chicken or a pig. That's what they say."

"But you've never seen this yourself?"

"No. But I heard that Altimiro charges everybody fifteen cruzeiros for every card he gives out in line. That's what everybody says."

"Are you sure of that?"

"That's what everybody says," Seabra answered. "And I also heard that they have to sign a card saying that they will vote for Arigo or he won't treat them."

"What else do you know about Arigo?"

"He's got a big appetite, and drinks a bottle of wine with every meal."

"But you haven't seen any of this yourself?"

"No," said Seabra. "But a lot of other people have."

"I guess that's all," the inspector said. "If you'll just sign this statement, you can go."

Seabra signed the paper and left. Inspector Arantes knew that this wasn't much of a statement, but it indicated that he would be bound to get stronger direct evidence as time went on.

But the next few witnesses were all strangely vague, even though they included some of Arigo's enemies. One of the ticket agents at the railroad station brought word that someone had come into the station and announced that Arigo had charged him one hundred cruzeiros for a treatment. It turned out that the man was actually insane, and had paid nothing.

It wasn't until Dr. Carlos Cruz, the dentist from Belo Horizonte whose sister-in-law had been successfully operated on by Arigo for cancer of the liver, testified strongly in Arigo's favor that the obvious strategy to follow was revealed to the inspector. Many who had been saved from a fatal medical prognosis by Arigo were more than anxious to testify on Arigo's behalf. Parodoxically, it was in these defense testimonies that the real evidence against Arigo could be shaped.

Since Article 284 of the Penal Code provided that the simple act of prescribing, operating, or making hypnotic passes was illegal, all the success stories about Arigo would do nothing more than lead to his conviction.

Under the illusion that they would be helping Arigo, his sympathetic witnesses came forward in droves to give their buoyant testimonies, until the files were bulging. Still, it was somewhat rankling to the prosecution that no one could prove that Arigo had ever accepted money or that anyone had been harmed, and further exasperating that practically everyone had to admit that Arigo was a good father, a good family man, and of the highest character. Even the rumors of his alleged assignations failed to come forth.

A series of mysterious incidents began happening at about this time that were never fully explained. On one occasion, late at night after a particularly long session with his patients at the Spirit Center, Arigo was walking home alone down the dark, narrow streets of the town when from out of the shadows of a doorway a man jumped at him without warning. Eventually, the massive strength of Arigo was successful in beating him off.

Word immediately went around the town that the hoodlum had been hired by Arigo's political enemies, but the incident remained unsolved. Later, government marshals raided his house several times. They were unable to find anything incriminating. In spite of this, Arlete reported to her friends that Arigo did nothing but continue to pray for those who were against him, insisting that they were misguided and should be forgiven. His supporters in the town felt no such magnanimity. They were up in arms, and Inspector Arantes could see that he might have his hands full if he moved too swiftly. Sitting down to make out his summary report on September 11, 1956, Arantes wrote:

"I tried to get witnesses who could give very complete information in the prosecution of the case, those that would back up our charges. We have many witnesses who discussed operations they have seen, including the use of cotton, and the removal of 'meat' from the patients' bodies. Some claimed that no scar was left. I think we have an ample number of these witnesses.

"I think it's possible that we are confronted with a case of the use of hypnosis and psychotherapy. In many hypnotized persons, hallucinations are built up so that they have no concept of the reality of the situation. Many licensed doctors use these methods for some of their patients. It's not at all surprising to scientists. Many people have been cured by the power of suggestion.

"But regardless of this, there is no question that Arigo has been practicing illegal medicine, without a license. He is clearly, by the penal law, practicing a profession without having a license for it. It must be said, however, that Arigo does not accept any remuneration for what he does."

There were, however, some delicate questions of law involved. While Article 284 made spiritual healing a crime, it was only because Arigo stood head and shoulders above all the hundreds of other healers throughout Brazil that he was singled out. The others were not important enough for the courts to bother with.

Another complication lay in the fact that Article 141 of the Penal Code guaranteed the free practice of religion to every citizen, and further assured him that he would not be refused the protection of the law because of his religion. Also, the illegal practice of medicine brought a much lighter sentence than the practice of charlatanism or witchcraft. This would have an important bearing on Arigo's future.

The actual law against witchcraft made a great deal of sense. "Witchcraft," it specifies, "is made punishable in order to protect both the individual and the public. If a person who does not hold a medical degree diagnoses a disease by its symptoms; if, without being licensed, he operates on patients; if he claims to be in a trance, in the control of a 'spirit'; if he writes prescriptions or performs operations or administers herbs to the patient; if he uses 'passes,' or certain postures or phrases or prayers to facilitate childbirth, bring relief to the symptoms of a cold, snake bites, cancer, high fever, bleeding, cataracts, deafness, and other conditions—such a person creates a vast danger to the health and safety of many citizens who depend on the state for protection." If the law made good sense for the protection of the common citizen, the problem was that it failed to make any provision for a strange anomaly like Arigo.

Newsman Gabriel Khater, who lived in Congonhas, found that after several years of close observation, he had swung almost completely around, changing from a total skeptic to a firm believer. While he looked at spiritism with a jaundiced eye, the rationale for his new belief rested on what he felt was the validity of parapsychology. Khater found himself returning again and again to the Spirit Center to watch Arigo in action. He was finally forced to acknowledge from his many interviews with visiting medical men that Arigo could do things that modern science could not do.

Khater was convinced that instead of being prosecuted,

Arigo should be supported by funds for a special scientific study. In this way, Arigo would be placed under the control of licensed doctors—a necessary step to prevent uncontrolled charlatanism from proliferating— but he would still be able to do the manifest good for society it had been all but proved he was doing.

Reporter Khater's articles on this track produced a growing ground swell among medical men throughout Brazil. But this was not enough to stem the tide headed by Inspector Arantes and his state police. They had bulldozed their way through the resistance, and were happy enough to get the case out of their hands and into the courts.

By October 5, 1956, the case was in the lap of Promoter Afonso Infante Netto, roughly equivalent to a district attorney. In his report to the court, he announced that Arigo was condemned by the penal law, charged with the crimes of charlatanism, witchcraft, and the illegal practice of medicine. Arigo was ordered to come to the court for a preliminary hearing. He would be faced with hand-picked witnesses who would testify most severely against him.

Sitting in front of a table in the sparsely furnished courtroom of Congonhas do Campo, Arigo, in a dark, short-sleeved sport shirt, made a sad and pathetic figure as he faced Judge Eleito Soares and the clerk of the court. The fight seemed to have gone out of him; he was unusually passive. It was an informal session, but the tiny room was jammed with spectators who leaned over the rail and watched anxiously as their local hero and international legend was questioned by the judge. Arigo, his deep, moist eyes glistening in sadness, answered as if he were half in the room and half out of it.

"Do you confirm your previous testimony?" the judge asked.

"Yes," Arigo said. "I confirm it."

The judge showed him a list of the witnesses who were to testify against him. "Do you know these witnesses?" he asked.

"Yes," said Arigo, as he looked over the list. "All except one. But I want to say that the accusations against me are not true."

"In that case," said Judge Soares, who was an impatient man, with little regard for the subtleties of the case, "I must ask you to give proof of why you say this."

"These charges are made against me, and have all been written on your official police papers, but I must say that I don't even know myself whether I practice illegal medicine or not. All I know is that whenever anybody comes to me for material or spiritual help, I must try to help them. I will not turn them away. I tell them to ask God for good health."

"And just how do you go about this?"

"I start to say a prayer. It is the Lord's Prayer. And from that moment on, I don't see or know about anything else. I don't remember what I do. There is no memory of it at all. The others tell me I write out prescriptions for people, but I do not remember that. I don't know what kind of drugs they are, and I do not understand why this happens. I do not see them as I write them."

"What about the operations that are alleged?" the judge asked.

"It is the same with them. I cannot give you any information about them. I am in a state that I do not understand. They tell me I have done these things. I would be happy if I knew how to explain this."

"Do you have witnesses in your defense?"

"Yes," Arigo said. "I have a lawyer who is going to present them to you." He named several: a well-known industrialist from Belo Horizonte, a group of doctors, and a few prominent public officials.

"Have you any criminal record?"

"I have been brought before the police only once," Arigo said. "I took a knife away from one of the customers in my bar. He would have killed somebody if I had not done it. I was innocent, and I was immediately set free."

"About the witnesses who will speak against you. Are

there any friends or enemies of yours among them?"

"There is one who is an enemy," Arigo said. "But I do not hold anger against him."

"Who is that?"

Arigo named João Hilariro da Cunha. "He is against me politically. He is a doctor who is the brother of the man who ran against me for mayor. We do not talk with each other."

"Have you seen this before?" the judge asked, showing him a copy of the only prescription of Arigo that the state police had been able to round up. It was unsigned.

"Yes," Arigo said. "It is one of the prescriptions that I have been told that I write for people."

"You are a Catholic, aren't you?"

"Yes," said Arigo.

"You are aware of the attitude of the Church toward what you are doing? That you are doing the work of a *curandeiro*—a charlatan?"

"But I am not a charlatan," Arigo said quietly. "I did what the priests wanted me to do. I went to doctors and psychiatrists. They said I was in perfect health. I just want to help the poor people, and I must do this."

"But you are doing what you are charged with, are you not?"

"I am not the one who is doing this," Arigo insisted. "I am just an intermediary between a spirit and the people. It is the spirit of Dr. Fritz. He insists that I help people, and I am just doing what God wants me to do."

"You are a spiritist, then?"

"I did not know anything about spiritism or about mediums. Some tell me I am a medium. I do not receive any payments or gifts for this work. I cannot do so, even if I wanted to, because it would not then be possible to help heal the sick. I would be very rich by now if I did this. I do not do this for any political reasons. I have tried to get away from this, and I thought I was going insane."

"You have been told by the police, have you not, that

you must close up the Spirit Center where you work?"

"I can only do this if the spirit of Dr. Fritz tells me I must do this," Arigo replied.

"You realize what you are asking us to believe, do you not?"

"I realize only what I must do, and how I must help people."

The judge was reaching the end of his patience. "If this is so, why don't you just make this Dr. Fritz of yours appear right here in this courtroom?" he snapped.

Arigo did not answer. A transparent cloud seemed to slide across his eyes. He sat in utter silence as the judge glared at him. Several moments went by.

Then the judge slapped his papers together and said: "The case will continue on a schedule to be announced."

The case dragged along as Arigo's lawyer, Dr. Alfredo Figueiredo, of Belo Horizonte, began to gather favorable witnesses for his *sui generis* client. This part was not difficult; there were more impressive and prominent volunteers than he could handle. What he did face was the problem of shaping a defense for a client who was a criminal in the eyes of the law and a saint in the eyes of the people. Judge Soares was obviously a total pragmatist, who would see none of the nuances. Further, there was no real defense in the conventional sense of the law.

Just how to size up this unprecedented case was a riddle. The passionate defense testimonies of medical experts as to Arigo's prowess with a knife would be of dubious value. They might even bury him. Yet there was a remote chance that the testimony might help slightly, if only to soften the jail sentence.

The lawyer realized the probable futility of gathering such witnesses as Dr. Carlos Cruz, Dr. Ary Lex, and all the other doctors who were convinced of Arigo's legitimacy. Their testimony could only suggest the setting up of a scientific study to get at the bottom of this phenomenon. But the law was rigid, and such a suggestion would mean nothing. The law might be rational in clamping down on charlatanism, but it was also irrational if it would send Arigo to a miserable louse-ridden jail cell, where he would rot.

The penalties under Article 284 of the Penal Code were rough. Arigo was facing well over a year in jail and a heavy fine that would leave Arlete and his young boys practically destitute. The jail sentence would be utterly cruel on a man as sensitive as Arigo, who, in spite of his crudities, was easily moved to tears.

That the judge and the prosecuting attorney were emotionally on the side of the Church and of Arigo's political adversaries seemed obvious. The only thing that appeared to be slowing them down was the fear of public outrage.

As the fall (spring in Brazil) of 1956 slid by, the prosecution gathered more nails for Arigo's coffin as defense attorney Figueiredo pondered and worked on his strategy. He brought in an influential retired judge from Belo Horizonte who would be an excellent character witness: he was a fervent supporter of Arigo, and would not only testify that Arigo never accepted money, but that his work would have had to come from some higher power outside himself to accomplish the incredible results he had demonstrated.

Figueiredo also got the support of Dr. João Ranulf de Melo, the doctor from Congonhas do Campo, who would testify about the unbelievable ovarian-cyst and cataract operations he had watched and followed up on. He would state that the operations were something that simply could not be done by an ordinary human being, and that the court was dealing with events that were plainly supernatural.

Dr. de Melo was joined in this by the group of doctors from Lafaiete, who agreed that they would not hesitate to risk their professional standing by testifying in Arigo's defense. Their testimony would support that of the other doctors to the effect that a formal scientific study should be made, and that in any country other than Brazil, this would be done. They would also testify that when Arigo was performing his operations he was not himself, but possessed by a guiding power outside himself. Further, the doctors would confirm that Arigo had brought about many documented cures of terminally ill patients with cancer or leukemia whom medical science had given up.

All would testify that no evidence of any harm, infection, hemorrhaging, or critical adverse drug reactions had been demonstrated by any of the thousands of patients Arigo had treated. This figure was now conservatively estimated at far over half a million in the past five years. If there were any contesting of this figure, it would be that it was too low. They would add to this their conviction that parapsychology was involved, that this was a science that was only beginning to be properly explored, and that the study of Arigo would advance this science.

Technically, all this was tissue-thin legally, and Figueiredo knew it. The prosecutor had temporarily quit his job, which was the source of some comfort for the defense, but very little. The defense could do little but wait until the case came to trial months later in March 1957.

On March 17, Figueiredo had his chance to test his shaky theories. The defense witnesses testified well, and he pleaded simply and eloquently, in spite of the weaknesses of his case. In addition to Article 284, Arigo was charged with several other chapters of the labyrinthi-an Brazilian Penal Code. The laws in Brazil are patterned almost entirely on ancient Roman law, and they contain many ambiguities.

Facing the liverish Judge Soares, Figueiredo immedi-ately demanded that the case be dismissed on the grounds that charlatanism had not been proved and that on several occasions, he, as the defense lawyer, had not been notified when hostile witnesses had been heard. In these instances, neither he nor Arigo had been able to present a defense. In addition, he insisted that the prosecutor's leaving his job at the time made the trial automatically invalid.

"Further," Figueiredo continued, "definite harm and danger to other people must result from the acts of the defendant. No harm whatever has resulted from Arigo's acts, and therefore it is quite plain that a crime does not exist."

He was aware that Article 284 did not include such a provision, but there were other chapters in the law that did give this protection. He went on: "It is impossible to call Arigo a criminal. Aside from the fact that there is no crime—and even the adversary witnesses have agreed to this—Arigo has been shown to be an honest and hard-working citizen, a responsible member of the community, who is respected by all. Only one person has tried to call him a criminal, and that is the prosecutor of this court. He has failed to provide proof of such a charge, because no such proof exists."

Figueiredo then began moving onto less firm ground. He did so with great convolutional indirection and masterfully engineered eloquence. The only direct evidence that the court had been able to come upon was the one small slip of paper with Arigo's prescription written on it. It was unsigned.

"How can the prosecutor say that Arigo gave out prescriptions, when all he has is one small piece of paper that is unsigned, and totally lacks proof that this comes from Arigo?" he asked.

In spite of this flimsy physical evidence, there was hardly a newspaperman in Brazil who didn't know that Arigo gave out literally hundreds of prescriptions a day. It was not exactly a worthy defense, but the attorney was grasping at straws. He had one more important point, however. In order to prove witchcraft, it was necessary to prove that a defendant had personally distributed concoctions of roots and herbs. This was clearly a thing Arigo never did. Arigo had prescribed only bona fide drugs from standard pharmaceutical houses, most of which were known throughout the world. The mystery was why these prescriptions worked when Arigo issued them, when they failed to work for the ordinary doctor. One drug was known only in New York. It was in an experimental stage, and was hardly known there. Arigo himself did not know how he knew about it.

In pointing all this out, Figueiredo continued by saying that drugstores all over Brazil often administered shots of penicillin and other drugs, a technically illegal act that was never brought before the courts. Why was Arigo singled out?

Reminding the judge that Article 284 prohibited the use of gestures or passes with the hands, Figueiredo said: "We want to ask the court to take into consideration this fact: that if gestures and passes can be judged as crimes in Brazil, then throughout the entire great Catholic Church, all the members of the clergy are committing crimes every day. The priests constantly make gestures every time they pray.

"What's more," the defense attorney went on, warming up now to new emotional heights, "we like to call everyone a brother because we are all sons of God. If anyone—anyone at all—came to Arigo to ask for help because he was suffering, Arigo would pick up a little cross, look high in the sky, hold his hand, and he would ask the good God to have compassion on his brother. This is what Arigo wants to do. He wants only to help people."

True as this was, Figueiredo neglected to add that more often than not, Arigo would also pick up a battered penknife and slice it expertly into the body of a patient. There was no need to remind the judge of this. He knew it well.

"We want to ask the judge: Is praying for our brothers and wishing for their health a crime? Can it be so construed? If the judge says that this is a crime, we can draw the conclusion that all the innocent people are in jail, and all the guilty are out of jail. For do we not pray for the health and good of people? If this is a crime, we are all criminals."

By now, Figueiredo was piling it on a bit thick. He had little choice, in one sense. In strict legal terms, the case against Arigo was cut-and-dried. If the obdurate judge could not see beyond the law, and into the unique and totally unprecedented values of the case, there was little a defense plea could do. The only possible track to take would be to ask for a suspended sentence, with a court order placing Arigo in the custody of a group of competent medical doctors who would work with him in trying to unveil the mystery of his powers. No such defense was presented. With the judge's hostile attitude already manifested, such a plea would likely be given short shrift.

Realizing the weakness of his position, Figueiredo concluded: "If Your Honor does not accept these arguments, I ask one other request. Arigo is a gentle man, from a good family, a fine father, and a loving husband. If these arguments fail to move you, may I ask that your decision be weighed by these considerations, and that the lightest possible penalties be imposed?"

The plea finished, the case rested. Headlines all over Brazil brought a harsh spotlight on the case. It did not please the dour Judge Soares to have this happen. Readers flooded the newspapers with well-meaning letters in Arigo's defense. One housewife wrote to the *Diario de Minas*: "My husband was given up by the doctors. He had a perforated ulcer. He went to Arigo, who operated on him. Today, he is completely well. Arigo said he didn't do anything for him, it was God. But my husband wants to thank Arigo publicly in this newspaper, because Arigo was the only person who gave him back his health. Arigo gave him back his dreams, after the doctors and science told him that they could do nothing whatever more for him."

It was a splendid testimonial. But it amounted to one

more witness for the prosecution. Without insight on the part of the court, Arigo was trapped.

J. Herculano Pires, the prominent professor of philosophy, wrote his opinion vigorously in the press. "It is simply ridiculous," he wrote, "to deny that the phenomenon of Arigo exists. It is also completely unscientific to state that Arigo is a paranoid or a psychotic of any kind. Medical specialists, famous journalists, intellectuals, prominent statesmen, and those who have been cured from hopeless conditions, have all had ample chance to witness the phenomena at Congonhas do Campo. These simply cannot be denied or misrepresented. If no formal scientific committees have been organized to verify the many cases, there have been many verifications by many reliable scientists individually. Among these are the medical testimonies given at court. To deny the paranormal capacities of Arigo is simply an act of utter stubbornness.

"We may want to examine Arigo critically. We may desire to severely limit his activities, as several doctors on the witness stand have testified. What we cannot possibly deny is the total reality of his feats, and his complete sincerity."

When defense attorney Figueiredo filed an addendum to his plea on March 17, 1957, his arguments far exceeded the scope of his first brief. The problem with the entire case was that both sides were trying to deal rationally with the irrational. The court held the upper hand, because it was already set in a harness that kept the proceedings on a tight legalistic bridle path. Any literal interpretation automatically spelled Arigo's doom. The only question was whether some spark might disturb Judge Soares' clod to the point where he would allow special consideration. Arigo could, for instance, be given a minimal sentence, which could then be suspended in favor of putting him in the care of medical scientists.

Figueiredo did everything but handsprings and a

tumbling act to push the judge in this direction. The ability of a healer, even if illegal, has to be taken into account, Figueiredo pleaded in his new brief. The wealthy and the prominent would never stampede to Arigo's humble clinic, as they were doing, unless he had ability. Arigo was obviously more than able, he was super-able. Arigo accomplishes what he does without even knowing he is doing it. He is not responsible for these acts, as benevolent as they are. The Catholic Church acknowledges the validity of parapsychology. The only possible solution to the problem is to set up a scientific study at the court's direction. Arigo helps only those that the medical world cannot help. He acts through an invisible element that is possessing him, helping other people for God. The Catholic Church recognizes the reality of possession. In Arigo's case, this is benign possession.

Arigo does his work without incantation or screaming. He practices none of the ritual of low spiritism, of the Umbanda and Quimbanda ilk. Arigo believes that the spirit of Dr. Fritz is the spirit of Christ. He believes that he must act to do everything through the light that God has given him. He wants us to become less materialistic, more spiritual, and to be parascientific.

Arigo doesn't want or ask for this spirit that possesses him, the defense attorney went on. In fact, he willingly fought it with the help of doctors and psychiatrists, who pronounced him normal otherwise. His gradual trend toward spiritism is protected by the Brazilian Constitution. It is a legitimate religion, protected against attack by public authorities.

The only thing he has done is to give people who have their days numbered, their lives back. People whom modern science has given up. He helps them without charge or harm, and is the exact opposite of a criminal.

Figueiredo continued with quotations from the Latin poets, from William James, from Conan Doyle, from Pope Leo XIII. He concluded with words from St. Paul, to the effect that he who judges his brother is judging himself.

It is doubtful that in all the history of jurisprudence there has been such a strange and twisted brief. Actually, though, it matched the intricacies of the trial itself. Throughout the plea, Judge Soares sat like a sphinx, frozen in time and space, and faced with almost arcane imponderables—just as everyone else was.

The plea failed to make a dent in the facade of either Judge Soares or District Attorney Netto, now back in harness again to complete the case. Nor did the last-minute appearance of the Secretary of the Treasury for the state of Minas Gerais, who voluntarily appeared in Arigo's defense. He told the judge that he had witnessed Arigo remove a cancerous growth from a friend who had been given up as hopeless, and that a group of the finest doctors in the state had confirmed the condition, the operation, and the full recovery.

On March 26, 1957, less than ten days after Figueiredo's last-ditch stand, Arigo was summoned before the court. With him was Arlete, this time her hair neatly in place, his father and mother, and friends and well-wishers who packed the small courtroom to its minuscule capacity. Newsmen and photographers scrambled as best they could for a vantage point, to record the final decision.

Arigo was ushered to a wooden chair in front of the judge. He was wearing a black suit and a necktie. In the heat of the courtroom, he opened his collar and loosened the tie. He sat with folded hands and waited for the judge to speak. He was quiet and subdued, a sad and very lonely figure, his shoulders slumped in resignation. As the judge reached the bench, Arigo's eyes again clouded. He looked, his friends reported, just as he always did at the times that Dr. Fritz was said to enter into him, in an indefinable trance state that wiped out his crude and jovial personality. But instead of being commanding and Germanic, he was passive and unseeing.

The judge, his bearing stern and unyielding, briefly

reviewed the case. The defendant had admitted his wrongdoing before the court. The witnesses, both of the defense *and* the prosecution, had substantiated the charges. In fact, the strongest witness for the defense, Dr. João Ranulf de Melo, had offered the most damaging evidence against the defendant. He had admitted to watching several operations.

Arigo would still be guilty, even if he were not aware of what he was doing, even if he were possessed by this strange spirit. Nothing in philosophy or religion can defend Arigo. The law is not interested in this in the slightest. The only issue at hand is to apply the Penal Code, which is very specific. Arigo has been committing crimes, and he is guilty. He is not excluded because he is a mystic or a medium or an idealist or a charitable person of good standing. In the eyes of the law, Arigo is a criminal.

The courtroom was hushed and silent. Arigo, still in his trance, did not respond at all. He stared vacantly into space, his bulky form hunched in the chair. The sobbing, beginning with Arlete, spread throughout the gallery. The judge rapped for order. Then he said:

"I hereby sentence you to one year and three months in jail, effective immediately as of this day. I further levy on you a fine of five thousand cruzeiros, plus all the court expenses, the same to be paid within three days, by March 29, 1957."

The decision was unbelievably harsh. No one had expected anything like this. Arlete broke down and had to be ushered from the room. Some of the sobs elsewhere broke into open crying. This was augmented by hostile murmuring among the men.

Arigo continued in his trance; he failed to respond at all. His lawyer leaped to his feet, protesting that the terms were incredible, that he was asking for an immediate appeal, that the sentence must be stayed, and that the fine and costs were totally out of reason. Arigo had a wife and family to support, and the amount levied came to almost an entire year's earnings for Arigo at the pension and welfare office.

With obvious reluctance, the judge said that he would grant a stay until April 1. Regardless of any appeal, the fine would have to be paid by that date.

Figueiredo, furious, faced the judge and said: "I remember a prayer I learned when I was studying law. It said, 'Dear God of Grace, is this a dream or is it the truth that so many horrible things can happen in front of God's eyes?'"

The judge turned and left the room. Figueiredo took Arigo by the arm and led him out of the court. Among the spectators, many of whom had not moved from their seats, there was still the sound of crying.

7

There were two places in the village where news traveled most swiftly: the barber shop of Ferando do Santos and the railroad station. But that day every street corner, store, and bar was abuzz as the news of Arigo's sentence swept through Congonhas do Campo. Judge Soares remained as inconspicuous as possible; he was the enemy of the people. The town's mood was like that of a mutinous vessel at sea. Even those who felt that Arigo should be curbed rose up against the utter harshness of the decision. Dissidence within the Catholic Church rose to a high level. The state medical society was splitting at the seams.

Both the Church and the medical society had stayed in the background during the trial. This fooled hardly anyone. Most knew that both organizations were lustily behind the prosecution, if not the cruelness of the sentence. The spiritists in town immediately rallied behind Arigo. With fresh support from unexpected quarters, they raised the inordinate fine that had been levied on Arigo by the court.

Arigo, calm in his hour of despair, urged his fellow townsmen to keep cool heads; he stubbornly insisted that the court must be forgiven. Figueiredo and his staff lawyers rushed swiftly to appeal, reiterating their arguments, as technically weak as they were. Attorney

---

148

Figueiredo appealed directly to the Minister of Justice of the state with an impassioned plea to spare Arigo from total ruin.

The prosecutor countered this by declaring Arigo guilty to the teeth, and accusing him of base political motives. He was relentless in his charges, to the point where many suspected a personal vendetta.

It took two months for the decision to come down from the Court of Appeals. Arigo and his supporters waited anxiously for the results. When the decision came through, it was not good. The higher court upheld the conviction, but ruled that the sentence was too harsh under the circumstances. The jail term was reduced from fifteen months to eight, and the fine considerably cut back. Most important, there would be a little more than a year's grace before beginning the jail term, provided Arigo remained on probation in the custody of the court.

In spite of the breathing spell, the specter of going to jail and leaving his family hung over Arigo's head. The terms of the custody were almost as confining as prison.

He would immediately have to stop treating patients. He could not move anywhere or leave town without the authorization of the judge. He had an early curfew. He could not go into any hotel, café, or restaurant, or sit at any outside tables in any of these locales. He could not consult with any strange person from out of town in his or any other house. He would have to get the permission of the judge to attend any spiritist meeting. He would have to report to the judge at the end of each month. He was further warned that the police were going to keep their eyes on him, wherever he went and whatever he did. He literally became a chattel of the court.

Arigo seemed like a lost man. He went to his job at the pension office, continued with his real estate work, tended his roses, played with his young sons. And he still went to Mass with Arlete, but unlike her, he did not take communion. He would have until the middle of August 1958 before he would be sent off to jail, like any ordinary criminal. Arlete tried her best to comfort him, again took in sewing to buttress their income, in preparation for the time when she would be left without support.

The year went by slowly. By the following May, 1958, it was obvious that the little savings they had put aside from Arlete's sewing work would be totally inadequate to tide them over the long months Arigo would be spending in jail. The children had now increased to six, all of them boys and under the working age, all of them needing food, shelter, and education.

In addition to the worries about what would happen to his family, Arigo's compulsion to serve the sick was almost too much for him to bear. The entire complexion of the town had changed. No longer did the buses full of patients rumble into the narrow streets from Belo Horizonte, Rio, São Paulo, or far-away Argentina—the last an event that had become almost a weekly routine.

Arigo rankled under the terms imposed on him by the court, but he had nothing to say against his enemies. His headaches returned again, as they always had when he tried to stop before. While he forswore his operations, he gradually began seeing those who sought him out for help, keeping this as inconspicuous as possible. The police knew immediately that he was beginning to resume nonsurgical treatments, but they looked the other way. Nearly all were friendly to him. They were aware, too, that he had little freedom left, as the starting date of the jail term approached.

The last two months before the jail term were the hardest for Arigo and Arlete. There was nothing to look forward to but despair.

In Rio, President Juscelino Kubitschek had his hands full, with a plethora of problems. The critics of the building of Brasília, in the remote state of Goias, were vociferous in their condemnation of it. But the new capital was already rising in sparkling majesty in the middle of nowhere, some six hundred miles from Rio,

São Paulo, or Salvador—the three nearest metropolitan centers. It was a concept of planned urban creation that had no parallel anywhere in the world. Kubitschek knew it, reveled in it. Its striking modern architecture was dramatic, breathtaking—and expensive. Determined to have the city finished before his five-year, nonrepeatable term was up, Kubitschek poured money, sweat, and dreams into it, even to the extent of air-freighting heavy construction materials. The new city was sprouting like a mirage out of the reddish scrubland waste of the country's empty center. It was a glorious obsession for Kubitschek and architect Oscar Niemeyer; to their opponents, it was an impossible drain on the economy.

Kubitschek had other troubles and preoccupations: the threat of a coup by the military, an unprecedented program for economic growth, and a new highway system that was to outdistance all the progress made since the country began. With inflation on the rampage, the military restless and hostile, and the treasury groaning under the new burdens, Kubitschek had little time to put his mind on anything but the affairs of state.

But in May 1958 President Kubitschek learned that Arigo was waiting for the ax of the jail sentence to fall on his neck. Kubitschek lost no time going into action. Within minutes, a presidential pardon was dispatched to the Congonhas do Campo authorities. It stated that as President of the Republic, Article 87, Number 19 of the Constitution gave him the power to pardon José Pedro de Freitas, more commonly known as Arigo, and that the defendant was to immediately be relieved of his jail sentence by presidential order.

The official pardon was received by the dour prosecutor Afonso Netto on May 22, 1958. For reasons that were never explained, the pardon lay fallow in the office of the prosecutor, without any action being taken on it. It continued lying there, as the time for the jailing grew closer. It wasn't until July 29 that Prosecutor Netto saw fit to pass the news of the pardon along to Judge Soares.

It wasn't until August 6 that the judge saw fit to pass the news along to Arigo.

With the sword of Damocles removed, there was great rejoicing through most of Congonhas do Campo. The jubilance was not confined to the town; it spread through Brazil and into Argentina. Arigo, who had been continuing to experience his strange symptoms and headaches since he had stopped or reduced his healing work to almost nothing, began to pick up the threads. The buses began to roll into the town again, and the patients began to line up at the center. Arigo, who never could refuse anyone who came to him for help, fell back into the routine. Within a month, the volume of patients had returned to an almost-normal figure of over three hundred a day.

But with one eye on the police, Arigo did not perform any major operations. He was content for the most part to offer his unorthodox prescriptions, to bless his patients, and to sternly advise them to go with God. It is said that he actually did operate at times, but never openly as he had before. He seemed to consider as nonoperations: cataracts, abscesses, lipomas, hydroceles, skin cancer, and others where the viscera were not involved. These he did, along with his unconventional "eye checkup," where he stirred the knife within the socket to remove pus or even a malignant tumor.

Kubitschek, as a surgeon as well as President, along with a growing number of other statesmen, intellectuals, scientists, and medical men, spoke openly on the line that Arigo was not a police case.

Commenting on Arigo in later years, President Kubitschek said: "It was impossible in Brazil for him to be alone. The people went where he went. If he had gone to the wildest reaches of the Amazon, they would have followed him there. I just don't understand his strength and his extraordinary powers. The most important people in Brazil sought him out."

As the months flowed into a year and more, Arigo's return to his old pattern bothered none of the more enlightened, except that they wanted control and observation of Arigo. But the smoldering resentment of the Church and the medical societies still burned with a glow. These fires had been banked by Kubitschek's pardon and the public elation at Arigo's release from the threat of jail.

But Juscelino Kubitschek's term was finished. Although he was an inordinately popular man, he could not succeed himself in office. If he could have, it is said, he would still be President, without uttering a single campaign speech. He had completed Brasília, a lyrical and extravagant monument to his courage and imagination, and even his adversaries came to acknowledge the city as a needed catalyst to the full development of Brazil's interior.

But he was no longer President. Jânio Quadros was swept in in 1960, sweeping himself out again after only seven months in office, by resignation. Vice-President João Goulart took his place, and was to last until 1964, when a military regime took over. Arigo's top-level support was gone. Again, the opposition went into action. Again, the press stories were beginning to flow out of Congonhas do Campo with monotonous regularity. Again, Arigo was beginning to slip back into doing a few major operations. Again, the stories of their success could not be held in check.

Not the least of Arigo's new successes came from an incident with the infant son of singer Roberto Carlos. Carlos was the toast of Brazilian entertainers, rivaling, if not exceeding, the popularity of the Beatles in that country. If there had been a popularity poll taken in Brazil, it is likely that the first three figures to be named would have been Pele, the world-renowned soccer player; Juscelino Kubitschek; and Roberto Carlos—with Arigo himself running a close fourth.

The new son of Roberto Carlos was born with a serious

fulminant glaucoma condition, an intensely acute form of inflammation with total loss of sight and light perception.

Roberto Carlos and his wife rushed the baby to specialists in Europe, where the child's condition was diagnosed as incurable. On his return to Brazil, Carlos chartered a plane and flew to Lafaiete, and took a car to Congonhas. The details have not been revealed about the surgery that Arigo performed, but within days the infant's sight was restored.

Carlos became a close friend of Arigo's from that time on, and the incident thrust Arigo's new activity into more blazing public attention across the country.

When pressed about what he was doing after his close brush with jail, Arigo would explain: "I believe in love and charity. I cannot deny anyone who comes to me for help. The Bible tells us that when someone knocks, we must open the door to him."

Distressed and frustrated about the persecution Arigo had faced—and might continue to face—was the assistant mayor of Congonhas do Campo, Dr. Mauro Godoy. He had studied both internal medicine and psychiatry at the University of Brazil in Rio, and continued to practice both specialties. He had had a much better chance to observe Arigo in action than all the scores of Brazilian doctors who had investigated him. Godoy's office was within shouting distance of Arigo's clinic, and he often dropped by in his effort to find a scientific rationalization for what he saw.

He knew the dangers of drawing attention to Arigo's new, post-trial activities, yet he was determined to persuade his colleagues in the medical society to shift their emphasis from persecution to study. He had recorded case after case of Arigo's surgery—many of them on operations that were successfully completed in one-fortieth or one-fiftieth of the time required by conventional surgical procedures.

As a psychiatrist, he believed that the modern school could benefit greatly by studying primitive techniques. While Arigo was anything but a primitive, and stood completely in a class by himself, beyond any known discipline, Godoy was convinced that only an extended, well-funded study could possibly make a dent in solving the puzzle. He reasoned that Arigo could do little or no harm to the public because most of his cases had been given up by medical doctors.

Godoy had come about his acceptance of Arigo's work slowly. At first, he ascribed it to some sort of hypnotism, but after two years of almost daily observation and study, he ruled this out fully. Arigo himself obviously went into a trance state, but the patients were diagnosed and operated on almost instantly, without any eye or word contact, without any suggestion, without preparation—psychological, surgical, or otherwise.

Dr. Godoy was also intrigued by the personality profile of the man. He was aware that when he was near Arigo at his place of work, he felt a completely different ambience in the room. It was charged with inexplicable emotion. When the knife cut and the blood did not pour out, it was a scene that was impossible to believe. The simplistic answer was that it was a question of mind over matter—but what did that mean? And there was no way whatever of explaining why, of the thousands of cases of surgery Arigo had performed, there was not one instance of septicemia—blood poisoning. Dr. Godoy knew from his own practice that any lapse in surgical procedure inevitably brought about this condition.

Arigo was anything but a simple character. His on-stage and off-stage personalities were widely split. Yet there were no conventional signs of psychosis, whether schizophrenia or paranoia. He was in control of both personalities, depending on which one he became. His ordinary foibles were many and varied. But they did not depart measurably from the norm of acceptable neurosis. His fear of elevators and airplanes was not crippling or devastating to his capacity to work and love. His family life was reasonably normal when he had time for it; his devotion to Arlete was as genuine as hers to him.

The entire syndrome about Dr. Fritz and his alleged

spirit colleagues was a great imponderable. There were few yardsticks to measure it by. Arigo's personality change when he assumed this cloak of his psyche was marked and real. Yet when he did, his personality was level and consistent—and totally rational within those bounds. The concept of a band of discarnate spirits, all with great medical prowess, all with a capacity of helping Arigo with their specialized skills, was of course totally unacceptable in the light of modern science. To the Kardec spiritists, however, this was old hat. At times, Dr. Godoy was tempted to assume momentarily, on a provisional basis, that this could be the explanation. But if this assumption were made, where could he go from there? He agreed heartily with a statement Dr. Pires had recently made: "In Arigo's case, the prevailing aspects are *the objective phenomena*. It is much easier to blithely label Arigo as a paranoid than to look seriously into what he is doing."

These questions were begging for answers. But the information Dr. Godoy was gathering from his less interested colleagues would not help answer the questions. Again, the medical association headquarters in Belo Horizonte was stirring restlessly. Dr. Godoy began to regard the situation as a race between possible enlightenment about a rare, incredible phenomenon and the iron-heavy forces of closed minds.

The new thrust from the medical association was not long in coming. On August 29, 1961, some three years after Judge Soares had reluctantly notified Arigo of President Kubitschek's official pardon, Dr. Fernando Megre Velloso sat down at his desk in Belo Horizonte to dictate a letter to the Secretary of Public Security of the state of Minas Gerais.

Dr. Velloso was president of the Conselho Regional de Medicina of the state, equivalent to a regional office of the American Medical Association. He stated:

Senhor Secretario:
In line with my responsibilities with the medical

association, over which I have the honor of presiding, let me bring to the attention of Your Excellency the activities of the well-known citizen José Arigo, relative to the practice of *curandeirismo*—witchcraft.

Since this citizen is being widely and publicly accused of such practices that, truly, can threaten and demoralize the rights of the public, I beg Your Excellency to institute the necessary inquiry to determine the facts in the case. If true, the case against José Arigo should be reopened, and a new process begun.

I am sure that you will immediately give your attention to this matter. Allow me to extend to Your Excellency my greatest esteem.

Within days, the snooping began again. Police investigators began fanning out. The talk from the barber shop and the railroad station had preceded them. They were expected. The detectives received a chilly response from nearly everyone they interrogated. The new probe sprung out of Lafaiete, twenty miles away, a safer distance for the authorities to be, at least. The investigators, as before, had a puzzling time trying to get any copies of prescriptions out of the drugstores in either Congonhas do Campo or Belo Horizonte. "The druggist informed me," wrote one detective, "that the prescription that one patient of Arigo's said he would give us could simply not be found anywhere, and must have been lost. If he found it, he would send it."

Another had trouble getting any kind of information out of the druggist on the plaza in Congonhas. The druggist swore he had never seen Arigo's name on any prescription (Arigo of course never signed them). He never asked a customer about this. He knew nothing whatever about Arigo, even though he was only a block away.

Nearly every witness who could have offered anything of importance dodged and evaded the questions. But eventually the prosecution won the war of attrition and was able to gather ample evidence of Arigo's having reestablished his practice. "We first noticed," wrote a field detective, "that everyone was expecting us to arrive. We found several good witnesses, but they didn't want to talk and refused to give us any help. But with our careful and expert techniques, we finally broke down the resistance. We conclude that Arigo is practicing right now, in spite of his denials. Our results will show clearly that he is engaging in illegal medicine, even though he was once prosecuted and pardoned." If the results of the investigation failed to prove the case, it would have been a miracle: the crowds formed every day under the eyes of the police.

The prosecution now was aiming hard and straight to prove that Arigo was practicing witchcraft, not merely illegal medicine. Earlier stung by the rebuff of President Kubitschek's pardon, the authorities were determined to get the much larger penalty that the witchcraft charge would provide. All the new testimony that was elicited was shaped in this direction. If a witness said that Arigo raised his hand above his head, this was more than the practice of medicine, this was witchcraft, whether it was meant to be or not. If he read the Bible or blessed a patient, that was to be interpreted as witchcraft.

Beyond that aspect, the second prosecution was almost a carbon copy of the first. But it took time, and the legal machinery was slow, especially in view of the resistance of the witnesses. The process continued all through 1961, 1962, and far into 1963.

As the two full years went by, Arigo continued practicing almost as if nothing were happening. His denials that he was practicing were based on his firm conviction that it was Dr. Fritz, and not he, who was doing the medical work. This was his justification—this, and his belief that he could not turn down those who needed him.

"They might say I am wrong," Arigo told reporter Reinaldo Comenale, "but I am not wrong in the eyes of God. A lot of friends have come to tell me that they want to help me. I have a special place in my heart for them.

But I still pray for my enemies. They are the ones that need more prayer and more love. If they want me to go to jail, they can put me there. If the court wants to charge me with helping the sick, and judge me for that, I will go any time. But I am sure that God will give me freedom. I'm not pure, but I try to be. If I carry out charity and if I'm accused of the crime of charity, yes, they can take me to jail, and I will stay there."

Meanwhile, Arigo's supporters were not inactive. Over three hundred of them signed a petition and presented it to the implacable Judge Soares. It said that the petitioners came from all social classes, and pleaded with the judge to forgive and forget. It did not fall on fertile ground, and the prosecution continued.

By August 1963, the legal process was still creaking along and Arigo was still practicing, though somewhat mutedly. And it was then that Dr. Henry Puharich and Henry Belk arrived in Congonhas in their microbus, to be among the first North Americans to encounter the phenomenon of Arigo face to face.

After returning to the United States, Puharich and Belk were not inactive on behalf of Arigo. In their talks with the interested Brazilian doctors before they left Rio, they had been warned that Arigo's capacities were in imminent danger not only from the impending new prosecution, but from the indifference of science in aiding him to discover the source of his strange powers. The sympathetic medical men pleaded with Puharich and Belk to organize an outside study by American doctors that would buttress their own efforts in the face of the formal opposition of the medical societies. But it should be done quickly.

Puharich was somewhat of a maverick himself, often defying the sacred tenets of the AMA in his willingness to tackle unknown phenomena. What he could not be faulted on was his scientific proficiency. He had proved himself enough in the hard-line school of pragmatic laboratory research and advanced biomedical instrumentation to feel secure and confident in stepping into the unknown waters that lay beyond the norm. What Puharich was to find here affected his life to such an extent that he was later willing to plunge precipitously into further explorations of the paranormal, that some of his supporters could not follow. This, however, could not negate the massive evidence that was piling up in regard to Arigo's work.

Neither Puharich nor Belk had any interest in pursuing fantasy. But in Arigo's case, where did reality leave off and the fantastic begin? This was the key question, one that was both difficult to answer and impossible to ignore. If it were ignored, the entire etiology, or root cause, would go begging. Yet any attempt to answer it in terms of Arigo's own theories about Dr. Fritz and his confederates would cause the entire investigation to go up in a cloud of derision.

The problem boiled down to proving the obvious. A knife can be painful even when slicing away at a hangnail or wart, to say nothing of scraping a naked eyeball or scooping the eyeball out of its socket in a totally conscious, unanesthetized patient. Yet there was no dispute whatever that Arigo was doing this daily— along with much more complicated surgery.

Puharich knew he had to present his findings as convincingly as possible, or his recommendations for the expensive and painstaking research could be laughed off by his associates. Second- or third-hand reporting by Puharich on something as astounding as Arigo was not the ideal method of scientific presentation. The scientist must be prepared to challenge, and challenge hard, which is of course healthy.

Puharich himself had already challenged Arigo with his own lipoma operation. On the surface, this would be reasonably good evidence, if not proof, of the worthiness of further study of Arigo. So were the films. But these still would not be enough for the exacting requirements of scientific-journal publication, which demands, in addition to prolific footnote references of past practices and observations, some pragmatic frame of reference on which a theory could be built and accepted. It had taken centuries for acupuncture to be even considered worthy of scientific study. Arigo's practices went so far beyond acupuncture that they almost soared out of sight.

Arigo dealt with raw anguish, desperation, and hopelessness. Pain and disease are the basic reality of those who suffer from them. Here were such people— literally hundreds of them a day—who knew and lived with this intensely horrible reality. They had no other choice.

The great majority of those who made the pilgrimage to Arigo did not come to him out of curiosity, religious faith, or fetishism. They came because they were literally, practically, objectively, totally hopeless. Modern medicine had given them up; in some cases, the best specialists in the world. Where else could they turn?

Although Arigo prayed briefly with his patients each day and continually told them to "go with God," there was none of the faith-healing aspect or mysticism that accompanied the activity at Lourdes. In most respects, his treatment was as perfunctory and clinical as a resident physician in an emergency room.

In their desperation, many would not let themselves accept the death sentence that their doctors had flatly predicted for them. Within their scope, the doctors were right. There was no other objective course for them.

Arigo offered hope in the face of seeming lack of it. They came to Congonhas do Campo. The overwhelming majority of them were miraculously cured. A small percentage were not, and Arigo would not hesitate to tell them he could do nothing for them. Nearly all figured it was worth the risk.

It was a great tragedy that the inexorable forces of the law were marshaled against this simple and inexplicable man, thereby threatening to foreclose on any organized study of his work. The stumbling block was the precedent that might be set by letting Arigo off scot-free.

Without disciplined standards, any imposter could assume the cloak of benignity and presume to do what Arigo was doing. He of course would not last long. The first thrust of a pocketknife into the eyeball of a suffering patient by an imposter would, in a matter of minutes, bring him abruptly to the police and courts. If Arigo had caused pain or injury, he would of course have been out of business in as short a time.

Arigo's pocketknife or paring knife "eye examination" puzzled Dr. Puharich when he had returned to the United States almost more than anything else. Arigo did this often, even when the eye looked perfectly normal. It was something never seen in conventional medicine, totally bizarre. He would often scrape out a glob of pus from behind the eyeball, even when there didn't seem to be any condition that would warrant it being behind the eye. Puharich suspected that Arigo did this maneuver in the eye, stirring the blade so roughly in the eye socket, to dramatize that he could do things for the patient far beyond the normal, and thus build up the confidence of both the patient being treated and those watching and waiting their turn.

As part of his experimental work in cardiology, Puharich worked often with Dr. Luis Cortes, a research scientist in the Department of Surgery of the New York University School of Medicine. Before he had drawn up his first report on Arigo for Essentia Research Associates, Puharich had shown Cortes the films of Arigo's operations and filled him in on some of the background. Cortes was fascinated with the surgical work depicted in the film. As a surgeon himself, he simply could not believe that a knife could be inserted into the eye of a conscious person without literally strapping him down and practically raping the eye. It was an assault on the nerves of the patient that positively could not be done.

Both he and Puharich decided to make a tentative check of this with some of the laboratory rats they were using with their cardiological research. They each had long experience in handling laboratory animals under the most difficult conditions, and could accurately predict whatever fear or reflex reactions the animal would have under almost any condition. In a normal pattern, if they tried the same technique that Arigo had used with his eye probes, the rat would use every muscle in its body to avoid the assault of the knife blade in its eye.

Using painstaking care, Cortes held a rat firmly while Puharich tried to insert a small knife under the lid and up toward the sinus cavities. They found that it was literally impossible to do on a conscious, unanesthetized rat unless its head was held in a viselike grip. And then it was practically impossible to hold the rat still to do any maneuvering whatever, to say nothing of stirring the blade inside the eyelid. Even in an anesthetized rat, it was impossible to emulate the rough crude plunges that Arigo executed without seriously damaging the eye tissues. Whatever Arigo did was beyond the province of either doctor.

But Puharich and Cortes were faced with one more challenge. A young laboratory assistant who had seen the films insisted that she wanted to volunteer to let either Cortes or Puharich attempt to repeat the experiment on one of her own eyes. Neither doctor wanted to accept the challenge. But she kept on insisting, saying that if they were ever to get to the bottom of this mystery they would have to take some chances. Puharich had taken his chances with the lipoma operation. She was willing to take hers, because she was absolutely absorbed by what Arigo was doing, and convinced that it must be solved.

Since Cortes was a practicing surgeon, he was at least confident that he could try the experiment without harm, by using extreme care. But the girl must promise to give him a signal at the very first moment of pain or discomfort. She promised that she would.

Choosing a small, smooth table knife, and avoiding the iris and cornea of the eye, Cortes very gently began to slide the knife under the lid. She remained stoic and quiet, but only for a fraction of a moment. His first, slow upward movement brought a quick sign from the girl that the pain had become unbearable. The knife was only a fraction of an inch under the lid. He removed it as carefully as he had inserted it, and no harm was done. The knife had gone less than one-tenth the distance Arigo's blade penetrated, and Cortes had made no lateral or circular movement. The experience convinced all three that they were dealing with an extraordinary case in Arigo that would be a mammoth challenge to science.

On reviewing Dr. Puharich's preliminary report, as well as the separate one filed by Henry Belk, the interest in a full-scale research expedition to study Arigo was high among the members of the Essentia Research group. Coming as they did from different disciplines and varied organizations, from Stanford University on the West Coast to Massachusetts General Hospital on the East, there were many logistic and time-schedule problems.

All agreed that further preliminary investigation had to be done to avoid confusion and wasting of time when a full commission of a half or dozen or so members took off on the trip. There would be a considerable amount of preliminary reading and study to be done on the subjects of parapsychology, Brazilian customs, and the Portuguese language.

Puharich agreed to make another trip to Congonhas for a detailed feasibility survey, and to try to gather statistics that could be used for shaping a well-planned team effort. Just when he could get away from his own research work, now suffering from temporary neglect, was another problem. Yet with the legal action against Arigo threatening the potential success of the research expedition, speed was essential. The arrangements were cumbersome, the distances between the members great, and the necessity for funding of paramount necessity. Several foundations were approached, a slow and difficult job. The race to try to uncover the mystery of Arigo continued.

In Brazil, the legal proceedings were still bogged down in delays. The prosecution that was to lead to a second trial had begun in September 1961, on the urging of the medical society of Minas Gerais. When Belk and Puharich had left Congonhas do Campo in August 1963, the legal preparation for the trial was still foundering, chiefly due to inertia, to the resistance of the witnesses, and to the difficulty of documenting new evidence in spite of the fact that Arigo was continuing his work under the noses of the police. The people who were benefiting were the last ones who wanted to assist the prosecutor.

The news in August 1963 of Arigo's operation on Dr. Puharich, which had been spread across the front page of nearly every paper in Brazil, provided a fresh impetus to the sluggish prosecution. It was again a case of a success story that would be damaging to Arigo. And it was a stinging rebuke to Judge Soares and the prosecutor that the nationally famous operation had happened under the very noses of the police investigators.

Although the case had been lying rather dormant at the time, there was action within weeks after the prosecutor read the Puharich headlines. Arigo was called up before him. A Dutch Roman Catholic priest by the name of Anselmo Meindres had also seen the headlines, along with the officers of the medical society. All were up in arms about this flagrant operation on the American doctor's tumor.

A new judge, Marcio de Barros, of apparently the same dour disposition as Judge Soares, had joined forces, and handled the fresh interrogation of Arigo. The prosecutor was now Marcelo da Paula, another who seemed to be of the same stripe.

Arigo reiterated that he bore no malice against those who had testified against him. He freely admitted that he had operated on the American doctor. He also confirmed the other nationwide headline report that he had saved the eyesight of Roberto Carlos' infant son. Since Arigo claimed these were done on the intervention of Dr. Fritz, and since he had no conscious memory at the time of doing them, Arigo did not feel they were against the law. If the court felt they were crimes, that was up to the court. His conscience was clear.

Such a bland admission was of course explosively irritating to the court. The defense of shifting the blame to a German doctor who died in 1918 was probably one of the most ridiculous in the history of jurisprudence, but neither the judge nor the prosecutor saw any humor in it. They were still feeling the stinging indignity of having, in effect, been made fools of in the press.

The dawdling went on through the rest of 1963 and through most of 1964. Arigo continued to practice under the rules of his own philosophy, soft-pedaling the operations but nonetheless continuing to do them. By the middle of October 1964, the court felt it had enough evidence to nail Arigo on the witchcraft charge, with its more stringent penalties, than the simpler charge of illegal practice of medicine.

Prosecutor da Paula pulled out all the stops in his summary of the charges. He argued that Arigo was a critical danger to society. He was guilty of practicing witchcraft and black magic with all the enthusiasm of the *candomblé* rites in a macumba clearing. Arigo was, to put it bluntly, a criminal. It didn't matter if he was successful in his cures, or that he benefited any who came to him. It further was immaterial that no harm had come to any of the hundreds of thousands of patients Arigo had treated, or that he never accepted any money or gifts. A crime was a crime. For some reason, the prosecutor was touched off by evidence that dozens of women from high society came to see Arigo with veils over their faces, to hide their identity. The prosecutor saw in this a most sinister omen. And, to sum it all up, Arigo admitted himself that he was committing this crime against the people.

The second trial was really a charade for both sides as they strained to conduct the proceedings on the level of legal reality though the phenomenon actually was unclassifiable, undefendable, and unassailable, all at the same time. Neither the prosecution nor the defense knew how to handle it, nor would anyone else. Judge Barros was unable to fathom the overtones and undertones, saw none of the paradoxes and subtleties. On November 20, 1964, he sentenced Arigo to sixteen months in jail for the practice of witchcraft, effective at once.

Arigo was permitted to go home from the courthouse in Lafaiete with Arlete to say good-bye to his sons. He did not try to explain to them what was happening, because he did not know how to explain it. His own feelings told him that he was trying to do right, in the way that he saw it. How could he explain that to his boys in the face of the long jail sentence? Arigo loved children—all children. He was known for his expansive love of his own boys.

That evening he held each one in his arms, promised them that he would see them again soon, comforted them because they sensed, with the awesome intuition even the youngest have, that a tragic happening was in the air.

Arlete, for the sake of the children, was holding back her tears. They prayed before dinner, and ate in silence. Arigo tucked the boys in bed, and said the Lord's Prayer with them.

Then he went downstairs, where Arlete was waiting for him. She did not cry, but her eyes were moist. They did not speak to each other. Arigo dropped his forehead on his hand, and both of them waited in silence for the police car to arrive.

8

Arigo and Arlete were barely aware of the crowd that had gathered outside their house that evening. It was quiet and orderly—so quiet that it seemed almost ominous. Only the mumbling of subdued prayers among the crowd of several hundred signaled to Arigo that they were there. He went to the window and looked out. When they saw him, the crowd cheered. There was still no sign of a police car.

At the local police station, there was consternation. None of the men on the force wanted to take Arigo to the jail in Lafaiete. Neither did the police chief want to give the order. Nor did the state police of Minas Gerais want to drive up through the crowd. Both the local and state officials tried to find an answer. No one, in fact, wanted Arigo in jail, aside from the authorities who had ordered it. The time wore on into the evening.

Arigo was becoming impatient. Finally, he crossed the room and embraced Arlete, then went out the front door. An enormous cheer went up from the crowd. He asked them to keep quiet and orderly, and to pray. Then he got in his jeep, nuzzled it slowly through the packed street, and drove to the police station. Sheepishly, the police chief told him of the dilemma they were facing. Arigo replied that there was no problem. He would drive to the jail at Lafaiete himself. The chief agreed that, in the light of the large crowd, it might be a good idea.

On the road to Lafaiete, Arigo's jeep was followed by a caravan of well-wishers. Behind the caravan, a lone police car followed, gingerly, uncertainly, its occupants half afraid of the crowd. It was a strange sight, the long dragon's trail of a motley assortment of cars and trucks, sandwiched between Arigo's jeep in the lead and the police car at the rear. Almost a carnival atmosphere prevailed, as the cars in the parade began blowing their horns. The cacaphony became deafening, but the police were powerless.

At the jail Arigo was met by the warden, almost as if he were a visiting dignitary. The police pushed their way up from the rear of the caravan, to deliver to the warden the necessary official papers. But in the confusion, the papers had been left in Congonhas. The crowd broke out into laughter as the police car sped back to retrieve the documents. Arigo laughed with them.

The warden insisted that it would be better for Arigo to serve his term in the local hotel, in the custody of the police. Arigo would have none of it. If he were being sentenced to jail, he would go there. The warden almost pleaded with him to reconsider, but Arigo still refused.

It was a dank, ugly, crumbling jailhouse. Some of the cells opened directly on to a musty alley that ran alongside the building. Arigo was assigned one of these. The warden took a large, old brass key and opened the creaky iron-barred door. The crowd pressed into the alley, until there seemed no room to breathe. Someone began saying the Lord's Prayer. The rest followed. The warden and the guard bowed their heads and joined them. When it was finished, Arigo spoke. He said to the gathering that they were not to feel resentment against either the jailkeepers or the police. They were only doing the work they were assigned to do. He promised that he would be released soon, because his lawyers were immediately appealing. Slowly the crowd dispersed and drove back to Congonhas do Campo. The warden, almost on the point of tears, told Arigo how distasteful a job this was for him to carry out. The night jailer said the same. Arigo blessed them both, and they left. Arigo lay down on the rough wooden bunk, and prayed again.

Arigo's case had attracted the attention of some of the best lawyers in Brazil. Dr. Jair Leonardo Lopes took the lead in bringing the appeal to the higher courts. He had spent considerable time reviewing the case, analyzing Arigo, and studying parapsychology. Interviewed the day after Arigo's incarceration, he told reporters: "Arigo never harmed anybody. He has a true gift which does not depend on legal authorization to cure strange ills of the rich and the poor. He often cures people doctors have given up on.

"Arigo has extrasensory perception. He is a clairvoyant and has other exceptional faculties we can neither define nor understand.

"He diagnoses by clairvoyance. He 'sees' the affected organs inside the patient's body. Through telepathy, he knows what other doctors prescribe for the illness or he knows what has worked in similar cases.

"He has prescribed medicines for some patients which have long passed out of use, and he also has prescribed medicines which were so new that they had not yet arrived in Brazil.

"Only clairvoyance and other undefined powers can explain these things."

Arigo had tried to explain his own powers to reporters previously, when he said: "When a case is simple, I can diagnose and prescribe without going into a trance, since Dr. Fritz guides me. But for complex cases, I must enter a trance and call on Dr. Fritz directly."

As Dr. Lopes began pressing the appeal, Arigo's cell door on the little alley next to the jail was swarming with reporters the next day. Arigo said he was glad to be in jail in one way, because he was badly in need of rest. He would be able to review his past and future. He said he was still praying for his enemies, and he hoped the journalists would do so, too.

Then he said a strange thing: "Perhaps being sent to jail is a gift of God. You know I drive very fast on the road. It is something I do without thinking about it. If I were not in jail now, I would be driving along the road, and I would be killed."

The remark was puzzling, and was generally passed over in the press. To the reporter who knew Arigo best and had studied him most, Gabriel Khater, the comment had something ominous about it. Arigo, he felt, did not make statements like this without good reason. He included it in his story, but then forgot about it.

Attorney Lopes was determined to bring the case to the Federal Supreme Court, if necessary. The appeal, labeled No. 2334, went anything but swiftly. Aside from pleading that there was not one iota of evidence that Arigo had ever harmed anyone, and that he was anything but a *curandeiro*, Attorney Lopes struck out for a writ of habeas corpus, on the grounds that Arigo had been tried twice for the same crime. But this process was burdensome and involved, having to pass through various panels of judges who would ponder the merits and demerits of the case endlessly before voting a decision.

Not the least damaging to Arigo was the aggressive attack of prosecutor Marcelo da Paula. Although some said they detected a softening in his attitude toward Arigo outside the courtroom, the brief he filed against the appeal failed to show it. He fought against even the temporary and provisional release the writ of habeas corpus would bring. He hit the Court of Appeals hard with a review of the case, emphasizing that Arigo did not even try to defend himself. He was unrelenting in his condemnation.

But Arigo did not exactly languish in jail. Action began almost as soon as he arrived. The other prisoners, long disgruntled by the appalling conditions in the jail, seized on Arigo's presence, with its attendant publicity, to stage an open revolt. They began burning everything in sight made of wood. They demanded less work and more food.

They terrorized the guards with knives that had been smuggled in, and held them as hostages. Finally, the guards broke away and ran from the jail, leaving Arigo alone with the rebelling prisoners.

He lost no time in quelling the riot. In his most commanding voice, he told them that they must not only stop what they were doing, but clean up all the damage they had done. He said if the food was good enough for him, it was good enough for them, and they had damned well better settle down, repent their sins, and start a new life for themselves. He faced the ringleaders directly with the demands. Strangely enough, they acquiesced. By the next day, most of the debris had been cleared, the guards had returned, and lumber and materials were supplied for the prisoners to rebuild what they had damaged.

But Arigo went beyond that. He asked the warden for paint, and began painting the dingy walls himself. Before long, the other prisoners joined in. The buildings began to take on a new life.

In gratitude, the warden offered Arigo complete freedom to leave the jail any time he wished. He actually left the key in his cell. Arigo used it on rare occasions, but only to visit the sick outside the prison, while the warden and guards looked the other way. They did everything possible to be kind to him. He took advantage of this in one respect: he began treating the prisoners in the jail. When word of this got around, crowds began lining up again outside his barred gate in the little alley. He even performed minor operations. Suddenly, the jail in Lafaiete began turning into another Congonhas. It seemed impossible to keep people from flooding into the town. The police and warden knew it; they did nothing to stop it.

Jorge Rizzini, who had tried futilely to support Arigo during the trial—anything he said about Arigo's medical success only helped seal his doom—came to see Arigo. He took motion pictures of the crowds as they filed by the cell in the little alley. Rizzini found Arigo alone in the cell when he arrived, reading the Bible. He looked well, and kept insisting this was the rest he needed. He again defended the people who had judged him, asking Rizzini not to condemn them in his press reports.

H. V. Walter, the British consul, made his way from Belo Horizonte to the jail, where he found Arigo resting on his bunk. He brought him two cheese sandwiches. Arigo ate one ravenously and passed the other to a prisoner across the hall. Arigo tacked the consul's calling card on the wall of his cell, referring to him as "Mr. Ambassador." He took great pride in his diplomatic visitor, whom he introduced to his fellow prisoners.

Esko Murto, Finnish-born reporter-photographer for *Manchete* magazine, the Brazilian equivalent of *Life*, arrived to do a picture story on Arigo's languishing in jail. Instead, he found Arigo in his cell performing a cataract operation on an old man who was almost completely blind. He photographed the surgery in a fast series of stills on his Leica, but Arigo quietly asked him not to print them, because of the impending appeal. Murto agreed not to, and later came to visit Arigo several times on the basis of friendship alone. Like so many reporters who interviewed Arigo, he became more interested in the man than in the story. Arigo told Murto he tried never to operate when reporters were present.

On December 11, 1964, not long after he had been jailed, Arigo received one of his most unusual visitors. He was an aged Catholic priest, Francisco Alves Correa, who had been ordained back in 1913. He had come to Lafaiete from Belo Horizonte, arriving early in the evening. He claimed that Arigo had removed his cataract, saving him from almost total blindness, but Arigo had no recollection of it. "If I did," Arigo said, "it is not I who did so, but Jesus."

The priest went on to explain that he had always mocked Arigo, but that after his treatment his own doctor was amazed at the results. The doctor had asked where the operation was done. "I explained," said the priest, "that it was done in Brasília. He would not have accepted the truth if I had told it to him."

Then he added: "This is why I came here to thank you. I hope God will give you the strength to bear this trial. You will leave here to perform still greater things. Be strong, for suffering is part of the law of evolution."

Arigo did remain strong, but the weeks in jail had now turned into months, and still no progress had been made in obtaining even the temporary habeas corpus release. He yearned to be home with his family again. The separation from Arlete and his boys was most painful. He longed to take care of the roses in his aunt's garden. Only the fact that the warden and police permitted him to treat the sick kept his sanity. In fact, the warden would often pick him up in the prison jeep to visit many of the sick and ailing in Lafaiete, returning him to the cell afterward.

As the appeal dragged on, the patience of Arigo's supporters grew thin. Pressures mounted in many spiritist centers throughout Minas Gerais until finally several hundred people, if not a thousand or more, literally tried to storm the prison and remove him bodily from it. They were not aware that Arigo could have left any time he wanted to. The police had no control over the protestors, but Arigo silenced them and told them that he was confident the process of the law would soon rectify the situation. The crowd left grudgingly.

There were other vigorous protests. One woman wrote to a Rio newspaper that unless the appeal was settled in Arigo's favor and he was released from jail, she would kill herself. What Arigo's burning advocates did not realize was that even if he were freed temporarily under the habeas corpus, there would be no real certainty that he would remain free. The legal review under Brazilian law would be in two long-drawn-out stages: the decision to free him, if at all; and the decision as to whether he should be resentenced if he were freed.

The irony and tragedy would be if he were freed and then sent back again to the jail. This was a distinct possibility, especially with the type of narrow-spectrum thinking of such judges as Soares and Barros. There were plenty like that in the wings.

News of Arigo's plight had traveled slowly to the United States. Belk and Puharich, each working on the long-range plans of organizing the research expedition, did not hear about Arigo's being jailed until he had been there for several months. Belk immediately wrote the Brazilian consul in New York and offered to pay all expenses to fly Arigo to the United States, where a study would be made. His request was of course refused.

Dr. Puharich and his associates, intent on preserving the possibility of studying one of the most convincing medical phenomena yet encountered, were concerned. The group sent their attorney to Brazil to double-check on Arigo's availability for research under the new conditions. Sidney Krystal, the attorney, found the outlook dismal. Arigo told him that any attention from American doctors at this point might aggravate the situation and create strenuous protests on the part of the Brazilian Medical Society. Arigo still felt confident that he would be released, however. Thousands of letters and telegrams were being sent on his behalf to President Castelo Branco, many of them from prominent government officials. If he were freed, Arigo assured the American lawyer, he would more than cooperate in the research.

Puharich sat down and wrote a long letter to the chief justice of the region that included Congonhas do Campo and Lafaiete. Judge Filippe Immesi had just entered the case, and would be the chief factor in determining Arigo's ultimate fate. In sharp contrast to the judges of the lower court, Immesi was an intelligent man of wide perspective and considerable warmth. Puharich wrote him:

March 14, 1965

Your Honor:
    I am taking the liberty of addressing an appeal to you on behalf of José de Freitas, more popularly known as Arigo.

Let me introduce myself. I am an American physician, and a long-time student of parapsychological phenomena. In my own country, I am equally known for my espousal of genuine psychics, as well as for the exposure of charlatans and frauds. With these credentials, I now address myself on behalf of Arigo.

During August of 1963, I spent several weeks studying the healing work of Arigo. I observed hundreds of patients being treated by him, and interviewed about a hundred of these patients.

In the first place, I could not find any case in which he did any harm to any individual. I also spent some time traveling around Brazil trying to find cases in which he had been a failure, or could be accused of malpractice. I could find no such case. I also witnessed many positive results of his treatment, both with drugs and with surgery. Needless to say I was most impressed by the therapeutic benefit that Arigo brought to people he treated. I was also impressed by the fact that Arigo does not charge any patient for treatment, nor will he accept any gratuity or contribution from anyone he treats.

In order to convince myself of the genuineness of Arigo's treatment, I had him operate on a tumor on my right forearm. I can affirm that his cutting of my flesh was painless, that he excised the tumor skillfully in five seconds, and that in spite of not using any antiseptics or antibiotics, my wound healed without any sign of pus or infection. This operation was reported in the Brazilian press, and shown on motion pictures on Brazilian television. My personal experience with Arigo, and my observations of many patients, convinces me that not only is Arigo's healing intervention safe, but also shows positive therapeutic benefits.

Brazil should be proud that it has an extraordinary man like Arigo at work among its people. I feel that his work is so unusual that it deserves intensive scientific study in the years to come. I shall do everything in my power to bring Arigo to the attention of scientists. I beg your honor to consider his case with compassion and justice in the interests of humanity.

Sincerely,
Henry K. Puharich, M.D.

Judge Felippe Immesi was impressed that a North American doctor would make the effort to write on Arigo's behalf, and especially that he had risked an operation on his own body. But he knew little about Arigo aside from what he had read in the newspapers, and still less about the intricacies of the legal case at this point. As a newcomer, he was intrigued with the unusualness and subtleties of the process. But it did not take him long to realize that Arigo sat on very thin ice as far as the law was concerned.

A panel of five judges was already reviewing the question as to whether Arigo should be provisionally released from jail, while Judge Immesi studied the case to determine if he should be resentenced. From his preliminary study, Immesi knew that he was in for an agonizing and complex decision. On June 24, 1965, seven full months after Arigo had entered the jail in Lafaiete, the five-judge panel agreed that the Congonhas judges were correct in declaring Arigo guilty, but ruled that he should be temporarily freed while Judge Immesi carried out his extensive review.

The news of his temporary release came almost as an anticlimax to Arigo. It was not an occasion for rejoicing, because the ax could fall any time in the near future. There was no assurance, no security, in a precarious release that left this possibility wide open. The respite would be welcome, of course. He would be able to be home with Arlete and the children, and to breathe the aromatic air of his rose garden on his aunt's farm. Beyond that, the suspense would be almost as painful as the possible reality of returning to the sweltering jail cell.

His first days at home were quiet, but both he and Arlete knew that the tranquility could not last. As President Kubitschek had said, Arigo could never be alone in Brazil, even if he went to the Amazon jungles. Convinced that he was doing right, Arigo returned to the Spirit Center, where the crowds collected again, just as they always had. Everyone knew it; it was no secret. The police ignored him as he worked with the new crop of patients; the court concentrated on trying to come up with a definitive decision that would settle the matter once and for all.

It wasn't long before Judge Immesi realized that he was sitting on top of a case that he dreaded to make a decision on. The more he learned about Arigo, the more he realized that he was dealing with something beyond the ken of normal jurisprudence. His reading of the facts convinced him that this was not a police case. But the law was clear. Arigo was wrong. As a judge sworn to uphold the law, he would have to condemn Arigo, regardless of his own feelings, which had swung widely to sympathy for Arigo and his family. Arigo emerged from the pages of the legal briefs and court records—hundreds of pages in thick, bound copies—as a warm and charitable human being, a sad and perplexed man, confused by his strange powers, and consciously unable to cope with them and the people who sought him out.

When he first came to the case, Judge Immesi had no belief whatever in the scattered reports about Arigo he had read in the papers. As a good Catholic, he simply could not comprehend the stories that came out of Congonhas do Campo. As he got more and more into the case, he realized that he would have to observe Arigo at first hand. Like everybody else, the judge knew that Arigo was back at his medical work shortly after he had his reprieve from jail. Arigo never tried to sneak his work with the ill. Except for the operations, he did it openly. And even with his surgical work, he was never that muted. He often explained that he didn't carry on his work in opposition to the authorities; he did it because he had no other choice. Whatever practices he engaged in now, in the interim period between his stay in jail and the ultimate decision by Judge Immesi, would make little difference. The evidence was already in. Further practice, even surgery, would simply be more of the same thing.

Arigo knew that the two men who came into the clinic that day were authorities from the law. He did not know exactly who they were, but he invited them to come forward and observe as he went to work. If they were going to be there, they should at least have a chance to see that he could bring about cures without harm to the patient.

One of the men was Judge Immesi. The other was a district attorney from another part of the region who was not involved in Arigo's case. One of the first patients to reach Arigo's table was a woman who was nearly blind in both eyes from cataracts, a frequent condition that Arigo faced because of his reputed expertise in the ophthalmic field. He asked the judge to stand by and hold the patient's head. The judge felt queasy and awed, but he did so.

"I saw him pick up what looked like a pair of nail scissors," Judge Immesi described the scene later. "He wiped them on his sports shirt, and used no disinfectant of any kind. Then I saw him cut straight into the cornea of the patient's eye. She did not blench, although she was fully conscious. The cataract was out in a matter of seconds. The district attorney and I were speechless, amazed. Then Arigo said some kind of prayer, as he held a piece of cotton in his hand. A few drops of a liquid suddenly appeared on the cotton, and he wiped the woman's eye with it. We saw this at close range. She was cured."

After the operation, Arigo smiled at the judge. "It is not I who do this, you understand. It is Dr. Fritz."

The judge and the district attorney from Belo Horizonte returned to Arigo's clinic several times. "I went there to convince myself that what I was seeing was true," Judge Immesi said. "I have great difficulty in believing anything like this. In spite of his bizarre explanation of Dr. Fritz, Arigo was a tough, hard realist, which he combined with a paradoxical sensitivity. From what I learned in studying the case, he was far from being a saint, and at times unbelievably crude. For anyone brought up in a puritan tradition, this was hard to justify in a man who had special powers, as Arigo did. I watched him treat two hundred people in less than two hours. He would take seconds to prescribe, and the diagnoses were immediate, without asking questions. I had to check all this personally. I had to study this man whom I would have to decide the fate of."

The results of his close observations over a period of time made Judge Immesi realize that the case simply could not be judged in conventional terms. He made it a point to keep his personal feelings from dominating his role as a judge, although he admitted to himself that this was hard to do. If it was within his power, he would have ordered Arigo to undergo an intensive scientific study by a university, because he was now convinced that Arigo was perhaps the wonder of the century. But this step was not within his realm under the Brazilian law. He would have to find other ways.

Judge Immesi pored over the testimony day and night, in the hope that he could combine technical justice with justice of a higher order. He gave particular attention to the medical testimony of the doctors who certified, with before-and-after documentation, cures that Arigo had achieved in the face of ominous prognoses from the conventional medical point of view. The judge took into account the advances made by parapsychology, as faltering as those steps were, in spite of recent recognition by the American Association for the Advancement of Science. He analyzed the attitude of the Catholic Church, noting that parapsychology was becoming acceptable to the Church's tenets. He studied the works of Padre Oscar Gonsalez Quededo, a priest who was considered among the best parapsychologists in Latin America. The padre had stated openly that Arigo held the highest rank among all the healers on the continent. He reviewed the tolerant and interested attitude of William James, Gardner Murphy (of the Menninger Foundation in Kansas), and others toward the unexplored potential of the human mind in the paranormal area.

His thinking boiled down to this: Arigo was doing a job that he was not entitled to do. He was practicing medicine, and he was not a doctor. But at the same time, he was definitely not a criminal, as the harsh charge of witchcraft suggested. Arigo's crime, if that was the word for it, was not against the public, but against the structure of legal medicine. The public had not been harmed. There had been no witnesses to testify to that, even among the hundreds of thousands whom Arigo had treated. Nor were there any among his most intense adversaries who claimed that he had harmed anyone. The public had not even been bilked; no one could testify Arigo had charged a penny.

There was no question that he would have to condemn Arigo, to send him back to jail, much as he hated to do it. If Judge Immesi did not condemn him, he would be a legal heretic, a position that no responsible judge could afford to hold.

The law was brutally cut-and-dried, exacting and specific. Judge Immesi would have to follow it, regardless of his leanings. Yet being the first judge who had done comprehensive field research on Arigo (Judge Barros was said to have read the testimony in one day and then made his decision), Immesi felt that in the broadest possible sense, Arigo was innocent.

As a result, Judge Immesi went through what he called "procedural calisthenics" to try to reach the fairest possible answer to an unanswerable problem. Since there was no choice but to condemn Arigo again, the judge sought ways to reduce the sentence and make it as light as possible. The first thing to consider was the public prosecutor's charge of *curandeirismo*.

Immesi was convinced that this was unfair in the light of both Arigo's character and practice. Arigo never used any ritual whatever, never practiced any of the mumbo-jumbo of primitive rites, said only simple prayers of the conventional Christian category, and these he said half to himself. The judge's brief but intensive study of Arigo at work had affected him strongly. "It gave me another vision of life," he said. "Very subtly, it seemed to validate the very essence of the Christian belief—the belief in life after death. If the existence of Dr. Fritz—whether real or illusory—were postulated as the root cause of Arigo's objective and verifiable miracles, I felt it did not conflict with the Christian ideal. In fact, it supported it. Arigo was not working against the Christian ethic."

Judge Immesi recalled watching Arigo perform an eye operation in which he extruded the eye visibly out of its socket with his kitchen-knife leverage. Medically, this was impossible without pain. How could Arigo do this? He recalled another operation during which he stood directly next to the patient. The incision started to bleed profusely. Arigo put his finger directly on the wound and said: "Jesus does not want this to bleed." The bleeding stopped. It was so unbelievable that the judge and the district attorney had to confirm it with each other.

Immesi searched the archives of Brazilian law on the subject of witchcraft. He turned to a favorite jurist of his, a former judge named Nelson Hungria, who was known as the "prince of penal jurists" in Brazil. It was Hungria who, in a famous decision, had determined that to reach a finding of witchcraft, the defendant must be found guilty of not only prescribing herbs and roots, but of personally concocting and dispensing them to the patient.

Arigo of course was not doing this, with his use of modern pharmaceuticals. This might be malpractice, but it certainly wasn't witchcraft. Because of this, Immesi found that he could, with full legal justification, shift the charge from a crime against the public to a crime against the public administration, bearing a far lighter sentence.

Further, the evidence showed clearly that Arigo had never harmed anyone, and the Brazilian Penal Code stated that there cannot be a crime without harm, injury, or damage. The only party, therefore, who could claim to be injured was again the public administration, specifically the office that grants licenses to doctors for the practice of medicine. This too would shift the case from a crime against the public to a charge of contravention, with an appropriate reduction in the severity of the sentence. The main thrust of the judge's thinking was that the only thing harmed was the medical profession.

When Judge Immesi sat down to write his opinion, he felt deep sorrow that he would have to return Arigo to jail. "I have to admit," he said, "that I felt just a little like a judge who handled a case about two thousand years ago, and I didn't like it at all. I had spent hours, days, and weeks trying to find a way I could free this enigmatic man, who should have been placed in a university for serious study. I was doing the best I could for Arigo, I knew that. It was tragic to separate him from his family again, to see him go back in that jail."

The only bright spot was that Immesi was able to reduce the sentence to only two months more of incarceration, whereas Arigo would have been facing nine more months under the witchcraft charge.

The judge signed the papers with great reluctance. On August 20, 1965, Arigo drove himself to Lafaiete, entered his waiting cell, and began more months of prison life.

Meanwhile, the Federal Supreme Court continued to review the case, on Judge Immesi's urging. There had been many irregularities in the prosecution, many oversights. In a strange about-face, Prosecutor da Paula recommended that the sentence be canceled. The court finally voted unanimously that the charges against Arigo should be dropped. He was freed from prison on November 8, 1965.

The rejoicing was again overwhelming. The warden and the guards embraced him. Many of his fellow prisoners cried. Several thousand gathered outside his cell to greet him on his release. Arlete was waiting for him, with all the boys. Arigo was crying openly. He waved to the caravan of cars that had come to greet him on the Rio–Belo Horizonte road. Newsmen's flashbulbs were popping like fireworks.

He arrived home, went to the refrigerator, took out a

piece of meat, and called his dog Tostao over to his favorite chair. He was home again, this time without the immediate threat of a new jailing.

Where the future would lead was uncertain. By the next morning, they were lining up outside the Spirit Center again, as if nothing had happened over the past year. Rising early, Arigo went out the door, walked down the cobblestones in his muddy shoes, and into the clinic. He went into his small inner room for meditation, then came out again, his deep eyes glazed and his voice thick with a German accent.

Arigo was back, and the hopes of thousands of sick were rising. How long it would last was anybody's guess.

9

With Arigo released, Dr. Puharich and his group of American scientists renewed their efforts for the research expedition to Brazil. They would still have to move cautiously to avoid drawing inordinate attention to Arigo's fresh start at his practice. Several preliminary probes were made by Puharich, including continual contact with many Brazilian physicians who were sympathetic to Arigo and wanted the extra support of North American research.

On learning that former President Juscelino Kubitschek was living in New York, out of favor with Brazil's new regime of President Castelo Branco, Dr. Puharich and Maria Treen, an interpreter, visited him at his office on East 57th Street, in Manhattan. They were interested in any authoritative information he could give them. Kubitschek greeted them cordially, and confirmed his friendship and experiences with Arigo. He told them that he would never have pardoned Arigo if he had not had firsthand knowledge of his healing powers or if he had had any information that Arigo had ever harmed anyone. He felt that a full-scale medical research program on Arigo was not only desirable, but urgent.

Encouraged by this verification from a Brazilian who was both a doctor and a statesman, the Medical Commission on Arigo, as the group within Essentia

Research Associates was named, contacted several Brazilian doctors as to the best method of approach and the timing of the expedition. The Brazilian doctors suggested holding off until they had explored the conditions of Arigo's work, now that he had been freed from his legal troubles.

By July 1966, some eight months after Arigo had been released from jail, the doctors in Brazil advised that Arigo was back at his usual routine and that he would do everything possible to cooperate with the American researchers. Arigo had suggested, however, that Puharich come alone for a preliminary survey, as inconspicuously as possible, to avoid arousing the hostility of the medical society.

Puharich arrived in Congonhas do Campo during the first week in August, 1966. With him was his research assistant, Solveig Clark, a fair, tall, slender, and efficient American woman of Norwegian extraction. The immediate job at hand was to quietly explore just one factor of Arigo's skill: his ability to diagnose disease. This study would attract the least attention on the part of the anti-Arigo faction of the medical society, and provide essential groundwork for the fully equipped scientific team that was to arrive later.

It was the first visit to Brazil for Solveig Clark, and she was captivated by the charm of Congonhas. She sat with Puharich in the small café at lunchtime, waiting for Arigo's inevitable appearance on the Rua Marechal Floriano, on his way to the clinic.

"You can sit here," Puharich told her, "and let the town come to you."

But from her view of the street outside Arigo's clinic, it looked as if the world were coming to Congonhas. Several chartered buses were parked down the street from the clinic; the people were waiting patiently on the sidewalk, ignoring the hot sun, wearing a motley variety of clothes, from elegant to tattered, and at times looking anxiously around the corner for Arigo to appear.

It wasn't long before a battered truck swung around the corner and into the carport of the Hotel Freitas. It narrowly missed a post as it screeched to a halt. A powerful, thick-set figure jumped out, who Solveig knew immediately was Arigo. Buoyantly, he bounced across the street toward the café. He was wearing his usual sport shirt, collar open, and a dusty pair of slacks. He looked as if he were on the opposite end of the spectrum from a mystic. Solveig was most impressed with his eyes, however. They were warm and deep, and seemed to have great command.

He shouted a loud hello to Puharich, then embraced him warmly. Together, Arigo and the two visitors crossed the street and went into the clinic. Within moments, Arigo was at work.

By the next morning, Solveig and Puharich were ready to begin their study on Arigo's method of diagnosis. They found a young Peace Corps girl who was willing to interpret for them, although she later became so awed by watching Arigo at work that she would often forget to translate.

Solveig's organizational ability was legend, and she immediately put it to work. The plan that was worked out was simple. Arigo agreed to give an immediate verbal diagnosis for each patient, as he stepped up. He would ask no questions of the patient at all. Arigo's diagnosis would be tape-recorded. Solveig would then interview the patient to find out if he had brought medical records from his own physician. This diagnosis would be matched against Arigo's. If there was a difference of opinion between the two, the diagnosis of the physician would be accepted over Arigo's. This admitted bias was used only because it was impossible to reexamine the patient.

Puharich and Solveig worked three full days beside Arigo. They took the first thousand patients as a sample base for the preliminary study.

It was recognized that this would not be a definitive study, but the results would be invaluable in assessing the potential for success of the full research team. After the third day, Puharich and Solveig went over the records and summarized the results. They were impressive:

Preliminary Study
Diagnostic Capacity of José Arigo
Congonhas do Campo, Brazil
August 2, 3, 4, 1966

Cases diagnosed by Arigo	1,000
Cases rejected by Arigo:	
ordered back to own physician	35
Final sample base, cases	965

Number of patients with medical records out of above	545
Cases rejected due to lack of medical records	420
Sample total	965

Correct match between Arigo's diagnosis and physician's	518
Disagreement between Arigo's diagnosis and physician's	27
Valid sample	545

Percentage of diagnoses made by Arigo that matched diagnoses of physicians	96%

Beyond the diagnoses, the unorthodox pharmacology continued to defy rational analysis, yet a follow-up on several cases showed measurable success. One example was a forty-two-year-old American woman, the wife of a successful lawyer, who had been plagued for most of her life with various allergies that were believed to trigger severe migraine-like headaches. After consulting specialists in both the United States and Europe, the couple flew to Brazil in desperation to see Arigo. The course of drugs prescribed was, as usual, medically irrational. It included an obsolete form of streptomycin known as Garomicina; the rarely used German drug Olobintine, supposed to increase biological defense mechanisms; a Brazilian anti-allergy drug known as Piro-vac; an enzyme preparation called Pankreon; an antacid, Alcalitrat; and massive doses of vitamin B$_{12}$.

Puharich was later able to follow up on the case back in the United States. There were no adverse reactions from the drugs, although this would seem highly likely in the quantities prescribed, which were large. The course was continued for over two months, during which time the migraine headaches subsided for the first time in over twenty years. Mild attacks would occur at rare instances after that, but were insignificant compared to the former intensity of the attacks. Within six months, the attacks had completely disappeared.

Puharich summarized in his report: "It is reasonable to conclude that Arigo has paranormal medical diagnostic talent." Admittedly, over 95 percent was an outstanding accomplishment, but it still failed to explain how or why Arigo was able to do all this. Further, it was obvious that when the American team arrived, they would want to add their own diagnoses to this record where possible, in order to establish further verification.

In the course of his routine, Arigo treated several ophthalmic cases. Puharich, along with everyone who saw it, could never get used to this part of Arigo's technique. Regardless of how many times he watched Arigo plunge the knife up into the sinus cavity or behind the eyeball, he could not conceive how a conscious patient could stand the pain or overcome the fear. The cases where Arigo would leave the knife sticking out of the eye while he turned to pick up some cotton or another instrument were particularly graphic. The patient Puharich had seen on his previous trip, who had brushed away a fly from his cheek while his eye was extruded from the socket, had remained in his mind all during the time he was back in the States.

When Puharich was least expecting it, Arigo turned to him while he was stirring a knife blade in a patient's eye and said: "Every good American doctor should be able to do the same thing." He was continuing to manipulate the blade mercilessly. "Here," he said to Puharich, "take hold of the knife yourself."

Before Puharich was hardly aware of it, Arigo had grabbed his hand roughly and squeezed it around the knife handle. Puharich felt weak and faint. He took his hand away. Arigo pressed it back on the knife handle again, this time forcing Puharich to shove the knife in to the limit. Puharich was horrified. But he noticed one thing: there seemed to be some kind of repellent force that inexplicably worked for Arigo but for no one else when it came to this maneuver—except when Arigo guided his hand.

At dinner at Arigo's house, they found him relaxed and voluble. The change from the stern and brusque manner at the clinic was marked. Arigo joked with Arlete, played with his cats, rough-housed with his sons. It was hard to believe he was the same person they had been studying clinically all day.

Puharich was determined to find out how Arigo was able to give his diagnoses in modern medical terminology. Even though Arigo had stated the condition of the patients in Portuguese, the tapes were easily translatable into articulate medical terms. Dr. Mauro Godoy had been on hand to help in this regard, and continued to help at dinner.

"How are you able to know modern medical terminology in such detail if you haven't studied it?" Puharich asked.

Through Dr. Godoy as interpreter, Arigo laughed and replied: "That's the easiest thing to do. I just listen to what the voice tells me, and I repeat it."

"What voice are you talking about?" Puharich assumed

that the answer would be the alleged Dr. Fritz. But he wanted to hear Arigo's own response.

"It's the voice of Dr. Fritz," Arigo confirmed. "I always hear it in my left ear. If the people in the room are making too much noise, I can't hear the voice. So I shut them up."

"Does the voice speak to you in German or Portuguese?" Puharich asked.

"I always hear it as Portuguese," Arigo said. "I don't know German. If someone who is curious wants to talk in German to Dr. Fritz, I simply mimic what Dr. Fritz is saying to me. But I don't understand what I am saying."

"Do you understand the medical words?" Puharich asked.

"No," Arigo said. "I just repeat what I hear."

At the end of the conversation, an easily grasped explanation was as far away as ever. There was only one pragmatic thing to go on. That was to analyze the massive statistical evidence of accurate medical diagnoses. This much could be checked, although it still left many tantalizing questions.

On the long, eleven-hour flight back to New York from Rio—one of Pan Am's longest legs—Puharich had plenty of time to mull over the visit. He had studied German for six years in high school and at Northwestern, and although he was extremely rusty in the language, he was not too impressed with the few phrases that Arigo threw out from time to time during his work. Others, however, who had made it a point to check Arigo's capacity in the language, found that his use of it was more than acceptable.

Arigo had seemed bored when Puharich pressed him about the language syndrome. Puharich didn't follow up at the time, because the main basic questions were: Could Arigo diagnose accurately without even examining the patient? Could he actually heal? Everything else was peripheral.

The whole question of the possibility of a deceased personality possessing the motor-sensory equipment of a living being was almost totally unexplored in modern psychology. Parapsychologists had done intensive study on mediums, with some evidence—but not proof—that pointed to the legitimacy of certain mediums as channels for communication with discarnate personalities. But the research was spotty and difficult to carry out in the laboratory. It could not, however, be totally ignored, especially in a case such as Arigo's, which defied any conventional explanation.

Whether new explorations into the area, attempting to forge some of the instinctual prowess of primitive medicine men with the discipline of modern science, would shed more light on the matter was unpredictable. On the other hand, before Freud there had been no such concepts as the id and superego—except in ancient mythology. Was Arigo a symbolic expression of bypassed ancient lore?

In Brazil, the possibility of possession—for better or for worse—is taken almost as a matter of course in all levels of society. The Brazilians have a tendency to accept such a potential phenomenon as part of the culture, and therefore it becomes in their eyes either a literal or metaphoric truth.

Puharich reasoned that the human mind is built like a filter. It is constantly focusing on certain subjects, constantly filtering out others. It has to do this or, like a computer, it would be overcome with random information bits of no cohesive value. In Brazil, where many minds permit the concept of possession to filter through, it is therefore culturally acceptable at least to *consider* such a phenomenon as a viable postulate.

A reflection of the easy acceptance of this idea is shown in a routine Brazilian school English examination labeled "Proficiency One Comprehension and Composition," which reprints an article by John Francis-Phipps that appeared in the British publication *The New Statesman*.

The article concerns a healer in Brazil and a festival in his honor. It begins: "Sometimes bizarre things happen to be true, and are therefore worth investigating ..."

The questions at the end of the examination reflect the atmosphere in which the student is brought up. They include:

"Do you believe these cures took place?"

"What is your explanation for them?"

"Are modern medicine and this kind of healing necessarily in conflict?"

"What is this 'metaphysical cocktail' the writer mentions?"

"Describe experiences you know about Umbanda."

"The writer mentions that socially and racially, the human friendliness and equality were taken for granted. Is this typical of Brazil?"

Young Brazilian minds, like those of their elders, are more conditioned to accept this sort of possibility than an American or a European would. But in Arigo's case, this cultural difference mattered little. His material accomplishments were fully obvious and observable to either foreign or domestic minds.

Anyone studying him could only go so far in rational judgment. When the full medical expedition came down to Brazil, it would be important to focus only on those verifiable facets of Arigo: the diagnostic ability; the successful treatment of incurable diseases by unconventional pharmacology; the ability to perform surgery without anesthesia, antisepsis, or hemostasis—the tying off of blood vessels. These objectives alone created a formidable challenge.

Back in New York, the elaborate plans for the expedition finally began to jell. There would be six medical members of the commission heading up the research. These would include William Brewster, M.D., senior research scientist at the New York University School of Medicine; Luis Cortes, assistant research scientist at the same school; Walter Pahnke, M.D., chief research psychiatrist at the Maryland Psychiatric Research Center; Robert S. Shaw, M.D., associate visiting surgeon, Massachusetts General Hospital; and Henry Puharich, M.D., who currently was heading up medical research for the Intelectron Corporation of New York City, the medical-instrument developer and manufacturer. None of the commission members would be making the journey in an official capacity for the organization he worked with.

The immediate goal would be the scientific rationalization of the phenomena of Arigo as they were directly observed by the group. Since the preliminary investigations had firmly indicated that there was validity to the claims made for Arigo's work, it would be up to the team to try to confirm this objectively by instrument and examination.

If the biophysical investigation accomplished this, an important vacuum in modern medical knowledge could be filled. Paramount in the plans was the study of those aspects of Arigo's work which could be explained and related to accepted modern medical theory and practice. These aspects would be clearly separated from those of Arigo's work which could not be explained by any known theory or practice in modern medicine.

The obscure and more occult phase would have to have special attention, but since it was in unknown waters, it would not have priority. The "voice" that told Arigo his amazingly correct diagnoses would be considered, but the statistics on the actual diagnoses and treatment would come first.

The research problem to be considered eventually would be trying to identify the nature of the "Dr. Fritz" intelligence. Was it a creative process, similar to a composer hearing the music he is about to create and score? Was it simply a form of articulating Arigo's unconscious thoughts? Or was it a paranormal manifestation of a source of intelligence outside Arigo's personal memory and experience, which he called Dr. Fritz?

Arigo's knowledgeable utilization of a broad spectrum

of pharmaceutical drugs was another tough nut to crack. How was he able to achieve successes with irrational combinations of drugs for diseases that were not clinically responsive to these drugs? Arigo had, for instance, brought about medically confirmed, five-year cures of leukemia with readily available commercial drugs. Why couldn't other doctors do the same thing? Even when they duplicated Arigo's prescriptions, the drugs failed to work. What was the boundary line between the known and the unknown elements of Arigo's practice? Was the prescription itself only part of the picture, with Arigo's own proclivities a vitally necessary adjunct to the total effect?

Even though Arigo's surgery could be easily studied and photographed at close quarters, and the patients objectively examined and tested before and afterward, how could these unusual procedures and end results be accounted for?

Further, how could Arigo locate unseen, deep-seated lesions without diagnosis, X rays, or examination beforehand? Even though his surgical procedure was readily observable, and pathological tests could confirm the condition, how could he get away with neglecting to tie off blood vessels or use sutures? Why wasn't there postoperative bleeding? Why was there no apparent surgical shock? How could a patient walk out of a room, unassisted, immediately after major surgery?

And how could Arigo himself physically withstand the ardors of treating some 1,500 patients a week, without full assistance and without periodic rest periods?

The American doctors would have their hands full even attempting to answer these and other questions. To back up the staff, other specialists joined the team. They included Cesar Yazigi, a professor of Portuguese on the staff at NYU, and his wife; Edward Hall, of New York, an experienced film-maker; and Paul Jones, a still-camera specialist. Medical records would be handled by Mrs. Edward Hall, and audio recording by John Laurance, who would combine his advanced engineering and scientific background in the NASA space program with his wide studies of parapsychology throughout all of Brazil.

The equipment to be brought to Brazil was complex and extensive. It would include a Nagra tape recorder, with a recharger and mike, along with five Norelco cassette recorders. Other audio-visual equipment included a black-and-white film processing kit; two Sunguns for battery-operated camera lighting; a 16mm Eclair camera with three 400-foot magazines; five Instamatics; a Spectra exposure meter; an Auto Micro-Nikkor 55mm f 3.5 close-up lens; a 200mm f 5.6 medical Auto-Nikkor lens; and X-ray copy attachments.

Other cameras included a Nikon F, 55mm f 1.2 photomic; a Honeywell Super-8 movie camera; a 35mm Pentax; a 35mm Canon; a Hasselblad 500; a Polaroid; a 16mm Bolex; a Nizo Super-8; and a Fairchild cinephonic 8.

The medical equipment of course was far from slighted. The team would be bringing a portable X-ray machine, a portable EKG, a portable EEG, bacteriological slides, stains, and cultures, an X-ray viewing box, blood-typing equipment, Formalin jars for specimens, blood-staining and white-cell-count equipment, and a microscope. Added to this were five thousand printed medical-history and examination forms for the patients, and an equal number of forms for Arigo. A special Minox microfilm camera and accessories were added to photograph the medical records. Everything was included to make the survey as comprehensive as possible.

Most of the coordination for the expedition fell on Solveig Clark's shoulders. Nearly all the members of the group took night courses in Portuguese at New York University, cramming in as much information on and practice in the language as they could in a limited time. Much attention was given to contingencies and exacting minutiae. One concern was what the reaction of the Brazilian legal and law-enforcement agencies would be.

Confirmation had already been obtained that Arigo would fully cooperate with the scientific investigation. He had again assured the group that he would demonstrate his surgical technique in selected cases in his own clinic, and that he would guide the scientific team to former patients and doctors who had worked with him. He would also grant interviews about his ideas and the *modus operandi* of his healing art. In addition he would assist in the inquiry as to the sources of his information. Further, he would reluctantly consider the idea of coming to the United States for a full investigation of his healing practice there. All the practical arrangements had been made.

There were of course imponderables. The chief threat was the resentment of the official Brazilian Medical Society, still stung and sullen about what it felt was the laxity of the courts. This problem would somehow have to be met and solved as best as possible. There was an implicit slur in the very fact that foreign doctors were taking over a job that many felt the society itself should be doing. Some of its most prominent members felt that way.

The most important factor was obvious: the United States team should try to make itself inconspicuous. The mere mechanics and logistics of the research made it imperative that conditions in the clinic remain as normal as possible. This was going to be a difficult job with over a dozen North Americans descending on the small town of Congonhas do Campo. The presence of so many researchers and their equipment in the crowded clinic would be bound to present problems.

One difficulty with any research work is that often the observer and his instruments disturb the observed, whether the subject is electrons or people. This would have to be circumvented. Another difficult condition arose from the fact that Arigo was enjoined from doing major surgery as a condition of his release from jail.

There was also the cultural shock for those of the

researchers who had never been to Brazil before, who had not been exposed to the Kardecist philosophy or the widespread belief in spiritism throughout the country. Except for Puharich and John Laurance, who had studied the subject, only a few of the group knew any details about psychic healing.

Two reputable psychic healers, Dr. and Mrs. Ambrose Worrall, came up from Baltimore to address the researchers several times on their well-documented, cautiously practiced healing work that had accomplished much in the field. Worrall, a highly successful engineer in industry, devoted all his spare time to the art of healing, either by absent healing or touch, but not with surgery. Both he and his wife were a far cry from the spook-and-kook department that throws up so much static in this field that rational minds hesitate to explore it.

By May 1968, the expedition was ready. A strategic decision was made to split the team up, to stagger both the dates and places of arrival so that the ubiquitous Brazilian press could be avoided. This strategy was of the utmost importance. Brazilian journalists can be so over-ebullient that their enthusiasm wipes out reason. Blazing headlines were the last thing the American group wanted. Nor did Arigo. His interest was in scientifically redeeming himself after the brutal punishment he had been through at the hands of the prosecutor and the state medical society. A sound and solid research program would help wipe away the stigma that had been forced on him. In spite of his lack of formal schooling, Arigo was an intelligent and rational man. He was also a good politician.

Some of the research group booked flights to Rio on Pan Am. Others came in on Varig Airlines to São Paulo. Still others came down on the flight to Brasília, and changed airlines. Up to this point, the strategy worked well. No press was on hand, and the group quietly reassembled at Congonhas do Campo in the middle of May. To further avoid drawing attention, they rented a ranch outside Congonhas in an attempt to reduce the inevitable gossip in the town, which would attract journalists like the vultures in the river.

In spite of attempts to keep things simple, the arrangements turned out to be elaborate. It was necessary to tap the outside poles for power, both for the X-ray machine and the floodlights that were needed for filming. There was no good vantage point for the camera to photograph Arigo at work, and it was necessary to break through a hole in the wall that divided Arigo's work room from another small, unused one. It took two full days to prepare and test the equipment, but it was a necessary step.

The appearance of so many strangers in town—those who were not patients of Arigo—drew a great deal of attention. Crowds gathered simply to watch the process of tapping into the power lines. It was not a good omen. Sooner or later the press would be bound to be attracted, and the glare of publicity would measurably reduce the effectiveness of the survey.

Solveig Clark, as the coordinator of the project, remained cool and unruffled. She arranged the medical-report forms, set up the routine of the process that would be followed, planned the flow of patients, and saw that each participant was supplied with exactly what he needed to do his job.

Patients were to be divided into three groups. For the first group, they would screen out a small number of patients who had classical and clearly identifiable symptoms. These would be determined by a thorough examination of Arigo's diagnosis and therapy.

The second group would consist of those who had seen Arigo prior to the arrival of the scientists. The effectiveness of Arigo's treatment of them would be measured in line with the diagnoses provided by the registered physicians who had referred these cases to Arigo.

The remaining patients would be taken from the other

groups, where cooperation could be obtained from the referring physician for a long-term follow-up of Arigo's success or failure. In this way, it was hoped to determine whether Arigo's treatments were transient, palliative, or permanent.

The surgical studies would be most intense, to determine the response of patients in the total absence of anesthesia. Patients would be examined before, during, and after surgery. They would be checked by electroencephalograph, electrocardiograph, and an instrument known as a finger plethysmograph, which measures changes in the volume of blood flowing through a single finger. Blood pressure and respiration rate would be charted. In this way, the presence or absence of the appropriate autonomic nervous system response to the surgery could be determined.

Other tests would be applied to the surgical patients simultaneously. Their psychomotor performance and capability would be continuously analyzed during the operation with specific tests, such as recent and long-term memory tests, audio-visual response, and deep and superficial reflex changes. Immediately after an operation, the patient would be observed for possible amnesia. This observation could check whether or not some type of hypnosis had been unknowingly utilized by Arigo. Films would be made of the surgery procedure, with oscillograph monitoring in real time during the operation.

There were many other considerations. Every specimen of tissue removed from a patient would be subjected to gross and microscopic pathology studies. Arigo's unsterile instruments would be cultured before use to determine the bacteria counts on the surfaces before he used them. The surface area of the patient's body where the operation would be made would also be cultured, since Arigo never used any preoperative precautions to sterilize. Careful study would be made of incisions, and how they were able to remain closed without sutures. Follow-up plans of the surgical patients were included.

As the research procedure began, attention was first turned to the study of Arigo himself. Was there anything about his physiological makeup that enabled him to accomplish what he did? Arigo, with the body of a sumo wrestler, was an active man whose brute strength and earthiness belied his inner sensitivity. He was as puzzled about his powers as the doctors who examined him. There was little evidence of his spiritual and lofty qualities most of the time.

He cooperated completely as the American medical staff wired him with the awkward and intricate EEG electrodes. He seemed eager for any practical test of his ability. After a complete physical, the doctors could find no unusual powers or anomalies. He could not control his brain waves, his blood pressure, or his body temperature —or any other physiological variables that have been described in some autogenic processes, including the practice of Yoga. The only thing discovered was that he had a slight heart condition that did not seem serious or threatening. Aside from that, he was normal and healthy.

One interesting aspect came out of the questioning during Arigo's examination. He revealed that he was never able to treat successfully any organic illness of his relatives. Nor could he treat himself.

For the beginning of the broad-scale research, a routine was set up where Dr. Puharich sat by Arigo, an interpreter beside him. All the key staff had walkie-talkies for quick communication within the center itself. Solveig Clark sat with Altimiro, along with photographer Paul Jones, who made a microfilm record of both written and typed prescriptions. Later, package inserts of the pharmaceuticals would be gathered and filmed.

Cameraman Ed Hall was posted in the newly made wall opening, opposite Arigo's table in his little room. Anno Hall would write up a medical-history card for each patient. The other doctors were assigned to pre-treatment examination, post-treatment examination, and analysis of the medical records that many patients brought with them from their own doctors. John Laurance handled the tape recording, stationed close to Arigo, where he could try to analyze just what made Arigo tick as far as the mysterious Dr. Fritz was concerned. Laurance's extensive studies in parapsychology excited in him an interest in how this particular "voice" worked to motivate Arigo. The others were concentrating on the observable, objective surgery, diagnosis, and treatment.

Although Laurance was a hard, tough, material scientist and researcher in his work with RCA, NASA, and the armed forces, he was one of the few scientists who felt that material science was approaching a closed frontier, and that sooner or later it would have to cross over the threshold of metaphysics. In his successful career of many years, he had dealt with some of the leading scientists of the world.

Much of his work with the space and military programs had involved advanced development of electronic sensors and photoelectric cells. His accomplishments in this field were many, varied, and widely recognized. John Laurance had given Arigo a great deal of thought, puzzling over the possible mechanics that might be involved in his healing success. Laurance had been experimenting with the use of photoelectric cells to measure human auras beyond that of infrared, a field that the Russians were quite advanced in.

Laurance felt that to understand Arigo, it would be necessary to join in the phenomenon as much as possible, just as some psychiatrists were doing with their schizophrenic patients. By participating in the fantasies and delusions of their patients, these psychiatrists had brought about marked improvement in some cases.

Laurance also felt that, with the human mind generally operating at less than 10 percent of its capacity, it was possible for anyone to extend his sensory perception beyond the normal limits, to a greater or lesser degree. His conviction was that it was possible to work in the nonmaterial field in the same way as in the material field.

As he observed Arigo at work from his close vantage point, he tried as much as possible to become part of the experiment. He studied Arigo as he would an instrument that had a broad spectrum of sensors. Arigo's sensors were obviously hooked in deeper than normal to an unknown reservoir. When Arigo found something wrong with a patient, he sometimes seemed to absorb the ill radiations from him. This was evidenced, and had been seen in the past, by several cases when Arigo appeared about to vomit, or actually did so.

One man of about forty-five approached Arigo in his turn in line. Arigo started to speak to him, then suddenly turned to his left and began to vomit. An enormous amount of bile gushed to the floor. An assistant came quickly over to clean it up.

Arigo immediately explained to the interpreter that this patient was not physically sick at all, but was possessed by evil spirits. Arigo insisted that he had taken over the spirits, and in doing so, relieved them from the patient. Whatever the story was, the patient perked up immediately, thanked Arigo fervently, and left the clinic. It was a startling, dramatic scene—but one that could not be analyzed in any rational way.

But perhaps this was part of the picture, whether the case was physical or psychosomatic. Could Arigo absorb the pathological radiations of a patient, and then create an input of additional energy that the patient was lacking? When the problem was beyond Arigo's own energy field, was he able to tap a computer-like energy field beyond himself, and impute it to the patient? Since all people are analogous to a complex series of sensors, the problem was to get them to function properly. Whether Dr. Fritz was a myth or a paranormal phenomenon, did he act as a computer feedback to make Arigo's work effective? With a problem as wildly speculative as Arigo, the questions posed would have to be speculative, too.

Arigo seemed to transcend the normal, but Laurance's

analysis was that he was merely an extension of normalcy. Arigo's work was, in effect, analogous to acupuncture, in that it worked in mysterious, uncharted ways. But it went far beyond acupuncture. Because his surveys in parapsychology convinced him of the legitimacy of reputable mediums, Laurance was willing to accept Arigo as an extraordinary medium who acted as a middleman to forces beyond himself. Since "spirit guides" were a common factor among all mediums, where the medium became a vessel for a personality of unknown dimensions, could Arigo's Dr. Fritz fit into this pattern?

The medical team was of course concentrating on the technical, material side of the picture. Arigo's capacity for making accurate diagnoses without previous knowledge of the patient's illness and without a physical examination was confirmed again as case after case was recorded and examined by the American doctors, before and after treatment by Arigo. A paraplegic arrived in a wheelchair. Arigo stated that at the age of fifteen, he had fractured his cervical spine, the result of a diving injury. This was confirmed in full detail.

A woman stepped up to Arigo. After a quick glance at her, Arigo told the Americans that they would find her blood pressure to be 230 systolic and 140 diastolic. The cuff and Tycos instrument readings showed exactly that.

A man was next in line. He showed symptoms of congestive heart failure with dyspnea, and a distended external jugular vein. Arigo immediately said to the researchers: "This man has renal hypertension with a systolic pressure of 280." The post-Arigo examination by the American doctors and the history supplied by the man's own physician confirmed that reading and condition.

The next man spilled out his story to Arigo. He said he had Chaga's disease, a common parasitic disease in Brazil. Arigo glared at him, then turned to the Americans. "No!" he said. "This man has a four-plus Wasserman, and the diagnosis is syphilis, not Chaga's disease." This was confirmed both by the patient's medical records and a later Wasserman test. It seemed difficult to mislead Arigo.

What was noteworthy was the exactitude of Arigo's diagnoses. A patient would step up to the table where Arigo sat. To the American doctors, and even to the layman, it might be obvious that there was something wrong with the patient's eyes. But Arigo would not merely say that the patient had eye trouble. He would say that the patient had retinoblastoma, or retinitis pigmentosa, or use other modern medical terminology. He would invariably be proved correct by the technical follow-up by the American doctors.

The checking of Arigo's diagnostic ability continued. The statistics matched Dr. Puharich's preliminary survey, and continued to hold up as the assembly line pumped by Arigo at the rate of one patient a minute. Paul Jones, the still photographer, came over to the table to ask Dr. Puharich a question. Arigo stopped him by the arm and said: "You are taking entirely too much medicine!" The Americans laughed, because they knew Jones carried an overabundance of medicine with him.

Like nearly everyone who saw Arigo, Dr. Pahnke, the psychiatrist from Maryland, was interested in the threshold of pain when Arigo performed his seemingly brutal eye examinations. Hardly anyone seemed to be bothered by them, no one reported any pain. Out of dozens of these knife-in-the-eye examinations, two of the patients did show some sign of fear. It was on a day that Arigo himself seemed out of sorts. He had scolded the crowd waiting for him when he entered, saying that he would not tolerate anyone in the center who made noise or disturbed his work. He said he wanted to help all those who needed it, but that those who came merely to watch were not welcome. He said he knew that some of the people there had been drinking, and that they ought to return to their bars. He added: "I am not a saint. I am unclean and uneducated. I never called anybody here, and I won't put up with this drinking. Anybody who has been doing this, get out!"

Then he told the people to get in line and Dr. Fritz would take care of them. As they filed by, he often cupped his ear with his hand, explaining that he was having trouble hearing what Dr. Fritz had to say that day. Several times, he was heard to mutter: "I am very nervous today. Very nervous. And so is heaven."

In spite of Arigo's occasional mercurial moods, the filming went well. Making sure there were no reporters or police around, Arigo performed several operations for the motion picture camera. One difficulty was that the lights bothered the patients, and had to be reduced in order to make them feel more comfortable. This brought a corresponding reduction in the quality of the film. He did not perform any major operations for the camera, but did operate on a full spectrum of cataracts, lipomas, sebaceous cysts, a gigantic hydrocele, eye probes, and others. The legal situation was still hanging fire, and Arigo was obviously worried about it. Fortunately, up to this point, the press was not in the picture.

When the press did arrive, it hit like a tidal wave. It had been impossible to keep the survey confidential, of course, but none of the American team quite expected what was to happen when the flood of reporters stormed into the town, including radio, television, and print media.

All the meticulous, expensive planning of the research group was threatened disastrously. If there was one thing the American doctors didn't want, it was publicity. Nor did Arigo; nor did the patients. As the reporters and TV crews grew to over forty, the entire research project began sliding precariously to a halt.

10

The moment the press arrived, conditions for a scientific study became almost untenable. Everywhere anyone turned, a reporter or cameraman was on hand to squeeze out information on this first major medical study of Arigo. Headlines about Arigo and the North Americans blazed all over Brazil. The American doctors, interested only in serious medical research, simply could not and would not continue the project under such carnival conditions. Arigo pleaded with the journalists to refrain from the coverage, but to no avail.

Puharich called a hurried press conference with the reporters. He explained how publicity at this point would be ruinous not only to the expedition, but to Arigo. Many patients wanted to remain anonymous, but their pictures were being plastered on front pages across the country. Because none of the American doctors wanted anything but medical-journal exposure later, Puharich would not supply the press with any information on the identity of the group or on the methods employed.

All the conference resulted in was the resentment of the reporters, who labeled the expedition "the mysterious North Americans," and continued to badger the patients for any information they could get from them.

Arigo refused, of course, to do any further operations with the media men around. The patients, not knowing whether an interviewer was a reporter or a doctor, balked at talking to either. In a strange turnabout, the medical society of Minas Gerais issued a statement that the North American doctors were engaging in a purely parapsychological investigation; that this was praiseworthy; and that its own doctors should continue the work after the Americans had left. This radical change in the outlook of the organization brought protests from some of its members, but it seemed as if the tide had at last changed. Two Brazilian members of the society, in fact, arrived to observe the American researchers, along with H. V. Walter, the British consul, whose interest in gaining a rational explanation of Arigo never flagged.

The newspaper story that brought events to a crisis was one appearing on May 27, 1968, in *O Dia*, a widely circulated paper in Brazil. The headline to the story was: AMERICANS PLANNING TO TAKE THE MEDIUM TO UNITED STATES. PUBLIC UPROAR AGAINST IT. The story went on to say that the town of Congonhas do Campo was in an uproar with the news that Arigo might accept the invitation of the North Americans to go to the States for specialized research.

A large crowd gathered at the Spirit Center, and Arigo was forced to come out and address them. He assured the gathering that he had no intention of leaving Congonhas, that he would stay with his people and continue his work.

This seemed to relieve the pressure on Arigo, but a petition was actually introduced in the State Assembly that would set up a special commission to "defend Arigo from the foreigners" and prevent him from leaving the country.

There was no let-up from the pressure of the media group. Although considerable data had already been gathered, it was still inadequate for a complete study. Yet it was impossible to continue. At a meeting to deal with the problem, the consensus was that the only practical thing to do was to make a thorough analysis of the material already in hand, and to help a team of Brazilian doctors set up a similar study that could be done quietly, out of the glaring floodlights of publicity. Now that the Minas Gerais Medical Society seemed to be shifting its position, this plan might turn out to be a viable alternative. With doctors in residence in Brazil, the privacy of the research would be more likely.

Further, plans were already taking shape under the aegis of several Brazilian doctors to build a hospital in Congonhas, where permission would be obtained to have Arigo continue his work under the direct supervision of the Brazilian medical men. If there had been some way to foster this type of project at the time of the first court process, perhaps some real clue to Arigo's rare effectiveness would have already been available.

It was with a great deal of frustration and regret that the North American research group closed down their project at Congonhas. But there seemed to be no other answer. The reporters had even tried to storm Arigo's house. The work could have perhaps continued if the situation had not affected Arigo himself so acutely. He found it almost impossible to concentrate under the conditions, and became seriously concerned for the welfare of his patients.

Even with incomplete data, however, considerable information could emerge from the analysis of the material. There was, for instance, the case of a six-year-old girl, Maria Cristina Faleiro, of Rua Januaria 304-A, 13, in São Paulo. Her medical history showed that a diagnosis of leukemia was first made by her physician in São Paulo in March 1968. At this time, her white cell count had soared to 75,000, about ten times the count considered as normal. The prognosis given by her physician was grave.

The girl had been brought by her parents to Arigo on May 20, 1968. She had been given a prescription by him at that time, and began taking it on May 22.

She was riddled with the fatal disease, with the

leukocytes—the white blood cells—running out of control, and the lymphoid tissue of the glands and bone marrow enlarged and proliferated. Returning to São Paulo from Congonhas, the parents of the girl had found their own doctor willing to cooperate in administering Arigo's prescription, since he could find no rational way to retard the case in conventional therapy. He had held out little hope, however.

He administered the drugs, and watched the girl carefully. The key to any progress would lie in the telltale white cell count. This he took at regular intervals.

By June 18, the count had dropped from 75,000 to 20,000—about 12,000 above normal. It was a startling, unbelievable drop. By July 5, less than a month later, the white cell count had plunged to 10,000. By August 7, it was down to a normal 7,500, and the glandular system of the girl had returned to normal. A follow-up by the doctor half a year later showed that the white cell count remained within normal limits, and the glands were also normal, a condition which the Americans verified.

Another leukemia case studied by the North American researchers was equally dramatic. The patient was two-year-old Rosanna Canargos Ribeira, Rua Valdir Cunha 52, Congonhas.

The medical history showed that the baby girl had developed acute fulminating leukemia in April 1967, about a year before the American researchers arrived. Within three weeks after the onset of the symptoms, the child's glands, both external and internal, swelled massively. A month after her condition had been diagnosed, the glands in the abdominal cavity swelled to such an extent that they caused gangrene of the intestines, peritonitis. They further ruptured the abdominal wall with exudation of pus.

Rosanna was rushed to the hospital in Belo Horizonte. Her white cell count had risen to 110,000. Her fever skyrocketed, and she went into a coma. The doctors at the hospital conferred with the mother, and told her that

Rosanna's case was terminal. She had at best a day or two of survival time left. They indicated that in the presence of leukemia, nothing whatever could be done to control the runaway peritonitis.

The distraught mother refused to accept the verdict. As a last resort, she rushed Rosanna back to Congonhas on May 19, 1967, to Arigo.

Because of the severity of the crisis, Arigo took immediate charge. He personally administered the chemotherapy—a practice he very rarely followed. He prepared a mixture of cortisone, potassium chloride, and Puri-Nethol, an experimental Burroughs-Wellcome drug for the repression of cancer that had never been found to help in leukemia. He mixed an enormous dose—20 cc.— of the drugs in a syringe, and injected the medication directly into the peritoneal cavity—a procedure that would never be considered proper in conventional medicine. He told the mother to stay close by the child, and to give her water by mouth for the next twenty-four hours. She was to bring her daughter back the next day.

She did so. Arigo examined the child, and said that she had passed the crisis stage. There were still gaping wounds in the abdomen, draining pus. But Arigo did nothing to intervene. He told the mother that the wounds should be allowed to drain, and to close naturally.

Then he showed the mother how to grind up a mixture of 20 mg. of Meticorten (conventionally used for rheumatoid arthritis), 500 mg. of potassium chloride, and 50 mg. of 6-Mercaptopurina (a rather dangerous experimental drug for leukemia), and mix it with milk, administering it every eight hours for a month. To the physician, this is a startling, massive, and irrational combination. Under ordinary circumstances, it might even kill a child of two. The amount of Meticorten was a dosage that would be used for an adult twenty times the weight of Rosanna.

But the mother religiously followed the directions. The child began showing dramatic improvement. By the second week, the abdominal wounds had stopped draining pus and were beginning to heal. Within a month, Rosanna was afebrile—without fever—and the glandular swelling had disappeared. She was able to follow a normal liquid diet.

Arigo again examined the child, and said the same treatment should be continued for another month, at half strength. He asked the mother to get another blood count. She did so. The white cells had fallen from the original count of 110,000 to 12,000. By the end of the second month, the count had dropped to 7,000.

On May 20, 1968, almost a year to the day after Rosanna had first been brought to Arigo, the American doctors examined the girl and her medical history carefully. The white cell count was 6,700. Her abdomen still bore massive scars. Aside from that, she was normal.

There were many more leukemia cases with similar detailed documentation. In all of them, Arigo stated that he simply did what "the voice" told him to do. He never took blood counts, but they were often available from the doctors for verification.

Although the research project was abortive, there were scores of cases that had been recorded, and were to be followed up by the cooperating Brazilian doctors. There was also much work to be done on return to New York: assigning tapes to be transcribed and edited; making up a list of the Brazilian doctors for the follow-up; analyzing what went wrong on this trip, and how to avoid it in the future; analyzing Arigo's prescriptions; and, above all, planning a new expedition so that there would be minimum interference from the press.

The ideal situation would be to bring Arigo to the States, but this he finally would not consider. He felt he could not desert those who were depending on him, even temporarily. Because of this, the coordination of the research effort with the Brazilian medical men became of foremost importance. The key man in this regard was Dr. Ary Lex, the São Paulo physician who had first observed

Arigo six years before. With his cooperation, a meeting was set up in São Paulo between the American group and the interested Brazilian doctors. It was only through them that the plans for the dream Arigo had always had—the building of a hospital in Congonhas, where he could work with them clear of any legal harassment—could be fulfilled. In fact, it became a major obsession with Arigo; it filled his mind night and day. He knew he could not stop his work, in spite of the law or the Church. But he also knew he could not survive another assault by the courts, or another term in prison.

The meeting with the São Paulo medical group was held on May 28, 1968, at the art museum in that city. It allowed ample room for discussion and speculation about Arigo. From the point of view of most Brazilians at the meeting, the observations of Herculano Pires were among the most astute in trying to bridge the gap between the metaphysics and the material reality of Arigo's work. Dr. Pires' theory was that it was impossible to label Arigo as a paranoid case, as some tried to do, when he was able to perform verifiable physical operations successfully.

Arigo's detractors did everything they could to deny the reality of what they saw. But this was impossible to do in the face of facts, and Arigo remained above their barbs, except on legal technicalities. Pires also felt that it wasn't necessary to either accept or reject the bizarre concept of Dr. Fritz. Fritz could be explained in any number of ways, depending on the attitude of the observer. Fritz could be an element of mythology, of Arigo's unconscious, or of a clearly defined spirit personality, as the Kardecist spiritists believed. Whatever the truth, the fact is that it worked. It was that simple.

Dr. Pires was an intellectual Kardec spiritist, and he believed in the reality of mediumship under certain conditions that were as disciplined as any in formal psychology. Pires interviewed Arigo in a trance state, so ostensibly it was Dr. Fritz who was speaking through Arigo as a channel. In the session, the German-accented voice of Dr. Fritz indicated that he had been born in Munich, moved to Poland when he was four years old, studied medicine, became a fairly good doctor and surgeon, but made several bad mistakes. The voice claimed that he went to Estonia, where he lived from 1914 until his death in 1918. According to the voice, Dr. Fritz vowed before he died that he would continue his medical development after death, and return to cure as many people on earth as he could, to make up for his earthly inadequacies.

Attempts have been made by several students of Arigo to check out these facts, but have been unsuccessful.

In any event, the voice of Dr. Fritz speaking through the mediumship of Arigo claimed that he had become part of a group of other deceased doctors who decided to help people as best they could in the name of Christ. Dr. Fritz's voice claimed that he had studied Arigo for over a decade before he felt that Arigo was the ideal vehicle to carry out this work. At this point, Fritz continued, he was able to obtain perfect control of the medium Arigo, so that he could perform surgical operations through him. Further, Dr. Fritz's voice claimed, he served as a go-between for the other discarnate doctors in his group, each of whom had his own specialty.

Dr. Pires asked no one to believe all this; the phenomenon of Arigo stood alone without it. It is simply one way the Kardec spiritist might try to set up a theory, and it remained only a theory. But even the solid, hard-core rationalists were hard put to explain Arigo without some kind of postulate that seemed to go off the paranormal Richter scale.

An ophthalmologist of high standing, Dr. Sergio Valle, was fascinated by what Arigo could do in his field. His observations were important as the negative point of view of a specialist. His statement was emphatic: "No ophthalmologist could do what Arigo did in front of us. It is simply not possible to do an operation on the eye without previous study, preoperative preparation, full sterilization and antiseptic conditions, the quiet atmosphere of an operating room, and above all, complete anesthesia. It is literally impossible to understand how Arigo does what he does, so swiftly and under the conditions he works in. He moves with no thought whatever. No one can explain this, and no one ever will."

Dr. Valle had also spent considerable time studying hypnosis, and ruled that out as a factor.

Dr. Edoardo Basevi, a nuclear physicist, offered his theory. Like John Laurance, his feeling was that there was an analogy between Arigo's work and pure physics. He used the spectrum as an example, where the visual sensory equipment peeks in its confined way at the universe through a tiny slit in the spectrum between 356 millimicrons on the ultraviolet end and some 2,400 millimicrons on the infrared end. Light waves, or energy waves, move out to the infinitely small and the infinitely large in each direction, and our eyes do not perceive the rays on either side of the minuscule visual slit. Neither does our hearing extend beyond a tiny portion of the audio spectrum, with its own *ultra* waves. Dr. Basevi's concept was that Arigo was pure *ultra* in all of his work, but it was something the ordinary mind just could not perceive.

New studies exploring the human aura are just now beginning to be taken seriously with what is called Kirlian photography. Both Russian and American films show that more easily detectable and more brilliant auras emanate from the fingers of those who are considered to be psychic healers than from others. Since human cells, in the last analysis, are electromagnetic force fields, Dr. Carlos Cruz and Dr. Mauro Godoy felt this could be at the bottom of Arigo's prowess. "You could almost figure that this might have something to do with the soul of an atom," Dr. Godoy said.

There seemed to be as many theories as there were people. One medium, who was also the technical administrator of a large corporation in Brazil, tried to analyze the situation for journalist Reinaldo Comenale. He said: "The phenomenon I see is not just a simple one by Dr. Fritz, but a group of spirits under his direction. The diagnosis is already made by this group by the time the patient steps up to Arigo.

"Dr. Fritz passes the consensus of the group along to him before Arigo has a chance to look at the patient. The medical group around Dr. Fritz did not stop developing after they died. They only touched the surface of medical practice when they were alive. Their knowledgeability now has no limits.

"Not all mediums are possessed by their spirit guides. But when Arigo is practicing, he is completely possessed by Dr. Fritz. He remembers little if anything afterward. His whole body is possessed. He is unconscious. His person becomes that of Dr. Fritz.

"Spiritism on the intellectual Kardecist plane is a science, a philosophy, and a religion. Many people do not understand that. It is a religion when thought of as trust and belief. It is a philosophy when it gives to man the power of kindness, love, and the practice of religion. It is a science when the other two elements combine to bring about the observable surgery and cures Arigo causes.

"Both matter and spirit are energy forces. They are simply of different frequencies. They are not as far apart as might be thought. The spirit loses the shell of the body, as a caterpillar loses his cocoon. But the personality remains conscious and aware.

"To talk about the results of Arigo is like talking about rain in a wet place. There's no question of the facts. Nobody who has studied or observed the man has any doubts. But Arigo doesn't create miracles. He is merely a vessel for a higher form of energy, which you could say is ultimately God-given."

These concepts were interesting, but utterly useless for the medical researchers, who needed more statistical information on the hard, observable facts. It is one thing to be convinced by direct observation. It is another to articulate the facts in a form acceptable to the editors of a scientific journal, who must have precedents and previously documented material to fall back on.

With Arigo being unprecedented, the job remained as difficult as ever. Dr. Pires, who unquestionably had probed deeper into the mystique of Arigo than any other Brazilian, had searched long and hard among the medical and psychiatric professions to try to bridge the gap between the rational and the inexplicable.

His travels brought him in contact with Dr. Maria Pedroso, a psychiatric physician at the Municipal Hospital in São Paulo, and formerly assistant professor of legal medicine at the Medical School of the University of Brazil. She was internationally known, and had represented Brazil at the International World Convention of University Women.

Dr. Pedroso had participated in a study of university women in the United States, and been a forerunner in Brazil for women's rights. Her long list of credits included the vice-presidency of the Pan American Alliance of Women Doctors. She had practiced psychiatry for over twenty years in both São Paulo and Rio de Janeiro. She was most interested in the correlation between the paranormal and psychic abnormality.

The moment she arrived at Arigo's clinic, she noticed that Arigo turned and stared at her. Still looking straight at her, he said: "Anyone who is a doctor here, come forward." Dr. Pedroso, startled at the uncanny perception of Arigo, stayed in her place. Then he pointed his finger directly at her, and asked her to come close and observe from where she could see in detail.

She did so. The operation was another pterygium, at which he excelled. She was shocked at the violent movements made in the eye of a conscious patient, and at the lack of antisepsis. She was further shocked when the scissors seemed too dull to cut. She was thinking to herself that the crude strokes of the scissors would tear the tissues of the eye beyond repair. She also thought that if only he had a sharper instrument, there might be some hope.

At that moment, Arigo asked for a scalpel. He cut through the webbed structure, and the eye began to bleed profusely. She saw it flood down the cheek, and waited for it to drench the patient's shirt. The blood stopped exactly at the point of his lower jaw. There was no physical reason why it didn't flood over the jaw and down to his chest. The operation a success, Arigo swabbed the eye with dirty cotton, and called for the next patient. To Dr. Pedroso's utter surprise, he wiped the bloody scalpel on the blouse of the next patient—but the blouse did not show any stain.

"I was satisfied, and it was clear," Dr. Pedroso said, "that my trip was not wasted."

After watching several other operations at close range, plus the prescription procedure, she pondered long and hard about her experience. She found herself forced to conclude that Arigo showed evidence of paranormal manifestations, without any doubt. She agreed with Richet, Janet, Freud, and others that there is no organic substratum in a living individual that could be looked on as a center for paranormal functions. Yet she had to accept the theory that there is an element beyond the normal in an undetermined location. In some individuals this would come out either spontaneously or under stimulation.

Her technical rationalization was complex. She told Dr. Pires: "There are great silent zones in the brain which could possibly be the center of paranormal activities. The nerve cells are not inherent but adherent to the fibrillae. These act as batteries and distributors of potential energy. There are also magnetic and electrical forces at work within the atom. There are many forces that work on the central nervous system, either for good or for bad, that affect its protoplasm, by cohesion, electivity, or pressure. These can cause mechanical changes of the structure of the nervous system, which in turn affects the physiological basis of intrinsical associations. In doing so, either conscious or unconscious psychic phenomena would be included."

It seemed that anywhere anyone turned to try to explain Arigo, the attempt at an answer was hard to follow or believe, whether the effort came from a religious, spiritist, legal, or scientific source. The only thing all points of view agreed on was that Arigo's work was a cold, realistic fact.

Perhaps Dr. Oswaldo Conrado, the cardiology specialist from São Paulo, summed up the most interesting attitude from the point of view of the medical profession when he said: "If doctors were able to open up new hope for patients, it would be a wonderful experience. When I find that I am directly confronted with a hopeless case, and when every possible medical avenue is closed, I see no reason not to look for other means. We wouldn't be human if we didn't.

"The facts about Arigo exist. They have happened, simply and naturally. A commission of scientists, free from preconceived ideas *must* study him, and study him thoroughly. We might be on the edge of discovering entirely new and extremely beneficial therapeutic resources."

As frustrated as they were, the North American researchers agreed substantially with this premise. They formulated plans with the Brazilian doctors to follow up on their incomplete data, but with the conviction that it would be necessary to come back to Congonhas do Campo as soon as possible for a concerted effort.

The best hope for this lay in the establishing of Arigo's dream: a fully equipped hospital run by competent physicians and surgeons under whose observation he would be able to work free from the intrusions of either the press or the courts. It was a glorious dream because it would combine the best possible combinations: scientific and metaphysical; psychological and physical; religious and secular; practical and idealistic; shadow and substance; sickness and health—all amounting to a fusion of compatible paradoxes. And, as some thought, that is what life consists of.

As the Americans prepared to leave São Paulo for New York, there were signs in the air that the dream might be fulfilled. The medical society of Minas Gerais was softening, and markedly so. The Catholic Church had taken cognizance of the North American team's invasion of Congonhas, and was giving the potential of psychic healing a new look. It was even rumored that there were training courses in healing established in the monastery high in the mountains surrounding Congonhas that would compete with Arigo. Gabriel Khater, the journalist, was pushing hard to raise funds for the hospital. Puharich and his group made plans to try to raise money in the States for the same cause.

The last thing Arigo wanted was to be alienated from the Church. He believed in the Christian ethic, and shared Arlete's almost obsessive devotion to the Catholic rites. In the courts, his lawyers had emphasized that he was bringing his children up in the best Catholic tradition, that he put Christ above everything else. Only his almost demonic compulsion to heal the suffering and help the poor kept him from giving up his healing work.

This compulsion had been described as an obsessional neurosis, total psychosis, inspired evangelicalism, saintliness, profiteering, egocentricity, political machination, venality, naïveté, braggadocio, divine love, stupidity, charity, consummate skill, deviltry, unqualified citizen concern, black magic, sacrilege, pathological compulsion, humanism, and celestial skill. But there was no one who could say what Arigo really was. It is doubtful if he knew himself.

Arigo went back to his routine; the Americans returned to their more worldly jobs. There would be nearly a year of sorting even the incomplete statistics they had assembled.

Reviewing the color films of Arigo's surgery taken by

the medical team, Dr. Robert Laidlaw, director of psychiatry at New York's Roosevelt Hospital, screened the footage several times. It was thought his expertise might bring a fresh viewpoint to the research. He was a meticulous man, and he wrote a careful report of his observations:

1. Arigo's facial expression when he operates differs completely from that of his normal demeanor. During an operation, there is a trance-like serenity seen in both his eyes and face.

2. It is important to notice the precision with which his fingers work, especially in a delicate eye operation. They keep working in this extremely sensitive area, even when his head and eyes are turned away in another direction.

3. The movement of his fingers is extraordinarily fast. He uses a knife with extreme confidence and precision.

4. None of the patients have submitted to any pre-operative preparation. It is very odd that the conscious patients are completely calm, relaxed, and indicate no fear whatever, yet they have received neither tranquilizers nor anesthesia. There is no expression of tension; no muscular tension; the patients don't even move. They remain impassive.

5. There is very little blood coming out of the body. Almost nothing. There are no stitches. The edges of the incision seem to glue together. In the two lipoma operations, the incisions bind together immediately, with practically no bleeding.

6. It is documented that the knife used by Arigo was unsterile. There should be massive post-operation infection, but I understand this has never been reported. Many of the surgical routines observed cannot be done by highly trained surgeons.

7. The evidence shown in these films defies any explanation in terms of orthodox science.

Dr. Laidlaw's observations were echoed by many

members of various medical associations that Dr. Puharich showed the films to on his return to the United States. With the problems now anticipated and correctable, he was seeking support for another expedition to Brazil, convinced that Arigo needed a lifetime of organized research and study.

Back in Brazil, they continued to come to Congonhas do Campo for the pilgrimage to Arigo: statesmen, industrialists, actors, singers, peasants, miners, scientists, the whole broad spectrum of humanity. Roberto Carlos, the toast of the Brazilian entertainment world, chartered a plane to fly to Minas Gerais, just for the ceremony of thanking Arigo for saving the sight of his infant boy. Ex-President Kubitschek, now back in Brazil, would bring his wife and daughter to see Arigo, to thank him again for his help. Arigo, in turn, unabashedly kissed Kubitschek's hand for his pardon during his first pending sentence.

On his twenty-fifth wedding anniversary, Arigo went to Mass with Arlete and the boys. Here the couple had their wedding rings blessed. Asked why he went to Mass in the face of the censure of the Church against his work, Arigo said: "All my family are Catholic. I alone am a spiritist. But I believe that all religions take the people to God. So why not go to a Catholic Mass?"

What he didn't know as he entered the church was that almost the entire town of Congonhas had prepared a surprise anniversary party for him. Two bands were playing, and dignitaries from Rio, São Paulo, and Belo greeted him and Arlete as they came down the steps of the church after the service.

It was a festive anniversary. Uncountable telegrams arrived—some estimated as many as ten thousand. Some from Europe, Argentina, and the United States. One was from the Kubitschek family, in France. On facing the profuse enthusiasm of the crowd, Arigo surveyed the scene in disbelief. His eyes filled with tears. Then he broke down and cried openly.

After the gloomy oppression of prosecution and jail,

Arigo's life was taking a new turn. The newspapers and broadcasting stations gave absolute assurance of noninterference in any scientific studies that would be made on Arigo. Word came that Arigo would be permitted to operate under the controlled medical guidance of research surgeons. The new president of Brazil, Arthur da Costa e Silva, promised support to Arigo. Funds were mounting in the program to build a modern hospital where Arigo would be studied and would practice. The North American medical group's new plans for research were progressing swiftly, under foundation funding.

It seemed all Arigo's hopes were coming to fruition. But it was during this time that Arigo went to bed one night and again had trouble getting to sleep. He woke Arlete and said to her: "I see that terrible black crucifix again."

11

Whatever meaning Arigo ascribed to the image of the black crucifix, there were no sinister forebodings in the days that followed. Arigo was able to continue with his work free from interference, in a relaxed, fruitful atmosphere. There seemed to be a tacit truce between Arigo and those who opposed him. New support brought the hospital in Congonhas do Campo to the actual planning stage. "This is the dream of my life," Arigo told his friends.

Exhilarated by what now seemed to be a certainty, Arigo worked with fresh vigor, never leaving his clinic until the last patient had been taken care of—often well after midnight. If the mild heart condition uncovered by the American doctors ever bothered him, he never mentioned it, not even to Dr. Godoy, who was working closely with him in coordinating the medical plans for the hospital.

In the States, the Essentia Research group's plans were shaping up for the joint study with the Brazilian doctors. In September 1969, Dr. Cortes went down as an advance scout, to coordinate the arrangements. Being alone, he had no interference from the press, and he was able to gather more data. One case seemed particularly dramatic.

It involved Comtesse Pamela de Maigret, an energetic and adventurous geologist from Philadelphia, who was engaged in alluvial mining for diamonds on the

Jequitinhonha River in the mountains of Minas Gerais. It was a full-scale project, with heavy equipment and suction dredges. It was moderately profitable. Frequently she would be driven from Rio or Belo to her remote camp in the mountains by Jacques Riffaud, who headed up the vast Belgian and French iron-ore interests in the region, known as the Schneider Group.

Riffaud's chauffeur, Juvenal, was a dark-skinned Brazilian of middle age, a sturdy, squat man with a deeply lined, powerful face. He had been quite stout, but suddenly began losing weight at an appalling rate. On each trip, he looked sicker. Finally he was persuaded by Pamela and Riffaud to go to a hospital in Rio for an examination.

The X rays showed an advanced case of stomach cancer. As an employee of the Schneider Company, he was offered complete hospital and surgical care, but he refused flatly. He had a wife and six children, and he was sure the operation would kill him. The doctors at the hospital were irritated at his stubbornness, but their prognosis was that it was a terminal case, even with the operation. Further X rays and tests showed he was completely beyond medical help.

Shortly after this, in Belo Horizonte, Juvenal asked Riffaud if he could have a few days off. He would like to go and see a "healer" in Congonhas do Campo. Juvenal was a pragmatic man, but when he had learned that he was going to die, he simply felt obligated to try every avenue of escape. Neither Riffaud nor Pamela knew much about Arigo at the time beyond newspaper headlines. But they urged Juvenal to try anything that would help.

Juvenal later told them what had happened. He had arrived at Arigo's clinic, but the line was impossibly long. He gave up any thought of getting to Arigo that day, but sat down on the street with the others and waited with little hope. A few hours later, Arigo came out of the clinic and walked directly up to him. "You are very ill," Arigo told him bluntly. "Come with me immediately."

Without any examination, Arigo gave him a prescription and told him to take the medicine, and come back the next day. Juvenal followed instructions, and reported back promptly the next morning.

Arigo took him into the small, almost-vacant room behind his general working area. He laid him down on the crude wooden door stretched between two sawhorses. Then Arigo began pressing down on his stomach with both hands. Juvenal experienced no pain, just a feeling of heavy pressure and considerable discomfort. Arigo pressed with all his beefy weight, until it seemed as if the stomach wall would be pushed against the spinal column. Suddenly the stomach popped, with a clearly audible sound, like the cork of a champagne bottle. There was blood, but there was no hemorrhage. Arigo reached into the upper abdomen with his hands and literally pulled out a large quantity of what Juvenal described as "bloody things." Arigo used no instrument. Juvenal felt apprehensive, but still no pain.

When Arigo removed his hands, the wound closed immediately, with no stitches. Juvenal felt weak and shaken, but was able to get up and walk out of the room.

He drove back to the mining camp alone, over the grueling roads, on the next day. Riffaud and Pamela were open-mouthed when he told them the story. It contradicted every conceivable tenet of medical science, and they frankly felt he was fantasizing. The skin on the stomach showed only a slight mark, without any conventional scar. They remained unconvinced.

Several months went by. Juvenal recovered from his shakiness, and his health obviously seemed to be returning. He was gaining weight rapidly. Riffaud, his curiosity now aroused, finally persuaded Juvenal to have another X ray taken, at the company's expense. It showed no trace whatever of anything abnormal. The man regained his full health.

Another case developed after the initial North American research expedition. It involved a nine-year-old boy from Hartsdale, New York. He had suffered from major

Jacksonian epilepsy since birth, which creates massive involuntary, uncontrollable spasms, although the subject remains conscious. He had received the best possible medical attention in the United States, but he continued to have twenty to thirty epileptic seizures a day.

The parents were distraught and desperate. Learning about the American medical expedition to Brazil, and having been to that country several times in the past, the parents obtained Arigo's address, and decided to take the boy there.

He was treated by Arigo on May 20, 1969, and given a prescription immediately. It read:

First Treatment
Revulsun: 1 tablet each night
Antisacer: 1 tablet each morning
Neo-Combé   1 ampule, intramuscular every other day
             Treat for 100 days

Second Treatment
Tryvigenex: 1 tablespoon with each meal
Metioscil: Ditto
Testoforan: 1 tablet after each meal
Memoriase: 1 capsule daily
             Treat for two months

Third Treatment
Gamibetal: Inject 2.0 cc. daily, intramuscular
             Treat for one month

Again, the course of drugs was puzzling, though not entirely without logic. Revulsun is an anti-spastic sedative; Antisacer is a specific for epilepsy; Neo-Combé is a high-potency vitamin B–complex compound; Tryvigenex is used in cases of anemia; Metioscil is a fortified liver extract; Testoforan has a sedative action; Gamibetal is an anti-convulsant. It is doubtful that any conventional doctor would combine these drugs in these quantities, in fact almost certain that he would not.

The first treatment was begun on the same day Arigo wrote the prescription. The drugstore in Congonhas kept enormous stocks of Arigo's unconventional drugs on hand. All previous medication the boy had been taking, such as Dilantin and phenobarbitol, was discontinued at once.

Within two months, the boy was able to leave home for the first time in his life and go to a summer camp. By September 1969, he was radically improved. By a year after that, he was free of all epileptic convulsions and living a completely normal life.

Major successes of this sort continued, but Arigo would at rare times tell his close friends and family about the black crucifix that still kept appearing in his dreams. It seemed to plague him, unnerve him.

At other times, though, he was unruffled and confident, still a front-page figure in Brazil, still the subject of special news bulletins on television featuring some dignitary or celebrity who told about his personal experience with Arigo.

As Arigo's work became tacitly legitimatized, the more prominent people flocked to him, and the more his reputation grew. He received constant long-distance calls from many major figures in the country, not merely for medical advice, but for philosophical or spiritual sustenance. When he would go to Belo Horizonte on occasion, there were few persons, if any, who did not recognize him on the street, few who did not try to stop him and shake his hand. Passing the Hotel Normandie one afternoon, Arigo noticed a huge crowd gathered. He learned that President Arthur da Costa e Silva, with his wife, Dona Iolanda, were about to leave the hotel.

Arigo waited a few moments, and the President and his wife appeared, waved to the crowd, and started toward their waiting motorcade. Spotting Arigo in the crowd, the President went directly to him, drew him out from behind the police barrier, and embraced him "with fire," as the press put it. Dona Iolanda took Arigo's hand, and said: "So you are Arigo. I am happy that you can continue your work. We'll do everything possible to help." Arigo kissed the First Lady's hand, and the entourage drove off.

Support like this bolstered Arigo's hopes for the new hospital, and he waited anxiously for the day that construction would begin. Ex-President Kubitschek continued his support when he returned to live in Brazil. Anticipating his return, he had written Arigo from New York to say that he looked forward eagerly to seeing him again in Congonhas, and to be "in condition to pass the days with you I want." Like the others, Kubitschek seemed to draw spiritual as well as medical strength from Arigo.

Along with the analysis of the statistics and the time-consuming preparation for the follow-up survey, several of the Americans who had visited Arigo continued to probe the reasons why Arigo was able to do what he did. He was constantly being compared to Edgar Cayce, the widely known American mystic. But Cayce had never plunged a knife into the viscera as Arigo did. He was also compared to many "healers," but none of them had done so, either. Acupuncture was another comparison, but Arigo's surgery was far beyond it. The Philippine psychic healers, who continued to receive sporadic attention in the press, could not be equated with Arigo. There was too much evidence of pure fakery in their work.

Luis Rodriguez, the retired industrialist and author who lived in Rio, kept up a running correspondence with the Essentia Research group, including Belk, Puharich, and John Laurance, on his own extensive studies of Arigo.

Rodriguez was an intellectual Kardecist who had come around slowly to accepting the concept that Dr. Fritz's possession of Arigo was an outright reality. Many felt that Rodriguez had gone overboard in buying this, although his reasoning was quite brilliant and persuasive. His prose was ponderous, but his thoughts were extremely cogent. His studies of psychiatry were probably as extensive as those of many of the advanced specialists in the field, and his knowledgeability was unquestioned. What *was* questioned was his tendency to extrapolate too much from the evidence at hand. In a lengthy letter forwarding his theories about Arigo to the North American medical group, he wrote:

In all serious psychic research, we are basically directed to evaluate innate or native capabilities of every individual. This is because we do not find psychic manifestations in things, but in persons.

Every person is a naturally endowed individual with his peculiar psychic qualities. Arigo, for instance, is a man like any other man, physiologically speaking. Yet psychically, he is different from many others.

A great number of people, the immense majority, do not have the slightest idea as to what psychic virtues distinguish Arigo from many others. But a few do know the how-and-why of Arigo. To these, Arigo is not a mystery; to the others, he is an enigma. Arigo is only a vivid example of what others could do, if interest is taken in the adequate development of the specific psychic faculties required to repeat what he is doing. Research work does not admit of the existence of personal monopolies. Knowing this, our effort is directed toward the scientific study of mediumship; its onset, maintenance, expansion, and varieties.

This embraces the study of the spiritual nature of man as a psychic phenomenon, beyond the limitations and contradictions of religion and mysticism.

This study, however, is not possible employing the present-day limited or superficial concepts of ESP research. Arigo is not an ESP phenomenon. He simply represents a link in a close and intimate teamwork device manifesting itself in the mediumistic capabilities of a man, and the medical knowledge and experience of discarnate entities working in the respective specialties and spheres. It is a method in which diagnosis, treatment, and prognosis perform their unifying routine.

This close collaboration between Arigo and his discarnate friends cannot be understood and cannot possibly be repeated by others unless these basic hard facts of life are taken into account:

1. That man is an incarnate soul.

2. That this soul was *not* created at the time of birth.

3. That it has had many other lives on earth and that others will consequently follow.

4. That contact between the incarnate and discarnate persons has been taking place since man appeared on earth for the first time.

5. That the psychic faculty known as mediumship is the method devised by nature to establish this necessary and enlightening contact.

6. That primitive peoples all over the world are well acquainted with these simple facts of life.

What I have learned is that it behooves us to improve the nature of this contact by enhancing its reliability, and separating it from the superstitions involved in religious creeds, doctrines, or dogmas, from rites and rituals. Likewise, not to waste time with obdurate skepticism that retards progress by postulating pseudo-scientific explanations that explain nothing.

Rodriguez went on to explain that he had developed a form of hypnotism that he referred to as the "hynometric trance" to bridge the gap. He was conducting extensive experiments with it, and was planning to organize the results in another book. His theme was that psychiatry under Freud, Adler, Jung, or any of the other pioneers in the field simply did not go far enough. He continued in his letter:

I have been preoccupied for many years with the failure of psychiatry to identify the etiology, or origin, of functional neuroses and psychoses, which in more than 80 percent of the cases is nothing else but symptoms and syndromes revealing the flourishing of mediumship. [Author's note: In other words, possession.]

Failure to identify these syndromes for what they are has converted, and *is* converting, hundreds of thousands of individuals in the civilized world who are not sick, into schizophreniacs. Mental hospitals are filled with them. This happens when electric shock, insulin, or chemical shocks are induced in them, blocking the natural manifestations of mediumship, destroying the mechanism through which the faculty manifests itself. The same occurs with the wholesale use of tranquilizers.

He then referred to a Canadian study by Dr. Raymond Prince, of McGill University in Montreal, who had spent seventeen months with native healers in Nigeria. Dr. Prince had discovered that their recognition of the reality of mediumship made psychosis a minor problem. Rodriguez continued in his letter:

The so-called witch doctors and spiritists of the reincarnation school all over the world quickly recognize these symptoms for what they are. As a consequence of this natural knowledge, mediumship is developed instead of psychosis. The development eradicates the psychoneurotic or psychotic condition that heralded the flowering of the mediumship faculty. This is the reason why mental diseases do not exist among these people, who may be counted in the millions.

Mental diseases are, therefore, the fruit harvested by over-civilized man due exclusively to a condition of ignorance maintained by an exaggerated sense of sophistication and hallowed cultural superiority.

Whether anyone agreed or disagreed with Rodriguez's premises, he was putting an intense and deeply thought-out spotlight on the workings behind Arigo, and was articulate in presenting his argument. Where he lost some people was in his six categorical postulates, which demanded a gymnastic leap into the outright acceptance of reincarnation, to say nothing of the existence of a soul. Neither concept could be accepted scientifically; at least, not without hard evidence.

His arguments were provocative, however. He continued coming up from Rio to Congonhas to observe Arigo, to see if he could throw more light on the matter. He noted that Arigo himself was oblivious to any theories behind his own capacities. Arigo simply carried out what he was compelled to do. He wasn't really a Kardec spiritist. He had been pulled into this strange scene without asking for it. The question provoked by Rodriguez's theories was: Would Arigo have become psychotic if he had *not* given in to his mediumship?

Many signs—the blinding headaches, the hallucinations, and the gross insomnia—indicated that he might have. As strange as he was in his clinical working hours, Arigo was a normal, functioning human being, with all of his cluster of sons growing up as healthy and emotionally mature young men. And in spite of his lack of education, he had a shrewd, inborn intelligence that attracted some of the best minds in Brazil.

Kubitschek, back in Brazil, kept his promise. He came to Congonhas and spent long hours with Arigo. It was now late in 1970. The hospital project was almost ready to go on the drawing board. The North American medical team's plans for the follow-up research were at last jelling. This time, the group was determined to complete the work they had been unable to do on the first attempt. Kubitschek promised his renewed support—he still had wide influence in Brazil.

When Kubitschek went to Arigo's house to say he was on his way back to Rio, Arigo seemed disturbed. He was not his usual, extrovert self. Kubitschek pressed him for what was wrong.

Arigo did not speak for some time, then he said: "I do not like to say this, Mr. President, but I will soon die a violent death."

Kubitschek was shocked and disturbed. "You don't mean that," he said.

Arigo nodded, and repeated in a sad, soft tone: "I am sure I will die violently very soon. So I say good-bye to you with sadness. This is the last time we will meet."

Kubitschek reassured Arigo that he merely was tired from overwork, but Arigo smiled and shook his head.

It was the image of the black crucifix again. Arigo became almost obsessed by it. The day after his talk with Kubitschek, Arigo met Gabriel Khater in front of the clinic door. Khater had come to tell him the good news that fresh funds had arrived for the medical center. Khater noted the same look that Kubitschek had noticed.

"You are tired, Arigo," Khater said.

"I am afraid, Gabriel," Arigo answered, "that my mission on earth is finished."

Khater pretended to laugh, then asked about his mother, who was critically ill at the time. "You are right to ask about this now," Arigo told him. Khater was about to go out of town for several days on a story. "Ask me everything now, because I think you will not see me again."

Arigo wrote a prescription for Khater's mother, then embraced him warmly. Khater said: "You will be all right. I know it." Arigo didn't answer, and went back to his clinic.

Others heard strange things from Arigo. Paulos Soares, a brother-in-law of Arigo, overheard him saying that his death was near. A month before, Arigo had lent his car to a friend. It had turned over and been demolished, but the friend was not hurt. Arigo told his brother Walter: "This is the sign of the end."

No one quite knew how to respond to these omens. For the most part, they tried to ignore the remarks, or attributed them to the fact that Arigo's schedule would exhaust a superman, to say nothing of a man with a heart condition, however mild. The heavy routine could quite naturally leave him in a state of depression. He continued with his long hours, at both the clinic and the pension office, taking time off only on weekends to prune his roses.

Every January, Arigo would take on another gargantuan, time-consuming job for himself. He would collect clothing from those who could afford to give it away, and give packages to the poor of both Congonhas do Campo and the surrounding plateau. It had become a traditional, festive event.

Arigo was always in the best of all possible moods for these occasions. This year, 1971, was no exception. He gathered what clothes he could, and being an enormously persuasive man, he collected a bounty quota, on this, the tenth year of his special event. On the morning of January 10, over five hundred poor townspeople gathered by the clinic in a festive spirit. Arigo dispensed both the clothing and crude jokes, in equal proportion. Those who knew him well were elated to see him back in good spirits. He didn't seem to show the despondency that had been plaguing him over the past few months. The old Arigo had returned. He even took the day off from his patients, an almost unheard-of event.

On the next morning—January 11, 1971—he rose early as usual and walked briskly to the clinic, where already the crowd was waiting. He would have to be going to Lafaiete that day, to arrange for payments and licensing of a car that he was buying from a retired police lieutenant in the town to replace his own. It was an old, blue Opala sedan—a car made in Brazil by General Motors.

He explained to the patients who had gathered at the center that he would not be opening the clinic that afternoon until three, but that he would take care of as many as possible in the morning, and the rest at the later time. Then he went about his work. He finished well before noon, and broke for an early lunch.

The sky was black and ominous that day, and already the cobblestones were glistening with rain. At his house, Arlete had prepared a hot lunch for him, and two of his good friends were there to join him. One was Bejou, a warm and earnest man who did odd jobs at the Hotel Freitas. He had been a close friend of the de Freitas family for years. He worshiped Arigo, and made no secret of it. He was bright and witty, and constantly cheered Arigo up when he was in his dimmer moods. The other friend was Antonio Ribeiro, who had learned that Arigo planned to drive to Lafaiete that day and wanted to hitch a ride.

Arigo was delighted to have company, and the group sat down with Arlete and Tarcesio, Arigo's oldest son, in his twenties. The lunch was brief, and afterward Arigo had a few moments to play cards with the men before leaving. Playing cards was one of the few ways Arigo could relax.

By now the skies had burst, and the mountain rains were drenching the village. Arigo said he would wait for a let-up before going to the car. There was light banter, and occasionally Arigo would rise from the table to look out the window to see if the downpour had eased.

Earlier that morning, José Timoteo, a driver for the national highway department, had picked up João Felicido, who was treasurer of the department, to drive him from Rio to Belo Horizonte on a routine trip. They had left Rio at first light. The drive had gone smoothly enough, until they reached the town of Lafaiete. There, the rainstorm hit with a fury, blocking visibility and turning the twisting roads into a wet-slick glaze. It was about noon when they arrived at Lafaiete, and they decided to push on. Timoteo knew the roads well; it was his job.

By noon a crowd of about fifty, huddled under newspapers and umbrellas, had already gathered at the Spirit Center for Arigo's afternoon session. Even though they would have to wait until three for Arigo's return, they wanted to be sure they got a place in line. Some were pinning their entire hopes on him, and had come a long distance. Two were foreign: one from Spain, another from Chile. They were both girls.

At just about noon, Arigo decided that the storm had let

up enough for them to set out on the trip. Arigo's mood had lifted since the distribution of the gifts on the previous day. He gave Arlete a cheerful kiss, roughed up Tarcesio's thick black hair, and went out to the Opala with Ribeiro.

Waiting for the train at the railroad station was a well-known Brazilian doctor, who was leaving for Rio after a trip to observe and query Arigo in a search for an explanation of the man and his work. He saw the blue Opala as it swung around the curve from Arigo's house. Arigo, at the wheel, saw the doctor, and pulled the car over to the side of the station to talk with him a moment.

After a jocular greeting, Arigo said: "Have you got everything explained now?"

The doctor smiled. "If I ever explain you, I'll be a genius. I enjoyed your party yesterday, though." He was referring to the gathering in which Arigo had handed out the many boxes of clothing. No child had gone away without a gift.

"I'm very happy about it. Very happy," Arigo said. "I love the faces of the children. It went well."

"I thought so, too," the doctor said. "I'll be back to see you soon."

"I hope we'll see you," Arigo said. He put the car in gear, waved again, and spun off.

The rain was picking up again, and the wipers were straining against it. A short distance out of town, Arigo stopped at a gas station, filled up with gas, and tried to adjust the wipers a little better.

Coming out of Lafaiete, the pickup truck of the national highway department was having some difficulty negotiating the turns in the heavy rain. The roads in Brazil are marked off with small kilometer signs. Near K.370 on Route BR-135, Timoteo eased up on his speed a little to squint at the road, with its unrelenting curves. By the time he reached K.373, the rain had again eased off, and he pushed the accelerator down to highway speed.

237

Highway marker K.374 was just about three kilometers from the gas station that Arigo had stopped in. There is a particularly treacherous blind curve at the marker. Anxious to get the annoying red tape over with in Lafaiete, Arigo left the station and started down the road. He passed his rose garden, glancing at it fondly, although it was hardly visible through the rain and mist.

The pickup truck was nearing marker K.374, soon to appear around the curve. It had just come into sight when Timoteo saw a blue car start to move across the road toward him. It was not skidding, just coming directly across the road. Beside the road was a precipice four hundred feet deep. There was no possible way he could drive off the road to avoid the blue car coming at him. The road was too slick to stop suddenly. He applied the brakes anyway, and at that moment the two cars crashed. There was a terrifying metallic thud that was heard more than a kilometer away. There was silence in both cars.

Back at Arigo's house, Bejou had been invited to have some cake and a cup of coffee before returning to his work at the hotel. Arlete had gone off with her umbrella to shop. Tarcesio had taken his VW to check the rosebushes for Arigo. Bejou was finishing the last mouthful of cake when a neighbor opened the door and called: "Go to the highway quickly! Something terrible has happened to Arigo!"

Bejou dropped his fork and rushed out of the house. He ran like a wild man to a taxi by the railroad station. He told the driver to drive quickly out BR-135. Within minutes, they saw the blue Opala up ahead, in the center of the slick highway. The smashed pickup truck of the highway department was fused to the Opala. At the wreckage, all was silent; there was not even a groan. The door on Arigo's side was open, his legs still in the car, his body half out of it. His legs were mangled. A steel rod of some kind had plunged through his massive chest like a spear.

Bejou froze for a moment, then ran to Arigo and ripped the steel rod out of the body. It was covered with blood. There was a huge gap in the head and in the chest. For some reason, he noticed Arigo's watch. It was stopped at exactly 12:15.

Then a scream suddenly came from the pickup truck. It was the treasurer of the highway department. Bejou, knowing that Arigo was dead, ran to help him. He felt he was going mad. There were no sounds from Timoteo.

Seconds later, Tarcesio arrived. He looked at his father, and dropped beside the body, heaving with enormous sobs. Then the police arrived. And an ambulance. There was confusion and shouting.

Felicido, the highway department treasurer, died at the hospital. Arigo and Ribeiro were pronounced dead on arrival. Only the unconscious Timoteo survived.

Bejou walked all the way back to the hotel in a daze. "I will carry this terrible weight all my life," he told a friend.

Congonhas do Campo came to a stop. "The town has been orphaned," someone said. Another said: "With Arigo dead, Congonhas has been assassinated." The mayor declared two days of mourning, with the flag at half mast. The shops and the bars were closed until after the burial.

Dr. Mauro Godoy was not a man to cry, but he did. He went to the scene with the police and the men from the highway department, and studied the wreckage. There were no signs of skidding, although the wetness might have obliterated them. Arigo's car had crossed to the wrong side of the road. It appeared as if it had simply gone out of control.

Later, Dr. Godoy assisted at the autopsy. Signs that he saw in the brain and cardiac region convinced him that Arigo had died from a coronary moments before he crashed. With a dead man at the wheel, the car had gone out of control. The rest was inevitable.

They came from all over. A parade of special planes flew into Lafaiete. The press was everywhere. Special buses arrived, this time with mourners instead of patients. Arigo's shattered body lay in its coffin in his home. Arlete stood by it, tearless and numb, just staring at it.

Roberto Carlos, his long hair flowing, arrived with his wife. He was dressed in blue jeans and black boots, with a medallion of Christ pinned to his belt. With the help of police, he made his way through the dense crowd to the coffin. He embraced Arlete and kissed her hand. "My child can see because of Arigo," he said. Then he turned to the casket and said: "I am here, Arigo."

There was no Mass, no music, no service. No one counted the people who filed by the casket, and flowed silently along the packed streets, like a giant moving carpet behind the bier. Some said fifteen thousand; some said twenty. "The air was full of silence," one observer said.

The pall bearers drew the casket on a small cart to Arigo's beloved union hall. Then they tugged it by hand up the steep cobblestone hill to the cemetery. High on the hill, with the mountains rimming the horizon, the body was interred. Far across on another hill, the twelve baroque statues of Aleijadinho stood like guardians, some with hands outstretched, pointing across the valley to the cemetery. A lone Franciscan priest murmured a prayer that was barely audible.

The crowd, sprawled across the green hillside, moved like a great herd of sheep slowly back to the village. Whatever was said in words, the thought was the same: "Arigo is no more."

Another thought, a phrase from Arigo, was unspoken but implicit, for his body could not be taken to the church:

"Our Christ is the same. The rest doesn't matter."

Epilogue

I.

I have found that I cannot resist a story that is slightly far-out, as long as there is a rich fund of solid, down-to-earth, material documentation to go with it. Without the latter, the story is utterly useless. With it, it is intriguing.

I had a relaxed lunch at The Players in New York several years ago with Arthur Twitchell, an astute and erudite gentleman who had been co-producer of one of my plays that came into Broadway at the Helen Hayes Theater, faltered, and died unmourned. Twitchell was a member of the board of the American Society for Psychical Research, founded by William James in the late nineteenth century. He was also an avid student of what might be called the rational occult.

He told me briefly about the story of Arigo. If I had not known Twitchell to be a man of discernment, I would have attributed it to fantasy and forgotten about it.

I did tell him that a story of this sort would be utterly unbelievable, and that even if it were true, it would be an almost impossible job for a writer to convey.

Twitchell said: "You ought at least to look at the films."

"There are films taken of these operations?" I asked.

"They were taken by the team of American doctors who went down to Brazil to study Arigo," he said. "All you need is a strong stomach."

My curiosity was aroused; I was looking for a good story. Twitchell put me in touch with Dr. Henry Puharich, who was kind enough to show me the films at his home in Westchester County.

Twitchell was right about the strong stomach. When you see a paring knife go up under the eyelid, and pry the eyeball half out of its socket, and scrape the socket mercilessly, it's a bit of a shock. I looked at the films twice, complete with hydroceles, tumors, cataracts, sebaceous cysts, retinoblastomas, and all the rest. At times I had to look away. But their dramatic power was overwhelming.

I thought about the story for a long time. It was obvious that, in spite of the considerable amount of medical records available, I would have to go to Brazil and check the story in detail. Nothing could be second-hand in a story like this. It was a chronicle that would have to be verified in every aspect.

But there was another problem. If the story *did* check out, and the book drew wide readership, what would it do to Arigo and his work? Would people who were desperately ill in the United States spend large sums of money to go to Brazil—only to find Arigo so flooded and exhausted with additional patients that he could not handle them all?

When I decided to go ahead with the story after Arigo's death, I told Puharich that I would be unable to depend on his word or the records of the medical group alone. He quickly agreed with me. "You will want to check everybody in Brazil and here you can get your hands on," he said. "His enemies, as well as his friends. You must never take the word of a single source. On any aspect of the story."

I was still skeptical. But there would be very clear and important checkpoints for challenging the story when I got to Brazil. Most important would be the judges, the attorneys, and the court records of Arigo's long-drawn-out trial proceedings. Here the harshest spotlight possible had been turned on Arigo. There would be both character witnesses and expert testimony to draw on, all of it under oath.

Another important checkpoint would be former President Juscelino Kubitschek. Here was a tough realist, the man who had built Brasília, the most outstanding capital in the world. The problem was—would I be able to find him, and to question him in depth? Others to check would be the Brazilian doctors, as many as I could get hold of; government officials; the clergy; the local townspeople; the police officials; foreign service officers, who could supply an outsider's view on this incredible legend; former patients; Arigo's family; and any other leads that would be bound to spring up.

I was satisfied from my preliminary probing that the story at least could either be confirmed or challenged to the point where it would fall apart. I was intrigued enough to take the risk, and so were the publishers.

In the case of the Arigo research, there were often slightly conflicting reports. I had to weigh these carefully, and choose those from the source that appeared the most substantial. Whatever choice I made, it would not be made lightly.

II

I had one other problem, but it turned out to be an asset rather than a drawback. I had already contracted to write a book on the new, deadly Lassa virus that had suddenly sprung up from nowhere, deep in the Cameroon Highlands of northern Nigeria. In contrast to Arigo, this was a hard, tough, scientific, medical mystery story, with the most pragmatic and materialistic sort of documentation, including everything from electron microscopy to the entire staff of virologists at Yale and the government's Center for Disease Control in Atlanta.

Some interesting things happened in Nigeria which accidentally had a great deal of bearing on my attitude

toward the Arigo research later. The tracking down of the
Lassa virus story took me on a three-thousand-mile trip
through Nigeria in a Land Rover, on what literally could
be called a small-game safari, the virus being just about
the smallest possible to pursue.

The trip took me to lonely medical-missionary stations
from near Lake Chad—in the very center of the widest
bulge of equatorial Africa—to the Jos plateau. It took me
to government catering rest houses (vestiges of the British
colonial days), mining camps, tribal villages, small
African cities, provincial diplomatic posts, the medical
research sections of Nigerian universities, and other
places where tourists are not likely to venture.

It was in the off-hours in places like this where I
learned that the local medicine man of the villages was
held in the greatest respect by foreign diplomats,
missionary doctors, medical researchers, university professors, mining engineers—whatever the station of the
European or American ex-patriot. Far from being an
absurd cartoon character, the local witch doctor, medicine
man, ju-ju man, or do-do man—whatever the terminology
that was used—was feared and respected in the
community, and was not to be trifled with.

But not from fear alone. Some of the witch doctors'
medical concoctions were being seriously studied by the
University of Ibadan Medical School, one of Africa's
finest. One concoction reduced malignant tumors to zero
in laboratory mice. Further success in reducing psychosis
to an absolute minimum was being studied and lauded
by the World Health Organization of the United Nations,
in line with Luis Rodriguez's theories.

The attitude of reasonable and intelligent men in
Nigeria created an atmosphere that opened my mind
somewhat for the trip to Brazil.

When I arrived in Rio, I was filled with the cold, cruel
realities of the Lassa virus, and the burned and dry
famine-stricken savannas of the sub-Sahara. The contrast
was a welcome change. The shift to the Portuguese

language wasn't welcome, however. It made the research very difficult. Eventually I was able to find interpreters who went out of their way to be helpful. I had a long list of leads for information. With the language barrier, it was a painstaking job to follow them up.

My contacts with American and other journalists made it abundantly clear that whatever Arigo was, he wasn't a fake. Their personal knowledge was verified in the files of the newspaper morgues and the court records over a twenty-year period. This was a good foundation to work from, because I had planned to go directly back to the States if Arigo's life and work appeared even slightly ambiguous.

Kubitschek was most gracious when I called on him. He spoke in a deep, powerful, but labored English. He told me he was delighted that someone from the States was doing a book on Arigo, because he was utterly convinced that there had never been anyone in the history of medicine like him. He freely offered any information I wanted about his personal experiences with Arigo, and said that as a doctor and surgeon himself, he was dumbfounded by what Arigo could do.

It was a stimulating and fruitful interview. When I asked him about Brasília, his eyes lit up and he laughed. "Even my enemies admit that it has opened up Brazil today. I am proud of it." He chuckled over the story of how he had been trapped into building the city by the spectator in the crowd at Congonhas. "I had forgotten completely about that article in the Constitution that required the capital to be built. I could not go back on my word. So I built it."

III

From that point on, confirmation of the Arigo phenomenon came thick and fast. Jorge Rizzini's color films were startling, vivid, and unchallengeable. Dr. Ary Lex and the author Hernani Andrade welcomed me to their homes and provided me with full information and documents on their studies of Arigo over two decades.

I had lunch at the São Paulo Hilton with Dr. Antonio Ferrario Filho, an energetic, salt-and-pepper–haired radiologist, who not only confirmed Arigo's prowess in great detail, but introduced me to the background of the Kardecist intellectuals in Brazil.

It seemed there was no one who didn't have a friend or relative who had been successfully treated by Arigo. These included George and Susan Brown from the American Embassy; Joe and Kathleen Caltagironi, an American investment banker and his wife; Elaine Handler, from *Time* magazine; Fred Perkins, the McGraw-Hill representative in Brazil, and his wife; Dr. Raimundo Veras, of the Centro de Rehabilitacao with branches in several Brazilian cities, and his son, Dr. José Carlos Veras; Dr. Clark Kuebler, a former professor at Northwestern University; and Guy Playfair, a British journalist. They and dozens of others went out of their way to provide leads and dig up information that would have been impossible to find otherwise.

Particularly helpful was Mrs. Irene Granchi, of Rio, who supplied me with material from the exhaustive files on Arigo that she had kept since the beginning of his career. She introduced me to publishers and editors who, in turn, had their own stories about the healer. What I had thought would be a long, slow job of digging up scattered scraps of information turned out to be a problem of handling a tidal wave of material that was becoming almost unmanageable.

I was met at the Belo Horizonte airport by Lauro Costa and his wife, and Maria Lucia, a volunteer worker in Dr. Veras' Belo rehabilitation clinic. Whenever I needed any help in language or information, one or the other of them was always on hand. It is impossible to describe the predominating attitude of the Brazilian people and not sound as if you are overpraising them to the skies. They will do anything for a visitor, to the point where it is almost unbelievable. At first, it creates suspicion in you, until you find that their hospitality is utterly genuine and inbred. Although there must be exceptions, I never ran into any.

IV

Lauro and his wife drove me to Congonhas do Campo, translated interviews endlessly for three days and evenings, and never showed a sign of the exhaustion I felt. We were received so warmly by Arigo's widow, Arlete, and several of his grown sons that I felt like a prodigal son coming home. In addition to hospitality, they offered all Arigo's clippings, diaries, and correspondence, and hours of anecdotes they recalled regarding Arigo's life and work.

Arlete, her hair definitely in curlers, was a shy and diffident woman, with a quiet, infectious charm. She was preparing to move to Belo to live near one of her sons who had recently moved there. Tarcesio, who was a strapping, bronzed young man in his twenties, handsome as a movie star, arranged for photocopying of any of the material I requested.

He also drove me out to Arigo's grave, high on the hill overlooking Congonhas in a small walled cemetery. It was late in the afternoon, and an ominous mountain thunderstorm was gathering. The scene turned into a black and gray El Greco painting as Tarcesio, who obviously worshiped his father, placed several roses on the grave and told me about the tragic accident on BR-135. On the way back to the village, he stopped and pointed out the place where the accident had happened two years before, as if this ritual might ease the pain that showed clearly in his face.

Congonhas do Campo was as lovely as the tourist brochures said it was, although there were the poor and underprivileged that Arigo worked so hard in the service of. Even the awe-inspiring statuary of Aleijadinho could not erase that scar. At the little, open-front café near the Rua Marechal Floriano, I met Dr. Mauro Godoy, now the mayor of the town, who claimed that neither he nor anyone else could explain how Arigo did what he did, but that there was no question in his mind that Arigo had literally been the eighth wonder of the world.

He said that the more medical knowledge a person had, the more Arigo was appreciated. In fact, anyone who had *not* performed surgery would not be able to understand fully what it meant to cut into the deep organs of the body without tying off blood vessels and without anesthesia. As the one medical doctor who had had a chance to observe Arigo intensively over a long period of time, he was rather convincing.

I wasn't quite prepared for what happened the next day. The front-page headlines broke all over Brazil to reveal that Arigo's youngest brother, Eli, had suddenly declared that he had been visited by the same sort of hallucinations that had plagued Arigo in his early days, and that both Arigo and Dr. Fritz had appeared to him in the middle of the night to urge him to carry on the work of his departed brother.

By noon, the town of Congonhas was beleaguered with reporters from the press, radio, and television, and nearly all the members of the Arigo family went into hiding. Eli was a successful law student at the university in Belo, and had been highly regarded in his work. I was able to corner him in the dining room of the Hotel Freitas, out of the way of the rest of the press that was looking for him. He looked something like a slighter version of Arigo, with bright, penetrating brown eyes, and seemed very disturbed and confused about the recent visitation, which he claimed he did not seek or want.

Nearly all the rest of the family, including Arigo's brothers and his sons, were dead set against the idea. They simply would not discuss it. By the time I left Brazil, the situation was still unresolved.

One benefit that came out of the incident was that it

brought *Manchete* photo-journalist Esko Murto to town, who was as widely informed as anyone about Arigo, having covered the healer in depth in several stories over the last nine or ten years of Arigo's life.

Esko, a native of Finland, was an intense, vital, intelligent reporter. Like so many others, he had found that his journalistic coverage of Arigo had changed his entire outlook. After having photographed Arigo in action many times, he was extravagant in his wonderment at the man. But this was true of nearly everyone who volunteered information. I was a little disturbed by this, because I was convinced no man could have such a clean record. Even the padre at the Church of Bom Jesus was mild in his protest against Arigo, simply saying that the Church did not believe in what he had done. Most of the medical adversaries who had been against Arigo had softened.

About the only thing I could dig up were rumors that Arigo had taken kickbacks on the prescriptions sold. But I could not verify this, nor could anyone else. I could find no one who claimed he had suffered harm or injury from his treatments, nor anyone who even suggested that he used fakery of any sort. There had been psychics in the Philippines who claimed to do surgery similar to Arigo's, but they had been easily exposed as fakes, and had refused direct observation in full daylight.

On returning to Belo Horizonte, I was convinced that Judge Felippe Immesi would be able to give me a cold, flat appraisal of Arigo, including whatever drawbacks (beyond Arigo's barnyard crudities, which everybody admitted and laughed off) the court proceedings had revealed. I was able to arrange a dinner with the judge at the Hotel Del Ray through a bright young Brazilian lawyer, Dr. Paulo Zanini, who had taken his law degree on a Fulbright fellowship at the University of Michigan and who could speak fluent English. He was also responsible for getting me Xerox copies of the haystack pile of court records of Arigo's trial.

I was more than surprised when Judge Immesi recounted his own story, in full detail. He described his voluntary observations of Arigo at work with revealing conviction, told of his conferences with doctors who supported Arigo's position, as well as those against, and of his agonizing decision. He admitted that there was simply no way to describe the impact of watching Arigo operate, and that the man had to be accepted as a paranormal phenomenon that could not be defined.

V

Ouro Prêto, which translates as "black gold," is the Williamsburg of Brazil. It was once the richest mining town in the country, and its charming eighteenth-century architecture, so infinitely well preserved, reflects the intellectual and art center that it became. Some statuary works of Aleijadinho are here, in the baroque churches that guard the hillsides. From these heights, the dull-red tile roofs create a tapestry like that of a French village on the Rhone.

Along one of the steep cobblestone streets, I found the restaurant Calabouco, literally meaning "dungeon" or "jail." But its subterranean rooms, lit by bewitching candlelight, were a feast of colonial antiques that blended into a pastiche of charm. It was Esko Murto who had told me to introduce myself to the owner, a White Russian, formerly Canadian and now a Brazilian citizen, Gerry Kanigan. She had been a professor of Slavic history in Canada, had taken her Master's degree at the Sorbonne, had come to visit Brazil, fell in love with it, bought a farm, fostered an art center at Ouro Prêto, and now managed her thriving bistro with the hand of a master.

Esko had told me I could learn much from her about the whole ambience out of which Arigo grew. He was right. In her living room on the floor above the dungeon restaurant, she talked unstintingly about what had happened to her own outlook in the decade she had lived in Brazil.

"The whole exotic side of Arigo and his work is going to make you very confused," she said, "unless you understand the basic belief under it all: that reincarnation is a fact; that the law of life is eternal evolution from one cellular creature to the galaxies."

She had been a specialist in the dualistic heresies of the Middle East, in which good and evil are viewed as equal adversaries. "It took a long time for me to understand that this dualistic conception was a heresy, in fact," she said. "I am now convinced, from arduous study and long reflection, that a human being is a creature who continues to evolve indefinitely, that he sheds lives as he sheds clothes, and that the essential part of him continues.

"Once you are able to believe that, the whole thing becomes clear—especially in trying to understand Brazil. When a person dies, it is simply the shedding of a few atoms. We know from Lord Rutherford that atoms are principally empty space, anyway. You see, the phenomenon of reincarnation was turned into a coherent philosophy by Allan Kardec. I spent eight years in Brazil before I had any interest in this whatever. And although Brazil is mostly Catholic, you'll find that eighty percent of them, when they are really in a pinch, off they go to consult a medium of some sort."

She went on: "You can look at a medium in two ways. Either he or she is a super-multiple schizo, or you begin to accept *possession*. You have an absolutely tumultuous interchange with what we call reality—what our eyes can see—and with what the Kardecists regard as spirits. Actually, this doctrine is superlatively Christian when you think about it. The followers of Kardec regard God as an immensely powerful accountant or computer. Its memory banks are infinite. You simply cannot get away with anything, so that whatever you do that is malicious or harmful in this life, you'll pay the bill sooner or later, today or tomorrow."

When I tried to steer her more on course, to relate this to Arigo, she said: "We'll get to that. But to understand

Arigo, it's good to understand some of this. The different levels of spiritist belief in Brazil are simply manifestations of the same thing, depending on the scope and mind of the person involved. People who are more intelligent, who don't need the ritual of Umbanda and Quimbanda, become Kardecists.

"Arigo was amazing because he cut right across the entire spectrum. He was a god of the most important people in Brazil, as well as the poor and needy. I knew personally the wife of the director of the largest German mining combine, with enormous interests in Brazil. She was miraculously cured, after being given up as hopeless by the best doctors in Europe and America. But Arigo was only one—perhaps the greatest, because he could be so clearly confirmed—the only one of hundreds of others here in Brazil who work in spiritist hospitals, and achieve at least part of the success Arigo reached."

I went with Gerry Kanigan to an Umbanda meeting that night. It was far out in the country, in a little tile-roofed house that was totally dark as we approached it over bumpy ruts, far off the main road. We stumbled along a twisting path, tapped on the door, and entered.

It was hard to see in the large room, in spite of the candles flickering on a wide table at the opposite end. There must have been about fifty Brazilians, apparently farmers and their wives, and children, sitting on wooden benches along the plaster walls. In the center of the room, a tall, handsome black man in a white robe was pacing back and forth, alternately chanting and speaking in Portuguese, which I could not understand. On the table that served as an altar were figurines of many Catholic saints, but, surprisingly, mixed in among them were an Old Black Sambo type of thing, and what seemed to be some African totems. The men and women sat separately. On chairs in the center of the room were two women, dressed in white, their heads slumped on their chests, arms drooped to their sides, obviously in a trance.

After more chanting, the congregation spontaneously burst into a hymn in Portuguese, which sounded for all the world like those sung in any Presbyterian or Methodist church in the States. The leader led the group, his eyes tightly closed, interspersing sermon-like phrases between the stanzas. Then he moved to the altar and took down a lantern sort of device, similar to the incense carrier used in Catholic and Greek Orthodox services.

He lit a black powdery incense in the lantern, and swung it precariously around the room. There was no ventilation, and the smoke filled the room like a sudden fog rising on a mountain road. The leader moved along the benches, waving the lantern and continuing to chant. As he approached, each person stood up and received a generous bath of the smoke, turning around in a circle to receive it. Following suit, I stood up too, turned a circle, fought back from coughing, and sat down again.

After the ritual was finished, the two women seated in the center of the room came to life, although their eyes were still closed, their heads still drooped. They began by snapping their fingers, then shuddering, then chanting, beating their feet on the stone floor all the while. Women and children came up to them, and as they filed by, the women ran their hands down the sides of their bodies, as if to sweep off any evil spirits that might be lingering. When the women were finished, the men came up to the leader, now seated in the center in a third chair, and the ritual was repeated.

On the way back to Ouro Prêto, Gerry Kanigan said to me: "You see, this is what Arigo was *not*. He used no ritual whatever, except for his preliminary prayers. Yet he was very close to these people in his artless, unaffected way. They have not shut themselves off from the springs of primeval origin. They are not encased in the cement overcoats we who are civilized surround ourselves with. I think we have much to learn from them."

VI

I met with Gerry Kanigan once more, this time in Belo Horizonte. She had urged me to go with her to see a spiritual prophet of wide renown, who lived on the outskirts of the city, and whose fame had spread throughout Brazil. He was blind, and he must have been well into his eighties. When we arrived at his modest house, he was sitting on the porch, his large, veined hands folded on the top of his cane.

His name was Henrique Franco. He claimed to be a distant relative of the Spanish dictator, but held no love for him. Gerry had never met him before. She explained that I was an American journalist interested in Brazil and exploring the background surrounding Arigo.

He said there were dozens of Arigos in Brazil, but none had Arigo's capacity for demonstrating the truth of the spiritual world so graphically and so incontestably. He insisted that we all had spirit guides, but that we do not listen and do not believe. Not all are good, however, and we must feel them out with discernment. He said that the reason doctors are amazed at some of the cures Arigo brought about is that they fail to recognize that there are no illnesses, there are only the ill.

"We come from mud on the way to God," he said, emphasizing that we constantly evolve through many reincarnations. "Our suffering is the lapidation of the spirit. Life after death is the same as it is on earth. You have the same structure on a different molecular plane."

In contrast to Henrique Franco, the attitude of H. V. Walter was of a different sort. I found him in his British consulate office in Belo Horizonte, relaxed and jolly as usual. He had been in the foreign service in Brazil for over a quarter of a century, and seemed to thrive on it. In his late sixties, he was dressed in a suit that must have come from one of the better London tailors, yet he loosened his tie and leaned back in his chair, and welcomed the chance to talk about Arigo.

"He was absolutely the most wonderful phenomenon of modern times," Walter said. "You see, hardly anyone thought of going to him until every doctor he knew had given him up. That's where Arigo's value came in, and why his cures were so dramatic. I followed the case of Dr. Cruz's sister. An absolute miracle. I'm going to take you downstairs to his office, and let him tell you about it firsthand. Both her father and her brother were fine doctors, very fine. Carlos Cruz himself is a dentist, and a graduate of the University of Brazil. They knew their professions, and they knew that Arigo had done what they could never do. I knew about Kubitschek's daughter, and many other leading diplomats and statesmen who have confided in me about their own cures.

"I don't go in for any of the mystical stuff. I'm a pragmatist, a realist. What happened in Arigo's case, happened. It's not to be believed—but it has to be."

Walter took me downstairs to Dr. Cruz's office. It was jammed with people waiting, and a woman was in the chair. As soon as the consul explained to him that I was in Brazil from the States to do a story on Arigo, Dr. Cruz left his patient open-mouthed in the chair and took us out to the corridor. He talked for fifteen minutes about Arigo, confirming everything that Walter had said, and claiming that the time wasted in the legal proceedings against Arigo had been an international tragedy. If Arigo had been placed in a university for scientific study instead of being prosecuted, Cruz said, we might have made major advances in medicine and surgery.

To get a North American point of view, I dropped by the United States Information Service office in Belo, first to touch base with compatriots after such a long absence, and second to see what the attitude toward Arigo was in these purlieus. There was the same confirmation, attested to either directly or indirectly by many of the staff, both American and Brazilian.

Back in the States, I reviewed my research and fattened it with additional interviews with Belk, Puharich,

255

Laurance, Cortes, and other members of the medical team of the Congonhas expedition. They were most helpful, especially because my mind was so full of what I had absorbed in Brazil that it needed better focus.

There were many new facets opening up in the study of the paranormal that they were all interested in exploring. As for me, it was all I could do to catch up on Arigo. Puharich had discovered Uri Geller, the Israeli phenomenon who promised to go far beyond Arigo in the realm of clairvoyance, psychokinesis, and other aspects of extrasensory perception. I had all I could handle in trying to reconstruct the Arigo story. Whatever else there was beyond that would be too mind-blowing for a journalist to contemplate.

Without ever having seen the man, Arigo became real to me from the meticulous research and in writing these pages. I hope the reader will be able to sense some of this in the book.

Afterword

by Henry K. Puharich, M.D.

I want to present a personal interpretation of what Arigo
means to me. To understand that, one has to have a
feeling for what it must have been like to be "inside" of
Arigo. Let's begin at an elementary level, namely, the feel
of Arigo's hand while doing surgery. If you take an
ordinary butter knife and gently run the edge across your
skin, you get an idea how this knife feels in the hand that
moves it. You will notice that there is a gradation of
pressure that can be applied, and that applying this
pressure gives you a feeling of frictional forces, resistance
of the tissues to being cut, control of the movement of the
knife, and so on. You could learn all these nuances of the
feel of a sharp knife by maneuvering it over other
materials, such as foods used in your kitchen. In short,
you would learn what every surgeon learns—the feel in
one's hand of a knife against tissue.

Now I thoroughly knew this feel of a knife in my hand
when it was used in surgery—human or animal. One day
when I was standing beside Arigo in his Congonhas
clinic, he asked a patient to stand against the wall—a man
of forty-five years. Altimiro, Arigo's assistant, handed a
sharp, stainless-steel kitchen knife with a four-inch blade
to Arigo. Arigo grabbed my right hand, thrust the knife
into it, and closed his hand around my hand, so that the
knife was doubly enclosed. Then he led my right hand
toward the eyeball of the patient and ordered me to put

the knife in the eye socket. I followed his orders and plunged the knife between the eyeball and the upper lid. As I did so, my right hand went limp—I could not proceed. I feared that I would slash the eyeball and do permanent damage. Arigo again grabbed my right hand and said, "Go ahead. Do it like a man!"

This order gave me the courage I needed. My fears vanished, as I plunged the knife deeply into the eye socket. Now I was in complete control of myself. As I moved the knife into the depths of the eye socket, I was amazed to discover that the tip of the knife had none of the familiar feel that a knife has against tissue. To give you the complete feeling of what my hand felt, do the following exercise: Take a pair of magnets and find the like poles of each. Then hold one magnet in each hand and bring the like poles toward each other. You will now experience repulsive forces between the two like magnetic poles, and these will be felt in your hands. This is a totally different sensation from that which you experienced with the butter knife against your skin.

Now when I moved the knife into the tissues of the eyeball and the eye socket, I felt a repulsive force between the tissues and the knife. No matter how hard I pressed in, there was an equal and opposite force acting on my knife to prevent it from touching the tissues. This repulsive force was the secret of why no one felt pain when Arigo did his famous "eye checkup." My patient did not feel any pain from my knife manipulations, either.

It is obvious to me that Arigo could control that repulsive force, so that he could go ahead and cut tissue. And this, of course, should cause pain. But it is known that Arigo did not cause pain. I have observed, and so have others, that Arigo could cut tissues without using the sharp edge of a knife. Often he would cut using the dull edge of the knife. He has been known, when in a hurry, to cut tissues without a knife. In these rare instances he would use his hands and fingers to go through tissue. It is my opinion that the actual cutting agency was the repulsive force, and not the knife or his fingers.

I have no idea as to the nature of this repulsive force. But from electrical field measurements I carried out on Arigo (EEG, EKG, and GSR), I do not believe that this repulsive force is in the electromagnetic spectrum. I believe it is an unknown form of life energy.

In September of 1967 I went to Brazil to continue my studies of Arigo. I had seen him many times since that lipoma operation in 1963, and it had never occurred to me to ask for help for myself. One day as I was working with Arigo, he suddenly turned to me and said, "You have otosclerosis." I replied, "I don't know about that but I have a chronic infection and drainage in my left ear from a cholesteatoma."

Arigo said, "Yes, you have had that for a long time, but the otosclerosis is new. Check it when you get home. I will give you a prescription that will cure both of your problems." In thirty seconds he had finished the following prescription:

Para Dr. Puharich

1° *Tratamento*

3 vidros de micotir
  vide a bula
3 vidros de hepadesicol
  tome 2 drageas apos cada refeicao
15 frascos de gabromicina
  apl. no musculo 1 frasco de
  24 en 24 dias

2° *Tratamento*

40 ampolas de olobintin
  apl. no muscolo 1 ampola de 2 en 2 dias
20 ampolas de Bituelue R de 1.000
  apl. no muscola 1 ampola de 3
  en 3 dias

There is not much need to explain the items in the first

treatment except to state that the first drug was an ear-drop solution, the second was bile salts, and the third, gabromicina, was a primitive form of streptomycin that had largely been dropped from use by physicians.

When I returned to the United States, I had the audiologist in my own laboratory run a hearing test on me with an audiometer. When the test was done, she volunteered the diagnosis: "You have otosclerosis." I checked the audiograms; Arigo was right. I did have otosclerosis—a hardening of the tissue over the small bones of the ear. I decided then and there to start Arigo's prescription.

Because of my odd working hours, it was easiest for me to give myself the injections just before I went to bed each night. I started the first treatment series on October 7, 1967. This meant that I gave myself the injection of the gabromicina once a day. By the fourteenth of October I had developed a reaction to this form of streptomycin. I had a swelling and tenderness in my hands and palms and in my feet and toes. Therefore I had to stop the injections and wait for the allergic reaction to disappear. By the twenty-fifth of October I was in good enough shape to begin the second treatment. I finished the second treatment on January 11, 1968. I was free of the ear-drainage problem that had plagued me all my life, and have continued to be so to this day. Over the next six months my audiograms showed that my otosclerosis had disappeared, and my hearing improved.

On January 11, 1971, I was working in my office at Intelectron Corporation in New York City when the telephone rang. I answered it, and a young woman whose name I don't now recall blurted out the following: "I am looking for Dr. Puharich."

I replied, "This is he speaking."

"Dr. Puharich, I just got a telephone call from a TV station in Rio de Janeiro, Brazil, asking for you to comment on the death of Arigo."

"Would you please repeat that? I don't think I clearly heard what you said," I stuttered.

She repeated her statement. I said, "Are you sure of what you are saying—that Arigo is dead?"

She replied to the effect that all she knew was what had been relayed to her. I told her that I could not reply because of my shocked state.

I sat back in my chair. It was not possible for Arigo, the greatest healer in the world, to be dead! He was too young, too vital. Besides he was the hope of thousands, perhaps millions of people who looked to him as the witness to higher powers. There must be a mistake, I thought. I had to check this out myself. I called friends in Brazil, who confirmed the dread news that Arigo had been killed in an auto accident.

I was personally despondent. The loss of Arigo to me was as though the sun had gone out; the planet earth and humanity had lost their great luminary. I had suddenly become impoverished. The shock was so deep to me that I decided to go on a fourteen-day fast and reexamine all my life, to weigh the meaning of Arigo, in life and in death.

Near the end of my fast, I came to some strong personal conclusions. The first was that I had failed both Arigo and humanity by not completing my studies of Arigo's healing work. I now realized that I should have dropped my other work in 1963 and concentrated all my efforts on him. I was sure there would never be another Arigo in my lifetime. But if there was, I would not fail the next time.

I looked back over the ten years since I had moved to New York from California. I had become a slave to my company, to my inventions, and to a complex, costly way of life. While it was true that I had been issued some fifty patents for my inventions which promised to help people with deafness, I could not really make any more creative contributions in this area. Others would carry on what I had started. But most of all I wanted to get into the full-time study of the mysterious powers of the human mind. One day I made my decision: I would resign from all my duties and jobs with foundations, companies, and laboratories, and give myself two years to find a place in full-time psychical research.

When I informed my family and colleagues of my decision, they groaned and tried to talk me out of it. By April 1, 1971, I had freed myself of all my professional ties and begun my new way of life. I had two goals: one was to develop a theoretical base for my research; the other was to find human beings with great talents who would cooperate as research subjects. With respect to the first, I spent two months pulling together all my ideas into the "Theory of Protocommunication," which I was to present at an International Parapsychology Conference in France in August 1971.

I had made contact with the startling psychic capacities of an Israeli, Uri Geller, by letter, and he agreed to see me in Israel the week before the conference and give me an opportunity to test his alleged talents. The result of this meeting was that I spent the next two years in an intensive study of this twenty-five-year-old man's powers.

Uri Geller proved to have power over inorganic things equivalent to what Arigo had over organic and living things. He was able to concentrate on metals and cause them to bend and split; he could repair complex devices like watches and computers; he could make objects disappear and reappear, and even translocate them over distances of thousands of miles. The probe for the source and nature of these powers has been fully covered in my book *Uri* (Doubleday, 1974). There are also other details about Arigo given in that book, details which John Fuller would have no way of documenting firsthand as he has carefully done in this one.

Today there is a Uri Geller. I am sure there will be other Arigos. It is up to mankind to cease and desist from persecuting these messengers from the higher powers of the universe and to learn the truth from them.

November 2, 1973

Bibliography

"Arigo: Curavo Mesmo," *Manchete* magazine, October 1972.

Bastide, Roger. *O Candomblé da Bahia*, trans. by Maria Isaura Pereira de Queiroz. São Paulo: Companhia Editôra Nacional, 1961.

————. *Les religions africaines au Brésil: Vers une sociologie des interpenetrations de civilisations*. Paris: Presses Universitaires de France, 1960.

Bettencourt, Gastão. *Os Tres Santos de Junho no Folclore Brasilico*. Rio de Janeiro: Agir, 1947.

Bourguignon, Ericka. *World Distribution Patterns of Possession States*, ed. Raymond Prince. Proceedings of the Second Annual Conference of the R. M. Bucke Memorial Society, Montreal, 1966.

————. "The Self, the Behavioral Environment, and the Theory of Spirit Possession," in *Context and Meaning in Cultural Anthropology*, ed. Melford E. Spiro. New York: Free Press, 1965.

Boxer, Charles Ralph. *The Golden Age of Brazil*. Berkeley: University of California Press, 1962.

Bozzano, Ernesto. *Popoli Primitivi e Manifestazioni Supernormali*. Verona: Europe, 1946.

Camargo, Candido. *Kardecismo e Umbanda: Um Interpretacao Sociologica*. São Paulo: Pioneira, 1961.

Carneiro, Edison. "The Structure of African Cults in Bahia," *Journal of American Folklore*, 53: 271–78, 1940.

Candomblés da Bahia. Rio de Janeiro: Conquista, 1961.

Cascudo, Luis da Camara. *Meleagro: Depoimento e Pesquisa Sobre a Magia Branca No Brasil.* Rio de Janeiro: Agir, 1951.

————. *Antologia do Folclore Brasileiro.* São Paulo: Martins, 1956.

————. *Dicionaria do Folclore Brasileiro.* Rio de Janeiro: Instituo Nacional do Livro, 1961.

"Catolicos Espiritas," *Realidade* magazine, November 1971.

Comenale, Reinaldo. *Ze Arigo: A Oitava Maravilha.* Belo Horizonte: Editôra Boa Imagem, 1968.

Crawford, M. W. J. *Experiments in Psychical Science.* London: Watkins, 1919.

An Evaluation of the Possible Usefulness of Extrasensory Perception in Psychological Warfare. Paper presented by ERA members to a conference on Psychological Warfare, Department of Defense, Washington, D.C., November 23, 1952.

"Faith, Hands and Auras," *Time,* October 16, 1972.

Fontenelle, Aluizio. *A Umbanda Atraves dos Seculos.* Rio de Janeiro: Organizacao Simoes, 1953.

Furtado, Celso. *The Economic Growth of Brazil.* Berkeley: University of California Press, 1963.

Galvão, Eduardo. *Santos e Visagens.* São Paulo: Companhia Editôra Nacional, 1955.

Gill, Merton M., and Margaret Brenman. *Hypnosis and Related States: Psychoanalytic Studies in Regression.* New York: International Universities Press, 1959.

Herskovits, Melville J. "African Gods and Catholic Saints in New World Religious Beliefs," *American Anthropologist,* 39: 635–43, 1937.

Hilgard, Ernest L. *Hypnotic Susceptibility.* New York: Harcourt, Brace & World, 1965.

Imbassahy, Dr. Carlos. *Freud e as Manifestações da Alma.* Rio de Janeiro: Editôra ECO, 1967.

Krestschmer, E. *La Structure du Corps et le Caractère.* Paris: Université Press, 1930.

Leacock, Seth, and Ruth Leacock. *Spirits of the Deep: A Study of an Afro-Brazilian Cult.* A publication of The American Museum of Natural History. Garden City, N.Y.: Doubleday Natural History Press, 1972.

Lhomme, José. *O Livro do Medium Curador.* Rio de Janeiro: Editôra ECO, 1965.

Lopes, Jair Leonardo. *Em Defesa de Arigo.* Belo Horizonte, 1965.

McGregor, Pedro. *Jesus of the Spirits.* New York: Stein and Day, 1966.

Morselli, Enrico. *Psicologia e Espiritismo.* Torino: Fratelli Bocca, 1908.

Physical Techniques for Increasing Telepathy. Paper presented by ERA members at a seminar sponsored by Armour Research Foundation, Illinois Institute of Technology, Chicago, December 4, 1953.

Pires, J. Herculano. *Arigo: Vida, Meiunidade e Martirio.* São Paulo: Edicel, 1963.

Ranieri, R. A. *Chico Xavier: O Santo dos Nossos Dias.* Rio de Janeiro: Editôra ECO, 1970.

Research in Extrasensory Perception. *Research Review,* Office of Aerospace Research, USAF, November 5, 1962.

Researches in Increasing or Decreasing Telepathy. Lecture presented by ERA members at the Aviation School of Medicine, USAF, Randolph Field, Texas, March 16, 1953.

Ribeiro, Hamilton. "Os Dois Mundos de Chico," *Realidade* magazine, November 1971.

Richet, Charles. *Traité de Métaphysique.* Paris: Felix Alcan, 1922.

Rizzini, Jorge. *José Arigo, Revolução no Campo da Mediunidade.* São Paulo: Edicão Cidade da Crianca, 1963.

Serrano, Geraldo. *Arigo, Desafio a Ciência.* Rio de Janeiro: Editôra ECO, 1967.

A Prece Segundo o Espiritismo. Rio de Janeiro: Editôra ECO, 1969.

Sharon, Douglas G. "Eduardo the Healer," *Natural History,* November 1972.

"Space Mind-Reading Tests Disclosed by U.S. Scientists," Washington *Post,* September 28, 1963.

Stainbrook, Edward. "Some Characteristics of the Psychopathology of Schizophrenic Behavior in Bahia Society," *American Journal of Psychiatry,* 109: 330–35, 1952.

"Telepathy—Boon for Spacemen?" *Electronics,* October 4, 1963.

"Testing for Extrasensory Perception with a Machine." Data Science Laboratory Project 4610. AF Cambridge Research Laboratories. Office of Aerospace Research, USAF, AFCRL–63–141, May 1963.

Transcripts: legal proceedings of the State of Minas Gerais *vs.* José Pedro de Freitas, known as Ze Arigo and José Nilo de Oliveiro, beginning Oct. 5, 1956 (indulto May 24, 1958); and second trial beginning Oct. 9, 1961, Congonhos do Campo, Brazil.

"U.S. Attuning ESP to Defense Purposes," New York *Herald Tribune,* August 31, 1958.

Valerio, Cicero. *Fenômenos Parapsicológicos e Espíritas.* São Paulo: Editôra Piratininga, 1962.

"Westinghouse Scientists Trying to Harness Mental Telepathy," New York *Herald Tribune,* November 3, 1958.

Worrall, Ambrose, and Olga N. Worrall. *The Gift of Healing.* New York: Harper & Row, 1965.

Index

Arigo, José *(cont.)*
   and Dr. Adolpho Fritz, *see*
      Fritz, Dr. Adolpho
   dreams of, 70
   enemies of, 124, 129, 131, 136
   exorcising of, 73
   expedition for purposes of studying,
      195-197
   extrasensory perception and
      clairvoyance in, 2, 51, 55-56,
      170, 230, 256
   faith healing and, 161
   fears of, 155
   as folk hero, 78
   found guilty and sentenced,
      145-147
   freed from prison, 183
   "German accent" or voice of, 25-26,
      33, 64, 70, 82, 86, 95, 112, 116,
      184, 191, 194, 202
   government dentist's opinion of, 31
   grave of, 247
   "green ray" of, 54
   hallucinations of, 67, 71-73, 82-83
   healing power of, 19-20
   home of, 31
   hospital "dream" of, 213, 219-220,
      224, 233
   "inside" of, 257
   jail sentence for, 150
   Kardec spiritism and, *see* Kardec;
      Kardecist
   "kickbacks" alleged to, 249
   lawsuits against, 21
   many personalities of, 91-92,
      155-156
   medical investigation of, 104,
      195-197
   mediumship and, 231-233
   as model prisoner, 172
   motion pictures of, 21, 32, 34-36,
      41-43, 51-53, 102, 160-162, 196,
      220-221, 241-242, 245-246
   new case against, 157
   nickname meaning "bumpkin," 63
   "nonoperations" performed by, 152
   nonpayment for services, 92, 130
   operative technique of, 6-7, 28-29,
      120
   pardoned by Kubitschek, 151

Arigo, José *(cont.)*
   personality changes in, 91-92,
      155-156
   physical attack on, 131-132
   police investigation of, 105-106,
      130-132
   politics of, 73-75
   popular support of, 142-143
   possession of, 73, 83, 144, 191-193,
      229-230
   prayers of, 24, 113
   premonition and clairvoyance of,
      104-105
   premonition of death, 233-234
   prescriptions and pharmacology of,
      10, 27, 45-46, 82-83, 87,
      121-122, 135, 140-141, 157, 189,
      194-195, 210, 211, 227-228,
      259-260
   press publicity and, 207-208
   priests and, 36, 72-79, 90
   in prison, 168-183
   probation of, 149
   "production line" of, 48
   prosecution of, 134-143
   as "Prussian officer," 25
   psychotic state and, 233
   Puharich's letter of support for,
      175-177
   pure physics and, 215
   in real estate and used-car business,
      91
   as receptionist in government office,
      30
   refusal of payment for services,
      47, 92, 130
   restaurant-bar of, 70
   Rodriguez's report on, 230-233
   rose-growing by, 102
   scientific study of, 187-188, 198-206
   second trial and sentencing of,
      165-167
   slander against, 102-103
   as staunch Catholic, 72, 74, 83,
      128-129, 136, 220, 222
   strictures on drinking, smoking,
      and gambling, 23-24
   supporters of, 159, 173-175
   temporary release of, 177
   trance states of, 24-25, 29, 32-33,